Steenstrup, Johannes C. H. R. (Johannes Christoffer Hagemann Reinhardt), 1844-1935.

The medieval popular ballad

THE MEDIEVAL POPULAR BALLAD

THE MEDIEVAL POPULAR BALLAD

BY JOHANNES C. H. R. STEENSTRUP

TRANSLATED FROM THE DANISH
BY EDWARD GODFREY COX

WITH A FOREWORD BY DAVID C. FOWLER AND A
BIBLIOGRAPHIC ESSAY BY KARL-IVAR HILDEMAN

UNIVERSITY OF WASHINGTON PRESS
SEATTLE AND LONDON

Library of Congress Catalog Card Number 16-27025

Original hardcover edition published by
Ginn and Company, Boston, 1914
First University of Washington Press edition, 1968
Printed in the United States of America

FOREWORD

Johannes Steenstrup first published this study of Scandinavian ballads in 1891, while Francis J. Child was still at work on his definitive edition of the English and Scottish popular ballads, an edition which was finally completed in 1898. Since that time, thanks largely to the influence of the great Danish collector, Svend Grundtvig, on Child's edition of the ballads, modern scholars have become increasingly aware of important connections between the English and Scandinavian ballad traditions viewed in the larger context of European balladry. Hence the present reprinting of Steenstrup's *The Medieval Popular Ballad* in Edward Godfrey Cox's translation is doubly welcome, as both a testimony to the enduring validity of the Danish scholar's work, and a reminder of the importance of Scandinavian balladry for students of the English and Scottish popular ballads.

Much has been written on the ballad since the time of Steenstrup, Grundtvig, and Child. F. B. Gummere's theory of ballad origins, his notion of communal composition, was contested by Louise Pound in 1921 and replaced by a theory of individual composition. A truce between the communalists and the individualists was declared by Gordon H. Gerould, whose study, *The Ballad of Tradition,* has been standard for the last thirty-five years. Less appreciated, but of greater value for medieval balladry, is the chapter on the ballad by E. K. Chambers in

English Literature at the Close of the Middle Ages (Oxford, 1945). In the last two decades books by Evelyn K. Wells, M. J. C. Hodgart, D. K. Wilgus, and Albert B. Friedman have continued and sustained the study of balladry. Interestingly, this stream of learned commentary is matched by a popular revival, in the 1950's and 1960's, of folksong and ballad, admirably sketched by Josh Dunson in *Freedom in the Air* (New York, 1965).

Works devoted particularly to international balladry are less numerous, but they are nevertheless important for seeing the relationship between the English and Scandinavian traditions. A pioneer in this field was Sigurd B. Hustvedt, *Ballad Criticism in Great Britain and Scandinavia during the Eighteenth Century* (New York, 1916), who also published a second volume, *Ballad Books and Ballad Men* (Cambridge, Mass., 1930). The entire international field was surveyed by William Entwistle in *European Balladry* (Oxford, 1939). In recent years studies of individual ballads have appeared which illustrate the relatedness of the European ballad community. By far the best of these studies is Holger O. Nygard, *The Ballad of Heer Halewijn* (Helsinki and Knoxville, 1958). As the preceding references indicate, much progress has been made in the study of international ballads. It is therefore all the more impressive that Steenstrup's book remains today a respected authority for English readers interested in learning about the canon of Scandinavian balladry.

It is true that the modern reader will find in Steenstrup an occasional attitude or technique that marks him as a nineteenth-century critic. In his preface, for example, he emphasizes the importance of distinguishing between medieval and modern forms of the ballad by asking these rhetorical questions:

> Since we otherwise lay such great stress on finding the proper time coloring, why should we then confound the songs that were sung on gentlemen's estates in the period of the Reformation with those that were current in the feudal castles of the Middle Ages? Why should we be content to look at a blank white wall, when it is possible, by knocking off the plaster, to discover lifelike pictures painted beneath the lime?

Modern criticism, of course, has long since disowned this antiquarian approach to the study of poetry. We are no longer confident that textual analysis is an appropriate tool for the "restoration" of the literary monuments of antiquity.

Surprisingly enough, however, Steenstrup's concern for chronology in ballad study turns out finally to be a strength rather than a weakness. It stands in fact as a major rebuke to modern scholarship which, dominated to this day by a mystique associated with the phrase *das Volk dichtet,* still scorns the dating of ballad texts, and looks with suspicion on any effort to deal with the ballads chronologically. Therefore I particularly commend to the modern reader such statements as the following one taken from the introductory chapter (p. 4): "In other words, the whole ballad literature has been regarded too much as an entirety; whereas it well admits of a division, not only according to subject matter, but also according to period of origin. Such a division would mark off the later elements from the older." It is an irony of literary history that this mandate for the advancement of ballad study has remained so long unfulfilled.

Steenstrup himself practiced what he preached, within the limits he set himself, and this is one of the reasons that his work stands the test of time so well. In discussing "The Soul at Heaven's Door" (No. 106), dated 1732, he lays down the rule (p. 146): "Here, in other words, we have every reason for insisting on the rules observed of all other historical sources; namely, that the age of a document is first and foremost determined according to the date when it first appears." On this basis he concludes that "The Soul at Heaven's Door," far from being a medieval text, is merely the product of a ballad monger in the "Grub Street" of eighteenth-century Copenhagen.

This judgment as to the modernity of a ballad may at times seem arbitrary, but more often than not Steenstrup gives stylistic reasons for his conclusions. Witness, for example, his discussion of "Agnete and the Merman" (No. 38), a ballad first appearing in the eighteenth century (pp. 224-25):

> Here we have parallelism carried out in full, together with what in the truest sense can be called antithesis; and herein we are again brought face to face with the purely artistic. We now stand on the exact border line of the rigid and the uniform, at the very threshold of the Learned Period; whereas our ballads of the Middle Ages speak in the fashion of children, or rather as a mother speaks to her child. The proof that "Agnete and the Merman" should be dated back to the Middle Ages, when its eccentric form and its late appearance certainly relegate it to the eighteenth century, has meanwhile not yet been brought forward, and he who is to adduce this will have his work cut out for him. Until that has been done, we ought to leave this ballad out of consideration when the question deals with the qualities peculiar to the ballads of the Middle Ages.

Steenstrup's common sense and his perceptiveness are

manifest in every chapter. In his reference to the ballad books of Harald Oluffson, Nils Larson, and Bröms Gyllenmär (p. 235), for example, we can see his sense of the importance of identifying sources, their dates, and the rationale of individual collections. And in citing Svend Aagesön's *Chronicle* as a source for "The Meeting of Kings in Roskilde" (No. 118), he exposes (p. 239) the fallacy of supposing that historical accuracy in a ballad is evidence of an early date of composition, a supposition still found in recent comments on the date of "The Hunting of the Cheviot" (Child 162).[1] It is thus with a great deal of respect that one rereads this early but reliable study of Scandinavian balladry.

I cannot conclude this introduction without a word of gratitude to the late Professor Edward Godfrey Cox, whose discriminating eye caught the value of Steenstrup's book for the English student, and who made for us this readable translation. Professor Cox well knew the close ties between Scandinavian ballads and those of his beloved Scotland, and so it was with some reluctance, I think, and certainly with too much modesty, that he disclaimed, in the translator's preface, the ability to translate the Danish ballads quoted by Steenstrup into the Scottish dialect, as one "not to the manner born." Because of his modesty on this point, the ballad texts are uniformly translated into plain English. Recently, however, Alex-

[1] See "The Hunting of the Cheviot and The Battle of Otterburn," *Western Folklore,* XXV (1966), 165-71. This is part of a book-length study by the present writer that will appear under the title *A Literary History of the Popular Ballad* (Durham, N.C.: Duke University Press, 1968).

ander Gray published his *Four and Forty: A Selection of Danish Ballads Presented in Scots* (Edinburgh, 1954), an experiment in translation which I feel sure Professor Cox would regard with the utmost approval. This volume, together with Gray's *Historical Ballads of Denmark* (Edinburgh, 1958), can be recommended to readers of the present volume who wish to explore further the riches of the Danish ballad tradition.

DAVID C. FOWLER
UNIVERSITY OF WASHINGTON

MODERN SCANDINAVIAN BALLAD RESEARCH: A BIBLIOGRAPHIC ESSAY

Johannes Steenstrup's book on the medieval ballad deals with a genre that is inter-Scandinavian. Very often a ballad found in Denmark has also been recorded in all other areas where Scandinavian languages are spoken, from Iceland and the Faroes in the west to the Swedish-speaking provinces of Finland in the east. The Scandinavian term for the ballad is *vise* (Danish and Norwegian) or *visa* (Swedish).

Although several of Steenstrup's conclusions and statements could be disputed today, it is surprising that most of them are still valid. Steenstrup was a historian fostered in the rationalistic 1870's and 1880's, and he approached his material with new and radical historical methods. These methods are obvious in his later contributions to the ballad field, his articles on the origin and the oldest period of the Scandinavian ballad, which were published in the Danish periodical *Historisk Tidskrift* (Copenhagen), Series 9, Volume I (1918-20), under the heading "De danske Folkevisers ældste Tid og Visernes Herkomst." Some of his insights, however, are already apparent in Cox's edition of Steenstrup's earlier work.

Today, several generations after Steenstrup, a ballad researcher in the Scandinavian field still has reason to use most of the ballad editions upon which Steenstrup's results depended, in many cases, of course, supplemented with new material. In most areas, modern and more complete collections have not made the older editions superfluous.

Denmark is the Scandinavian country with the greatest concentration of material on ballads. Not only were the Danes the first to record the ballads, but they have also preserved more old manuscripts than has any other Nordic group. Furthermore Denmark has produced the most important and the largest enterprise in the field of Scandinavian balladry, *Danmarks gamle Folkeviser (DgF),* a complete and annotated edition of the Danish ballads and a comparison of these ballads with their counterparts in other Scandinavian countries. The main sources are the old *vis*-books of the sixteenth and seventeenth centuries. Work on this project began around 1850, and it established precedents for similar editions, such as Child's.

DgF had famous predecessors. The Danish aristocracy had begun to record ballads by the middle of the sixteenth century, and in 1591 the historian Anders Sørensen Vedel printed one hundred of these songs, becoming the first to publish in the ballad field. The latest edition of his collection was printed in Copenhagen in 1926-27: *Anders Sørensen Vedels Folkevisebog,* edited by Paul V. Rubow.

When Steenstrup wrote his book in 1891, the fifth volume of *DgF* had just been published. The founding editor of *DgF* was Svend Grundtvig, who was succeeded by Axel Olrik and later by Hakon Grüner-Nielsen. Erik Dal, a representative of the fourth generation, completed the text work of the project by publishing the supplementary Volume X in 1967. Another volume with the melodies is forthcoming.

Because of the impact of archive material, ballad recording from oral tradition was slow in Denmark, and only in the later volumes of *DgF* does one find a heavy concentration of such material. The Danish oral tradition has been preserved mainly by a Jutland teacher, Evald Tang-Kristensen, who did not begin his work until the 1860's. But his harvest was immense: about three thousand examples. He has published some of them in *Jydske Folkeminder* (Viborg and Copenhagen, 1868-91), and the editors of *DgF* have also used many of his texts.

DgF has entirely dominated the field of scholarly ballad publications in Denmark. But researchers interested in the old manuscripts should consult another large edition of old Danish songs, *Danske Visor,* Volumes I-VII, by H. Grüner-Nielsen (Copenhagen, 1912-31), in which poems other than the *vis*-book ballads have been printed.

In Sweden similar manuscripts have been preserved to some extent from the sixteenth century. In the seventeenth century royal authority assumed the task of collecting ballads from oral tradition. But the first publications date from the Romantic period and a new interest ignited by Percy in England and Herder in Germany. In the first two decades of the nineteenth century enthusiastic amateurs began to collect ballads from oral tradition in the middle and southern provinces. The first Swedish ballad edition in print, *Svenska folk-visor från forntiden,* by E. G. Geijer and A. A. Afzelius (Stockholm, 1814-18), appeared in a third, luxury edition as late as 1957-60. However, the editing principles of this work were esthetic and are dubious from a scholarly viewpoint. A valuable contribution to the new edition is Sture Bergel's comments on the melodies. More scholarly, although still far from reliable, was A. I. Arwidsson's *Svenska Fornsånger* (Stockholm, 1834-42). His material can partly be found in the old *vis*-books of the archives, and was partly collected from oral tradition by such scholars as L. F. Rääf and the brothers Wallman. Quite different methods were used by A. Noreen, H. Schück, and others, when they published the old *vis*-books as entire units (instead of the individual ballads, each with its variants), and limited their comments to the manuscripts. Their work, *1500- och 1600-talens visböcker,* appears in the series "Skrifter utgivna av Svenska litteratursällskapet i Uppsala," Volume VIII (Stockholm and Uppsala, 1884-1925).

Some of the Swedish ballads are published in a modern and complete edition—those from Finland, where Swedish is often spoken in the coastal regions. These ballads were printed in *Finlands svenska folkdiktning* (Helsingfors), Volume V, Number 1 (1934), by Otto Andersson, who also participated in collecting the ballads from oral tradition.

In the 1950's Matts Arnberg and Ulf P. Olrog of the Swedish Radio recorded on tape old ballads from both Sweden and Finland. Their success was greater than had been anticipated. Part of their findings can be heard on a set of long-playing records, *Den medeltida balladen* (Stockholm: Sveriges Radios förlag, 1962). Included in this edition is a book with the same title, with extensive summaries in English of each chapter. The genre is introduced by Karl-Ivar Hildeman. The recording work is described by Matts Arnberg and Ulf P. Olrog, and the problems of music and dancing by Sture Bergel and Nils

Wallin. Several of the records have reconstructions of medieval ballad singing. The tape recorder has also contributed to our knowledge of Norwegian and Faroese ballads.

Denmark solved her text problem in the ballad field by publishing *DgF* and by founding the institution Dansk Folkemindesamling, a national collection of folklore situated in the Royal Library of Copenhagen. Sweden has not yet any complete ballad edition, but at Svenskt Visarkiv in Stockholm a huge edition is being prepared and practically all the necessary texts are ready.

In Norway a modern edition is also badly needed and is now under way in Oslo. The Norwegian counterpart of Dansk Folkemindesamling is Norsk folkeminnesamling. Most of the Norwegian texts were collected in the middle of the nineteenth century when an interest in the oral tradition arose, similar to that of Sweden one generation earlier and Denmark a few years later. Thus M. B. Landstad published *Norske Folkeviser* (Christiania [Oslo], 1852-53) and Sophus Bugge published *Gamle norske Folkeviser* (Christiania, 1859). In both cases the texts were often combined from different variants. The same methods have been used in the Norwegian collection, the three-volume set *Norske folkevisor* by Knut Liestøl and Moltke Moe (Oslo, 1920-24). A new edition by Olav Bø and Svale Solheim was printed in 1958-59. We do not yet have a scholarly edition of the Norwegian ballads, although a survey of existing Norwegian material, *Utsyn yver gamall norsk folkevisediktning* (Christiania, 1912), has been edited by Leif Heggstad and H. Grüner-Nielsen.

Of special interest are the Faroese ballads, since the

medieval genre is still sung and danced in the Faroes. However, these examples represent a type of their own, a further development of the Scandinavian ballad. They were first written down in the middle of the nineteenth century, and a few of them were published by V. U. Hammershaimb in his *Færøsk Anthologi* (Copenhagen 1891). This book is now difficult to obtain, but a modern and complete edition is being published by C. Matras and N. Djurhuus as *Føroya Kvæði, Corpus Carminum Faeroensium* (Copenhagen, 1941--).

In Iceland on the contrary the ballad does not seem to have been very popular, and most texts are to be found in manuscripts, the oldest dating from the seventeenth century. From 1854 to 1885 S. Grundtvig and Jón Sigurdsson published *Islenzk Fornkvædi* in Copenhagen. That title is preserved in a larger, modern edition compiled by Jón Helgason, director of the Arnamagnaen Institute in Copenhagen. Five volumes were completed by 1965, the first one published in 1962.

Recently Erik Dal's popular edition, *Danske viser* (Copenhagen, 1962), with a good introduction, has been translated by Henry Meyer as *Danish Ballads and Folksongs* (Copenhagen and New York, 1967). In his Danish edition Dal has chosen to publish existing texts, not corrected or altered in any way. The same method is used by his predecessor, Grüner-Nielsen, in his *Danske Folkeviser* (Copenhagen, 1925-57), and by Ernst Frandsen, *Danske Folkeviser i Udvalg* (Copenhagen, 1937). In earlier editions attempts to "restore" the texts were common. The most interesting Danish example is *Danmarks Fornviser,* Volumes I-IV (1927-29) by E. v.d. Recke, who makes many important comments. In Norway the collection by Liestøl, Moe, and their successors represents a similar approach. In Sweden *Svenska folkvisor i urval* by Sverker Ek and Erik Blomberg belongs to the same school (Uddevalla, 1939). The same methods as Dal's are used by a younger Swedish scholar, Bengt R. Jonsson, in his *Svenska medeltidsballader* (Stockholm, 1962).

Turning to scholarly commentaries on the ballads, we can consider "Scandinavian Ballad Research Today," a recent article by Erik Dal in the periodical *Scandinavica* (London), Volume I (1962). This article is actually a supplement to Dal's learned book, *Nordisk folkeviseforskning siden 1800,* which was published in Copenhagen in 1956. The book has an extensive summary in English which, however, does not include a most valuable and detailed chronological bibliography on Scandinavian balladry from 1591 to 1956.

The most useful ballad bibliography in Danish in competition with Dal's is found in *Den danske litteraturs historie* by Oluf Friis (Copenhagen, 1945), I, 561. In Friis's history the headings of the ballad warks are listed in groups according to content. A Swedish bibliography of the same type, but with a commentary, has been published in *Ny illustrerad svensk litteraturhistoria,* Volume I (2nd ed.; Stockholm, 1967). The ballad section is written by Karl-Ivar Hildeman. In all the works mentioned above, the whole Scandinavian field is treated to some extent.

Unfortunately there is no extensive modern introduction to the Scandinavian ballad to be found in English. In *Den medeltida balladen,* published by Sveriges Radio in 1962 and mentioned above, K.-I. Hildeman has a summary chapter translated from Swedish. In the English version of E. Dal's *Danish Ballads and Folksongs,* also referred to above, there is an introductory chapter on the genre.

In Scandinavian languages more complete presentations are published in all the modern histories of literature of the respective countries. Some of them have already been mentioned above. Thus O. Friis's *Den danske litteraturs historie,* Volume I, offers an extensive chapter on the medieval ballad. A newer introduction has been written in the Swedish *Ny illustrerad svensk litteraturhistoria,* Volume I, where K.-I. Hildeman comments on this portion of the literature of the Middle Ages. Volume IX of the series "Nordisk Kultur" (Copenhagen, Oslo, and Stockholm, 1931) is partly devoted to the Scandinavian ballad. The introductory chapter is written by Knut Liestøl, who also introduces the Norwegian, Faroese, and Icelandic ballads, while H. Grüner-Nielsen presents the Danish point of view, and Sverker Ek comments on the Swedish material. An extensive older work of the same kind, notable because of its methodology, is Henrik Schuck's *Illustrerad svensk litteraturhistoria* (3rd ed.; Stockholm, 1923), which has an important chapter on the ballads in Volume I. A more concise description with a useful bibliography is E. N. Tigerstedt's one-volume *Svensk litteraturhistoria* (3rd ed.; Stockholm, 1967).

After Steenstrup few attempts have been made to write monographs on the ballad as a genre with the stress on its history. The medieval sources are too rare for definite solutions. It was not until Sverker Ek published *Studier till den svenska folkvisans historia* in 1931 that a whole book on the matter appeared again (in "Göteborgs högskolas årsskrift," Vol. XXXVII). Ek's results, which previously had been partly published in his more popular *Den svenska folkvisan* (Stockholm, 1924), have been severely criticized, and his successors in the field have turned to other directions. Another book on the Nordic ballad and its development was offered by the Dane, Ernst Frandsen, in 1934: *Folkevisen* (Copenhagen). He tried to map the evolution of the ballad by using esthetic and literary analysis. Although his attempt was not entirely successful, his book is nevertheless valuable because of his methods. A similar analysis is used in K.-I. Hildeman's contribution to *Om visor och låtar, Festskrift till Sven Salén* (Stockholm, 1960), in which he discusses the development of the ballad in the late Middle Ages.

Single ballads and different groups of ballads have offered a less complicated base for research work. For those interested in single ballads the comments in *DgF* should be pointed to as far as Danish material is concerned—and the majority of Scandinavian ballads have been recorded in some Danish version. It should also be noted that supplementary comments are added in later volumes. The whole of Volume X (1967) is such a supplement. The commentators here are Grüner-Nielsen, Hildeman, Dal, and Jørn Piø. In their commentaries the preceding literature on each item is listed. Since parts of this supplement were printed as early as 1948, a few more recent studies must be sought in various periodicals.

Some of the scholarly Scandinavian periodicals are especially interested in ballad research. Most of the Danish contributions to the field are either published or reviewed in *Danske Studier* (Copenhagen). In Sweden they are listed in the annual bibliography of *Samlaren* (Uppsala), and quite a few have appeared in the folkloristic *Arv* (Uppsala). Important Norwegian articles have been printed in *Edda* (Oslo). During the last ten years most articles and some larger works on the Scandinavian ballad have also been published as offprints in the series "Meddelanden från Svenskt Visarkiv" (Stockholm).

Among the groups of ballads which are not to be found in *DgF* are many political and historical Swedish ones. They are the subject of *Politiska visor från Sveriges senmedeltid* by Karl-Ivar Hildeman (Stockholm, 1950), who also comments on various ballad theories in *Medeltid på vers* (Stockholm, 1958; summaries in English), Volume I in the series "Skrifter utgivna av Svenskt Visarkiv. The heroic Danish cycle on the rebellious Lord High Constable, Marsk Stig, at the end of the thirteenth century, is treated by the learned Danish medievalist Helge Toldberg in his last work, *Marsk Stig-viserne* (Copenhagen, 1963). Another of his contributions to the field is "Den Danske rimrønike og folkeviserne," an investigation of the Danish rhymed chronicle and its relation to the ballads (*Danske Studier,* Vol. LIII, 1958).

In comparison with the "knight ballads" *(riddarvisor)* of the Marsk Stig type, the ballads with folklore motifs have always received less attention. However, the Finnish scholar, Alfhild Forslin, has compared to the most famous of them—that of Sir Olof and the fairy dance—to its international counterparts in his article, "Balladen om riddar Olof och älvorna" (*Arv,* Vols. XVIII-XIX, 1962-63).

The Scandinavian ballad as a rule is not concerned with religious matters, but a few ballads—usually considered to be late—deal with saints as their heroes and heroines. The ballad about St. Stephen is one such ballad, still widespread in Sweden in a mutilated form. The last contribution to the topic can be found in Dag Strömbäck's article in *Om visor och låtar, Festskrift till Sven Salén.* The most famous by far of all these religious ballads is the Norwegian "Draumkvede" ("Dream Song") of the man who has come back from the realm of Death, a ballad that also belongs to the genre of visions. This ballad, commented on by almost all the great Norwegian scholars since Steenstrup's time, among them Moltke Moe and Sophus Bugge, is the subject of an entire book in English by Knut Liestøl: *Draumkvaede* ("Studia Norvegica" [Oslo], Vol. I, No. 3 [1946]). His theories and those of his predecessors concerning the age of the ballad are questioned by D. Stromback in *Arv* (1946) and rejected by K.-I. Hildeman in *Medeltid på vers.* Olav Bø is more inclined to trust Liestøl's conclusion about the age of the song in his review of Hildeman's chapter in the Norwegian *Historisk tidskrift* (1959-60).

Norwegian ballad scholars have also been very interested in the "songs of warriors" *(kampavisorna),* long epic ballads of battle and revenge. That this group as a genre is of Norwegian origin is proved by K. Liestøl, *Norske trollvisor og norrøne sogor* (Oslo, 1915), and by Sverker Ek, *Norsk kämpavisa i östnordisk tradition* (in

"Göteborgs högskolas årsskrift," 1921). The first scholars to launch that theory were Danish, for example, A. Olrik and Ernst v.d. Recke. A new contribution was made by Gun Widmark in her article on the ballad of Hagbard in *Arv,* Volume XV (1959). The arrival of this genre to East Scandinavia is the topic in a chapter of K.-I. Hildeman's *Medeltid på vers.*

A field of inquiry in the history of the ballad that is of special interest here is the connection between the Scandinavian and the English-Scottish ballad. K. Liestøl was interested in that question and discussed it in his article on Scottish and Norwegian ballads in "Studia Norvegica," Volume I, Number 1 (1946).

The language problem of the ballad—dealt with by Johannes Brøndum-Nielsen from Denmark in the periodical *Nordisk Tidskrift* (Stockholm, 1910), and by Elias Wessen from Sweden in another periodical, *Nysvenska studier* (Uppsala), Volume XIII (1928)—has interested the Danish scholar K. Hald, who has an article in progress on this topic.

In recent years the tradition itself—the way ballads have survived and been passed forward—has received considerable attention, as have the records. The manuscripts, the collections, and the collectors are the subjects for Bengt R. Jonsson in what is so far the dominating ballad work of the 1960's, his monumental study of 1967, *Svensk balladtradition,* Volume I (Uppsala; summary in English). Jonsson deals with Swedish material from the sixteenth century to the present, a field in which he has written many shorter articles now included in the larger work. There is no such investigation from the other Nordic countries, but a few old Danish manuscripts have been commented upon, for example, by Agnes Agerschou on Vedel's manuscripts in the periodical *Acta Philologica Scandinavica* (Copenhagen), Volume XV (1941); by Erik Kroman on the oldest Danish manuscripts in *Edda*, Volume XXI (1924); and by Kroman and H. Grüner-Nielsen in *Danske Studier*, Volume XX (1923).

The last two centuries of Scandinavian ballad research are covered by Erik Dal in *Nordisk folkeviseforskning siden 1800* and in his article in *Scandinavica* (1962).

KARL-IVAR HILDEMAN

TRANSLATOR'S PREFACE

Aside from the admirable books of Professor F. B. Gummere on the ballad, I know of no other work whose covers include such a comprehensive and fundamental exposition of the ballad, its origin, nature, subject matter, form, and age, as does the one which appears here in translation. Its peculiar claim to be placed before English students, that which distinguishes it from other works on the subject, is its purpose of making us see what the ballad of the Middle Ages was really like. In other words, using Grundtvig's mammoth collection of Danish ballads as illustrations, it sifts out, chips away, rubs off all impurities, in the shape of diction, metrical items, and ideas which had no legitimate claim to existence before the sixteenth century. In the residue thus purged and restored we have the genuine unalloyed ballad of the Middle Ages.

In another respect also this book merits consideration. While Professor Steenstrup's studies lay bare the make-up of the ballad as a universal form of literature, by the very fact that he uses largely the ballads of Denmark for illustrative material he enriches for English readers the study of the subject, in that they herein make the acquaintance of a ballad literature which, in importance and bulk, surpasses that of all other European nations. Then, too, the circumstance that the ballads constitute the only vernacular literature of early Denmark makes them of peculiar interest in a comparative study of literature.

The extracts from the ballads themselves I have endeavored to turn into suitable ballad measure with as close an adherence to literalness as possible. In many cases the baldness of the English rendering may be excused on the score that the original verse is equally bald. Naturally genuine ballad flavor could best be imparted to the translations by the employment of the Scotch dialect; but for one not to the manner born such a venture is hazardous. Where ballad stanzas are cited as bearing on questions of meter and diction I have given the original also. The numbers following the title refer, except when otherwise indicated, to Grundtvig's collection.

In conclusion I record with pleasure my obligation to Mr. Haldor Hermansson, the librarian of the Icelandic collection at Cornell University, for generous help in looking up references and in explaining passages.

EDWARD GODFREY COX

SEATTLE, WASHINGTON

AUTHOR'S PREFACE

In the winter of 1886–1887 I gave a series of lectures in the University on our popular ballads, in which, in addition to elucidating the cultural life manifested in them, I set myself to the task of pointing out what was peculiar to our ballads with respect to their form and their content. By this I thought to arrive at a sharper definition between those ballads and verses which were old and genuine and those which at a later date had come into being or had found their way into Denmark or else had assumed a wholly modern form.

It is this portion of the lectures that I am bringing out here. Our scholars and, after them, our poets, who have had daily recourse to this ever-flowing spring, have not, so it seems to me, rightly understood the style of the old ballads, which in simplicity and naturalness are still unsurpassed. Since we otherwise lay such great stress on finding the proper time coloring, why should we then confound the songs that were sung on gentlemen's estates in the period of the Reformation with those that were current in the feudal castles of the Middle Ages? Why should we be content to look at a blank white wall, when it is possible, by knocking off the plaster, to discover lifelike pictures painted beneath the lime? Now in this work I have attempted in various ways to separate the new from the old, the chance additions from the original, the slips of memory from the poet's own production. And here it is not a question of demolishing but only of removing the ugly so that the genuine and true coloring can emerge into view. Thus, I believe, those features which are individual and unique can more fully assert themselves.

In my studies I have used not only the ballads that have been published but also the entire great collection of ballads which Grundtvig left behind him, and which one can now find in the Royal Library.

I have sought to make the presentation of the material readable and intelligible to all, and to this end I have added throughout whatever explanation of words was needful. Since the interpretation did not require the old spelling found in the manuscripts, I have modernized the language of the ballads.

JOHANNES STEENSTRUP

COPENHAGEN, 1891

CONTENTS

CHAPTER | PAGE

I. Introduction 1

II. The Dance and the Ballad 9
I. The Nature of the Dance, 10. II. How the Ballad and the Dance began, 26.

III. The *I* 34
I. A Ballad will I sing to you, 40. II. Monologue within the Ballad, 49. III. The Change of Narrator in the Ballad, 53. IV. *I* Throughout the Entire Ballad, 58. V. This I say to you in Sooth, 66.

IV. The Refrain 81
I. Nature of the Refrain, 82. II. Ballads without Refrains, 95.

V. Rime, Rhythm, and Melody 125

VI. The Subject Matter and Purpose of the Ballads 170
I. Nature, 171. II. Religion, 178. III. Morals and Wishes, 194. IV. Fatherland, 202. V. Romantic Ballads, 210. VI. Ballad Style, 216. VII. Dramatic Structure, 228. VIII. Simplicity, 232.

VII. Some Remarks on Historical Truth in Ballad Poetry 237

VIII. Retrospect 252

INDEX TO BALLADS 263

SCANDINAVIAN BALLAD COLLECTIONS CITED IN THE TEXT 266

INDEX 267

THE MEDIEVAL POPULAR BALLAD

THE MEDIEVAL POPULAR BALLAD

CHAPTER I

INTRODUCTION

The scope of this book may be stated in a few words. It is an attempt to discover what our ballads of the Middle Ages were like originally, and to determine their proper form and subject matter. Perhaps the reader will say that this is supposedly well known already, since the greater part of our ballads are accessible in the model collection of Svend Grundtvig's. Here every one, so to speak, not only may see the ballads for himself, just as they were written down in the old manuscripts, but may also be led, through the highly enlightening remarks of the editor, to form his own estimate of the subject matter and different versions of individual ballads, as well as to compare our Danish and Scandinavian stock of ballads with that of other nations.

Nevertheless it may safely be asserted that very few people are really alive to the genuine form and spirit of our medieval ballads. Grundtvig's work bears as its title "The Old Popular Ballads of Denmark" (*Danmarks Gamle Folkeviser*) and, though it was his special endeavor to present to us the popular ballads that belong distinctly to the Middle Ages, still he included many ballads which he himself referred to the sixteenth and seventeenth centuries. Furthermore, Grundtvig is strongly inclined to dwell upon the changes which a ballad may have undergone in the course of later centuries, down even to our day, although this can possess but a transient interest in comparison with the great and weighty problem of settling upon the genuinely earliest version. In a large number — in by far the greater majority — of cases, the modern forms have not the slightest claim to literary notice. In the next place, none of the manuscripts in which the complete texts are recorded can be traced farther back than to the age of the Reformation, and only some few fragments of ballads are to be found in manuscripts that date from the Middle Ages. Thus it is clear that, along with what is really old, this great work contains much that is modern, that is, belonging to the period of the Reformation and to much later centuries. Obviously it ought to be one's task to separate the later additions from the original versions, and to set entirely aside the later poems of the sixteenth century and of the Period of Learning — provided that one wished to know the ballads as they originally issued from the poet's mouth. In several specific cases Grundtvig has given us suggestive hints that throw light upon this point, but nowhere has he offered us a general line of argument. He has nowhere classified the distinguishing features by which we may detect the new apparel — the new finery clothing the old body. In several respects also, it seems to me, Grundtvig's ear has deceived him; he has not caught the true ring of antiquity.

The general survey of the ballads which Grundtvig failed to give us has been attempted by others. In his "Intellectual Life of the Northern Peoples," Carl Rosenberg has entered into the spirit of ballad poetry with delicate appreciation and intelligence; he has strikingly illuminated many sides of the subject matter and the form. But he has taken virtually the same standpoint as did Grundtvig, and moreover he has made no attempt at a discriminating criticism. On the other hand, while Rosenberg has industriously studied Grundtvig's work, this cannot altogether be said of Professor Peter Hansen, though the latter has laid before us a pretty detailed exposition of the ballads in his "Illustrated History of Danish Literature." In place of a searching study of Grundtvig's *chef-d'œuvre*, Professor Hansen has contented himself with the popular books or discussions which Grundtvig published in addition to his great collection, in particular his "Selected Popular Ballads of Denmark" (1882). And one cannot help a feeling of resentment toward Professor Hansen when he passes so harsh a judgment as this: "So far as the needs of our literature are concerned, Grundtvig's edition of the ballads is a supererogation, and is based upon principles that are, to say the least, debatable." That such a work as this "Illustrated History of Danish Literature" should characterize Grundtvig's collection as a supererogation is indeed remarkable. At every point the author has called down punishment upon his head for these hard and other still more unreasonable expressions; and vengeance has not stayed her hand, for Professor Hansen's own sketch of the popular ballads has turned out to be an utter failure.

Though we may differ with Grundtvig in our studies in the ballads, and in our conceptions of how they should be edited,—the only charge that we can lay to him is that he has included too much,—we should be altogether wrong in misjudging the significance of his edition as a landmark in the history of Danish literature. For we have here a work that is distinguished by unique accuracy, by rare fullness of knowledge, and by great acuteness and far-reaching insight. Moreover, the way the material is shaped to the hand of him who is disposed to investigate further makes obligatory the study of a volume in which are preserved such precious relics of antiquity.

That there exists little real knowledge of the subject of our popular ballads is attested by the odd conceptions, ordinarily met with (especially noticeable in quotations from heroic ballads), of what the language of the Middle Ages is capable of expressing, and of what belongs to genuine ballad style. Even among our good writers—I name as ready examples the great works on Danish history by Niels Bache and Troels Lund—one frequently meets verses quoted which have absolutely nothing to do with the Middle Ages or with folk poetry, but which are, on the contrary, later reshapings and fabrications of Anders Vedel, Peder Syv, and others. In other words, the whole ballad literature has been regarded too much as an entirety; whereas it well admits of a division, not only according to subject matter, but also according to period of origin. Such a division would mark off the later elements from the older.

Now the present book has set for itself the task of coming to a clear understanding of the true form and nature of the old ballads. The investigation will first and foremost seek to solve the question of how the ballads were utilized; that is, what end they served, and how this end influenced their form. I shall investigate the changes the ballads necessarily underwent in the wear and tear of daily use, for memory constantly let fall the precious vessel to the ground only to pick it up again, though dented and cracked. In addition, my plan will be to pursue one course as long as I can; I shall, for example, endeavor to establish a general trait that will serve as a determining feature of ballad style or of choice of subject, by which individual ballads that appear as exceptions will be made to stand outside, or at least in the neighborhood, of the dividing line. After this I shall take up in a similar way another line of thought and continue on the chosen path as long as I can.

When by degrees all or the greater part of my separate investigations combine to set precisely the same ballads or group of ballads without the general circumference; when all lines gradually come to converge at the same place and to point, though with varying definiteness, to the above-mentioned class of ballads, then I shall believe indeed that I must have attained to a right understanding of what is native to the ballads of the Middle Ages, and of what is to be regarded as foreign and excrescent. At any rate, my researches will have laid bare what is in reality to be found in this borderland of literature, whether we confine ourselves to the age in which the ballads flourished, or whether we step outside of the realm of popular poetry and touch upon what is conscious and literary.

Meanwhile I wish to call attention to the following. As is well known, Denmark is by no means the only land that possesses popular ballads of the Middle Ages; on the contrary, they are to be found in nearly every country. Nevertheless our popular poetry has clearly marked superiorities which cannot be too strongly insisted upon. The Danish ballads of the Middle Ages have apparently furnished the only outlet to the popular imagination, to its creative power and its narrative impulse; for centuries they have served as practically the sole form in which the people gave vent to their feelings — at any rate outside of the church and the hours of prayer. This explains why such poetry has become so rich in various directions, and happens to contain so long and variegated a series of shadings.

Though the Faroes and Iceland, Norway and Sweden have preserved, to be sure, rich remains of old popular poetry, yet Denmark's store is far more important than that of any of these countries, whether in respect to numbers or to value. Then, too, Denmark's collection is characterized by the presence of a large number of historical ballads. However much one is obliged to shear away of what Grundtvig classes under this head, there still exists a large residue, which in numbers and worth, in beauty and illuminating power, far surpasses what is to be found of the same nature in the neighboring lands of the North. And it is clear that when the question turns upon the precise form and age of our popular ballads, the ballads that treat of historical subjects have a deep significance.

For the end I have in view there is one circumstance of even greater weight; namely, that Denmark possesses the earliest written records. However invaluable the literary material found lately in the living tradition of Denmark; however wonderful those objects unearthed in the heaths at Herning, or the songs heard in Telemark's fields, still I entertain no doubt that if we succeeded in gaining a knowledge of the genuine popular poetry of the Catholic Middle Ages, we should have to render our thanks exclusively to the noble ladies of the sixteenth and seventeenth centuries. To them it is due that we are acquainted with the old versions of ballads, and that we can see what changes the ballads themselves have undergone at various periods. To appreciate our wealth we need only to compare our sources of material with those of Sweden; for, while we possess forty ballad manuscripts of a period prior to 1750, Sweden has only about ten, the oldest of which are antedated by a number of the Danish. Of the Norse ballads there exist only a few that were written down in early times, and the same is true in a still more limited degree of the Icelandic ballads. In other words, the material to show what the ballads were really like three hundred to four hundred years ago is to be found solely in Denmark. Furthermore, the frequent recurrence of the same ballad in many manuscripts is of great importance in bringing about a knowledge of the true form of the ballad.

Finally, I desire to call attention to the fact that it is decidedly advisable, it seems to me, to be cautious in the use of Icelandic and Faroese ballads. Among the inhabitants of these islands the recollection of Saga and Edda poetry was constant and vigorous, and this recollection must easily have blended with and influenced the poetry of the Middle Ages. In Denmark, on the contrary, all knowledge of the poetry of antiquity had completely disappeared. While in the latter country there exist practically no poetical compositions in the vernacular, except the ballads, in Iceland the popular ballads form only a small part of a great poetical literature dating from the latter part of the Middle Ages. It lies in the nature of the case, then, that the one branch of poetry could not help influencing the other; that is to say, in Iceland and in the Faroes the ballads have acquired a more conscious and literary stamp than they have elsewhere. Moreover it happened that "learned men," in particular the clergy, throughout these islands contributed in a high degree to the flowering of this poetry, or at least to its preservation. Thus it took an impress which makes it less adapted to serve as a touchstone for what is genuine and ancient in the Danish ballads.

Having thus indicated the purpose and method of my studies, I shall pass on to the special investigations.

CHAPTER II

THE DANCE AND THE BALLAD

There is a marked difference between a poem as we ordinarily understand it and a ballad. The popular ballads of the Middle Ages are not poems which were written down in books and intended for reading; they are songs which have been preserved by memory and were sung by one or more persons in the presence of others, being accompanied at the same time by a dance of a mimic or dramatic nature. In the oldest poetry of every people there exists a close relation between these three things, says a well-informed writer: no poem that was not sung, no song that was not danced to, and no dance that was not accompanied by a song.[1] This statement admits of no question. Nowadays, in the majority of songs we sing, we lay only an infinitesimal stress, if any at all, on the text, which perhaps we do not even remember rightly, and which, at any rate, we seldom sing through to the end. We are never moved to embellish the performance with dramatic or mimic gestures, nor to mark the rhythm of the melody with the swaying of our bodies.

In earlier times song and mimic gestures were much more intimately related. As late as 1767 — as we can see from a poster of the Royal Theatre — a young Scotch lady

[1] Franz Böhme, Geschichte des Tanzes in Deutschland, I, 13, 229; cf. Böhme, Altdeutsches Liederbuch, p. xlvii.

appeared in various dances at the theater, singing at the same time, in accordance with the custom of former dancers, French and Italian arias. If we go back to Holberg's day we shall meet with a poster of 1726, which reads that during the performance of "the 11th of June" there will appear between acts "one of the best singers and dancers from the opera in Stockholm."[1] If we pursue the inquiry as far back as the Middle Ages, we shall find singing and dancing closely linked together; in Iceland, in fact, the term "ballad" signified a dance. For instance, Earl Gissur sang the *dance* "My sorrows are heavier than lead," and a man by the name of Berg was called "Dancing Berg," doubtless because he composed satirical ballads. Even in the word "ballade" we have an indication of its former connection with the dance.

The Icelandic sagas, which allude to so many amusements, games, and festivals of Norse antiquity, say not a word about the dance. It is not till the eleventh and twelfth centuries that we hear the dance at all commonly spoken of. At this period, however, as stated above, the dance meant also a popular ballad or a satirical poem, whose metrical form was identical with that of the Danish popular ballads.

I. The Nature of the Dance

It must now be our task to inquire into the meaning of the term "dance" as understood in those times, and whether or not we dare apply our modern conception of the term to the dance of our forefathers. The answer must evidently be "No"; the difference is too striking. The manner of

[1] Th. Overskou, Den danske Skueplads, I, 228; II, 400.

dancing with which we are generally familiar, namely, that of couples, who glide over the floor, whirling each other around more or less rapidly, belongs to a far later time. We can learn something of the period when the new fashion of dancing came into vogue from a study of the conditions existing in Germany. But I direct especial attention to "Chronik des Landes Dithmarschen," an account written in 1598 by the pastor Köster, called Neocorus. Here he relates that formerly the inhabitants of Ditmarsh had two styles of dancing, namely, "Trymmekendans," which was characterized by certain steps and imitative gestures (*Trymmeke* means a person with nice, affected ways), and a leaping or hopping dance. Finally, however, there was introduced from abroad about the time of the Ditmarsh wars (1559) "eine sonderlike Manere," according to which people danced in couples.[1] This mode of dancing, however, had come up from the South to other countries somewhat earlier than in the case of Ditmarsh.[2] Perhaps it was the appearance of this new fashion that gave rise to the following admonition, recorded in a book entitled "The Wreath of Honor of all Virtuous, Christian Maidens," which came out toward the close of the sixteenth century: "That they engage in a short, modest, and honest dance, doing the steps after one another in decency and order, without undue swinging and other indecorum."[3]

This older style of dancing brought to our notice in the Ditmarsh chronicle we can very clearly identify first and

[1] Johann Adolfi (called Neocorus), Chronik des Landes Dithmarschen, ed. by F. C. Dahlmann, I, 177 ff. [2] Böhme, Tanz, I, 49 ff.

[3] Fol. VII; cf. O. Nielsen, Copenhagen's Diplomatarium, VI, 157; Troels Lund, Danmarks og Norges Historie i det 16. Aarh., VI, 169.

foremost with the help of our popular ballads. Thus runs the ballad of "Proud Elselille" (No. 220):

> Midsummer night upon the sward,
> Knights and squires were standing guard.
>
> In the grove a knightly dance they tread
> With torches and garlands of roses red.
>
> In sable and marten before them all,
> Dances Sir Iver, the noblest of all.
>
> To the king in his tower strong
> Floats the noise of the dancing throng.
>
> "Who is yon knight that leads the dance,
> And louder than all the song he chants?"

Shortly afterwards the king enters the dance by the side of Sir Iver. From this ballad it appears that one walks the dance, that one steps it, that it takes place in the grove, that one person leads another by the hand, and that the whole is directed by a leader. Or we may cite "Hagen's Dance" (No. 465):

> The king he sits in Ribe,
> Quaffing the wine;
> He summons all his Danish knights
> Each to his home.
> *So stately dances Hagen.*
>
> "Stand up, stand up, my merry men
> And knights so keen;
> And step for me a beggar-dance
> In the meadows green!"
> *So stately dances Hagen.*
>
> Now longs the king himself
> To step the dance;
> The hero Hagen follows after,
> For them the song he chants.
> *So stately dances Hagen.*

Or "Knight Stig's Wedding" (No. 76):

> F 18. Gaily the maidens join in the dance,
> Each with crowns of roses and garlands.
>
> 19. There dances Sir Stig as light as a wand,
> With a silver cup in his white hand.

Here also the dance is held out of doors, in the grove, in the green meadows (that is, on the lawns), and always one "steps" the dance. So the refrain runs in No. 189: "She stepped so stately," and in No. 261:

> It was Mettelil, the count's daughter,
> She stepped the dance for them.

Among the Scandinavian peasants dancing in the open air is still kept up. In confirmation of this reads the account written by Jonas Stolt, a village shoemaker, setting forth the conditions existing in the region about Kalmar in 1820: "On summer evenings a dance was held on the grass-plots of the court-yards and on Sunday afternoons on the bridges that lead over the river" (p. 114).

The men can carry a cup, a ring, or a staff; the women a garland, or, according to ballads Nos. 364, 432, "she dances with mirror and wreaths of roses." In Germany it is said that the maidens dance with mirrors suspended coquettishly from a ribbon. Here, furthermore, the garland is most intimately associated with the dance, just as to-day it is used for cotillion favors and bouquets. Such may well have been the case in Denmark. In "The Maiden's Defense of Honor" (No. 189) occur the lines:

> 6. Fair Ingelil came to Thure's isle,
> Where ladies the time in dance beguile.
>
> 7. Lords and knights began the dance,
> Proud Ingelil sat still and wove garlands.

8. Then spake Sir Thure by the salt sea-strand:
"For whom do you weave those gay garlands?"

9. "I weave this garland for no other man
Than him, my brother, the best in the land."

We read in Article 32 of the statutes of a guild in Ny-Larsker on Bornholm (1599) that it was enjoined on all men and boys, members and guests, to be present in the barn while the preliminary dance was going on and the garlands were being distributed. He who declined the responsibility of the garland was fined one keg of beer. And in Articles 37, 38 of the same statutes we read that virtuous gentlewomen and modest girls were free to choose the May-king while the garlands were receiving their decorations of pretty herbs. Here, too, the member or guest who refused the garland made by honest folk, when proffered by the May-king, and in the struggle happened to tear it, had to pay for his obstinacy one keg of beer (The New Royal Collection, No. 399, Fol. C).

We can corroborate what we know of the old style of dancing by examining the pictorial illustrations of the dances performed by the nobility during the Middle Ages. A fresco painting from the fourteenth century in the church at Örslev on Skjelskör depicts a row of dancing men and women, led by a "foredancer," who directs those taking part with lively and emphatic gestures of his left hand, while in his right he carries a ring or some other object.[1] Some frescoes in Runkelstein Castle in the Tyrol represent a long chain of couples dancing under the trees in the garden. At their head dances a woman, followed by a

[1] For picture see *Aarböger for nord. Oldk.*, 1888, p. 135, and *Tidsskrift for Kunstindustrie*, 1890, Vol. I.

man clad in a thick doublet and wearing peaked shoes, holding his right hand behind him; he in turn leads with graceful steps the woman next to him.[1]

Similar to these dances thus portrayed we may conceive the dances in Denmark to have been. Besides these more decorous dances with tripping steps, there is found another, which the peasantry especially affect, characterized by leaping steps and wilder movements. At the memorable wedding of Solenta, sister of Iver Blaa, and Count Gunzelin (No. 16), which fell out so merrily and boisterously, there were present all those famous heroes, Vidrik Verlandsön, Didrik of Bern, Holger Danske, Master Hildebrand, Sivard Snarensvend, and Langben Risker. But the bride herself was an imposing figure:

> Six whole oxen she consumed,
> And five full flitches of bacon,
> And when the hiccoughs put an end to her bout,
> Seven barrels of beer she had taken.
>
> The rank began to leap and frolic (*Skrikke-Rei*)
> From Ribe to the bay of Sli;
> The smallest warrior in the dance
> Towered well five ells above the knee.
>
> Even the table and the benches danced,
> And fire flew from the hats;
> Out then ran the warriors good:
> "Now help us, Mother Scratch!"

Rei means "rank," "a row," "a train of followers" (cf. Asgaards-Reien, that is, Odin's Hunt, Arthur's Chase), and *Hoppelrei* was the name given in Germany to a dance which used to be popular with the peasants, who danced

[1] Böhme, Tanz, pp. 31, 320.

it "as if they would fly." On the whole, *den Reihen springen* corresponds to *den Tanz treten*. *Skrikke* means "to leap" or "gambol like a calf or kid." It may well be said, therefore, to have been a remarkable dance in which the merry revelers indulged.

Emphatic gestures were characteristic of even the more sedate dances. This we can gather from pictures, which almost invariably represent the arms, legs, and feet smartly extended and the head bent low, often combined with certain contortions of the body. At times the movements seem to overstep the bounds of grace. In the church at Hecklingen, Saxony, there is portrayed an angel dancing with the tips of the toes turned out on the right foot, and turned in on the left so that when the legs crossed the toes of both feet met. In several miniatures from a manuscript of Heinrich von Stretlingen ladies are represented with breasts and waists extended well forward, heads and arms sharply inclined, legs and feet forming acute angles, and the fingers spread widely apart and bent in various directions. In the church of St. Sernin in Toulouse is a picture of Salome, the daughter of Herodias, dancing with a bell in her hand before Herod Antipas; the right foot executes a curious step with the toes bent backward to the right.[1]

I am in some doubt, however, just how reliable to regard the evidence offered by these last mentioned pictures. The perplexing footboard on which several figures stand, together with the defective ability of the artist, however, may

[1] Puttrich, Denkmale der Baukunst in Sachsen, I, table 32. See Von der Hagen, Bildersaal, tables 16, 22, 39, 46; Böhme, Tanz, pp. 33 ff.; Schultz, Das höfische Leben, 2d ed., I, 550 ff.

explain away some of the oddities. But thus much is certain, that during the dance a very strong play of feature was called into action. In the Icelandic Vikivaki dance the participants stood on the right foot and swayed the upper part of the body to and fro. An account from East Friesland (1691) tells of an old dance, common among the peasantry, which was performed by two men and two women, accompanied by set movements of the arms, hands, legs, and head; distinct movements and gestures, in fact, existed for all the limbs, at the expense, it may be added, of much perspiration. The men struck their hands smartly together, first behind their backs, then in front of their legs, while the women went through the same motions after them. Their most individual postures they assumed toward the close of the singing, which was slow and mournful.[1]

Those were famous dances that were performed toward the close of the Middle Ages with so much dignity and splendor by the patrician families of South Germany. When King Christian I, in his travels abroad in 1474, made a stay in Augsburg, the families of the nobility held a dance in his honor, which seems to have been marked by a becoming union of mirth and gravity. As the old account reads:[2] "For the pleasure of the King of Denmark and at the wish of the Kaiser there was held soon after a merry dance, which was carried out with great pomp and dignity in the usual dance hall, lasting almost four hours, which the King mentioned as having witnessed with especial delight."

[1] Böhme, Tanz, p. 51.
[2] Werlich, Chronica von Augspurg (1595), II, 229.

A dance often spoken of in the ballads is the "Beggar-dance" (see Vol. II, 59, st. 8; Vol. III, 166, sts. 13, 27; Vol. IV, 365, 455, st. 1). In "Proud Signild and Queen Sophie" (No. 129) occur the lines:

> 27. When to the castle gate she chanced,
> She saw them dancing the beggar-dance.
>
> 28. Twice they danced the dance around,
> The queen stood gazing at her spell-bound.
>
> 29. Sad at heart then was the queen
> When Signelil danced by the side of the king.

From this ballad it appears to have been a figure dance. In Germany there was found a "Bettlertanz," in which all the couples formed a circle while dancing, with one couple in the middle, who assumed various attitudes and enacted a scene, somewhat perhaps after the style of the Polish "Going a-begging." In every instance song accompanied this dance, according to the old beggar ballad. This ballad treats of the same theme as the Danish drama "Karrig Niding" ("The Miserly Scoundrel"), in which the beggar, during the miser's absence, is received most courteously by the housewife and installed with all the privileges of the husband. The audacity inherent in the theme doubtless affected the dance, which became so hilarious that in 1580 it was forbidden by decree in the Electorate of Saxony.[1] The Danish beggar-dance must certainly have been identical with this. It is also called the "Beggars' dance" (and the "Begging-dance"), a name that is derived

[1] Böhme, Tanz, pp. 57, 103, 116. The German song has been printed by Birket Smith, Rauch's Plays, pp. lxxxii ff.

from *Bedere*, — a beggar, — which the old translators of the Bible rendered as "needy men" or "mendicants." The name "mendicants" was also applied to those inmates of the monasteries who journeyed about collecting the benefactions (see Molbech's and Kalkar's dictionaries). Our own time has preserved three distinct references to this term in the double refrain of "Peder and Malfred" (No. 278):

> Step ye well!
> Step and beg, an ye will!

or,

> Step up and beg, an ye will!

There seems to be good ground for believing that the refrain in its original form was an animating shout:

> Step up, beggar, an ye will!

One gets the impression that in Denmark also this dance was relegated to the more boisterous spirits. Perhaps it was a kiss that was requested; for that a kiss could be exchanged during the dance is scarcely to be questioned. In this respect the Germans never overstepped the bounds of propriety.[1]

In "The Rape of the Venedian King" (No. 240) there is named another dance:

> 1. So merrily goes the beggar-dance
> On the plain outside the wall;
> Maidens are stepping the luck-dance (*Lykke-Dans*),
> And knights are playing ball.

This last dance I am not acquainted with.

[1] Böhme, Tanz, index.

As is well known, the old dances are still kept up among the Faroe islanders. Men and women take each other by the hand and form a circle. The movement consists simply of taking three regular steps to the left, then, after balancing a little, bringing the right over against the left and kicking the left out, etc. Most frequently it is danced slowly and solemnly; but the youthful spirits of the circle often indulge in a faster step, leaping up in the air and raising their hands above their heads. It can also be executed in a lively, exuberant fashion. In the Hebrides, where they dance faster than in other places, is found a round dance which is taken at a very rapid tempo. This dance is considered to be their oldest. The participants form the usual circle. During the singing of the strophe they either remain in their places or dance back; but during the refrain they rush quickly forward. Throughout the dance the leader's song is heard above that of the others. The Faroe islanders make manifest, on the whole, that they are not indifferent to the content of the song; but that by their looks and gestures they endeavor to express the varying nature of the subject matter.[1]

All the above conditions must be borne in mind when we are considering our popular ballads. Beyond all doubt the style of dancing has influenced the form of the ballads, and vice versa. Moreover, that the ballads have been utilized by the dance does not follow merely from what has been stated above. Individual ballads themselves, so to speak, mention that they were danced to.

[1] Lyngbye, Færöiske Quæder, pp. 8 ff.; *Antiquarisk Tidsskrift*, 1846–1848, p. 259; 1849–1851, p. 279; N. Winther, Færöernes Oldtidshistorie, pp. 442 ff.

For example, note the refrain in "The Skipper and the Maid" (No. 241):

> Step lightly o'er the green plain —
> The maid must follow me;

and in "The Wounded Maiden" (No. 244):

> Step up boldly, young knight!
> Honor the maidens in the dance.

It must not be asserted, however, that the ballads served no other end than that of accompaniment to the dance; naturally they could be sung like any other song, and, to judge from several refrains, we must even think of people singing them while out riding or rowing.

So much is certain: the subject matter never interfered with the use of the ballads in the dance. To this the historical ballads, for example, testify. We know that the inhabitants of the Faroes danced to the ballad of "King Hans' Wedding" ("King Hans he sits in Copenhagen"), and the pastor Köster says that the inhabitants of Ditmarsh danced to a song on the Danish defeat at Hemmingsted. In the Faroes people danced to ballads that were religious in content, and in the preceding century even the clergy were seen in their ecclesiastical robes taking part in a dance, on such occasions as weddings, to the accompaniment of ballads like the "Ballad of Isaac" ("Ye noble bridal pair, give heed"), which was a psalm from the Book of Psalms; or the "Ballad of Susanna," which treated of Daniel and Susanna. In 1818 the pastor Lyngbye saw the congregation assemble in the churchyard and there carry on a pantomimic dance to an old mythological ballad — "Grane bore the gold from the heath."

At Danish manses solemn dances were permitted to the music of the Psalms of David.[1]

It goes without saying that erotic ballads took their rise in the dance. As far as satirical ballads are concerned, we know that in the Faroes lampooning ballads were danced to, and that he who was the subject of the ballad and the victim of the satire had to dance into the bargain, for he was seized by two stout men and held fast in line by either hand until the ballad came to an end.[2] In Bavaria there exists the so-called "Schnada-hüpfl" (*schnada* means "to babble," "to tralala"), which consists of a four-line stanza with one or two rimes, sung to well known melodies, and often composed offhand by the dancers. While these "Schnada-hüpfl" are often erotic, they are especially satirical. Two fellows seem to find amusement, for example, in endeavoring to outsatirize each other, being privileged in this sport, for the purpose of ridicule, to draw upon the faults and foibles of the whole valley side.[3]

This variety of petty satirical verse has found a home here in Denmark as well; mention of this fact is made in the sagas (see p. 10 above). An interesting specimen of such an improvised satirical ballad, which was danced to by those who composed it, is to be found in ballad No. 366. Here follows the greater portion of this ballad:

"All day my heart is heavy
With many a sigh and groan;
All because of those rich wooers,
Sir Lave's sons from Lund.
All day my heart is heavy!

[1] Vilhelm Bang, Præstegaardsliv, p. 272.

[2] *Skand. Litt. Selsk. Skrifter*, ser. 12–13, p. 265; Lyngbye, Færöiske Quæder, p. 14.

[3] Böhme, Tanz, p. 239.

"Stand up, stand up, my maidens all,
And dance for me a space;
And sing for me a ballad
About the sons of Lave's race!

"And sing for me a ballad,
And this your song shall be:
All how they wait outside my gate,
And no answer get from me.

"The first is hight Sir Ove,
The second Sir Eskel Hawk;
They 've served so long at the court of the king,
They stand neither heat nor smoke.

"The third is hight Sir Magnus,
A learned clerk is he;
There lies a jewel hid in my chest
Is worth more than all three."

Nought else thought Elselille
Than they two were alone;
But by stood Sir Magnus
And listened till she was done.

It was then Sir Magnus
He stepped within the door;
It was young Elselille,
Her face deep blushes bore.

"Stand up, stand up, my comely young men,
And dance with me a space;
And we ourselves shall sing a ballad
About the sons of Lave's race.

"Sing for me a ballad,
And sing it so for me:
They ride to proud Elselille's gate
And good the answer will be.

"The first is hight Sir Ove,
The second Sir Eskel Hawk;
They 've served so long at the court of the king
They stand both heat and smoke.

"The third is hight Sir Magnus,
A learned clerk is he;
There lies a jewel in the maiden's chest
Is worth more than we three!"

"Hear me now, Sir Magnus,
With your chaffing now let be;
Meet me the morn at the church door
And plight your vows to me."

Up then stood Sir Magnus
And leaned him on his sword;
"Men know well, proud Elselille,
The feast is more than you are worth."

He lifted up young Elselille
And set her upon his horse,
He led her out to the wild greenwood,
Where thick grow the broom and gorse.

. . . .

This is the reward proud Elselille got
For her scornful, bitter word:
For eight long years she sat a widow
Alone at her own board.

When eight years had come and gone,
He remembered honor and right;
He rode out to her father's gate
And wooed her for his heart's delight.
All day my heart is heavy!

To avoid misunderstanding, let me add in conclusion that while in by far the greatest number of cases one danced to the singing of ballads, yet instrumental music was also made use of. The simplest form of accompaniment was undoubtedly that of the drum alone. An account from 1570,[1] treating of the shopmen's guild in Randers, preserves the regulation that the drummer must not beat his drum longer than the master of the corporation allows. The drum was frequently heard also in the guilds of the peasants. In Article 32 of the statutes of a guild in Ny-Larsker on Bornholm (1599) there is a rule that "no one must be found playing the drum in our guild except our appointed drummer, unless the master of the corporation gives his consent thereto."

Further information on this point can be gained from a consideration of the "players" (*jongleurs*). These corresponded to the present-day musicians, and often in olden times most closely to ale-house fiddlers and jugglers. The "player" of the earliest day was an individual more or less defenseless and subject to ridicule, concerning whom the laws made various amusing provisions. Later he seems to have commanded more respect; at any rate, he is often mentioned in ballads as being attendant on weddings and other festivals. "No gold was grudged the player" is a standing ballad formula. There certainly can be no doubt that singing was one of his accomplishments. On the whole, his task was to furnish amusement, and listening to music was such a favorite recreation that singing and song naturally came under his jurisdiction. That the verb "to play" can mean "to sing" as well is evident from the expression "they played in the Danish tongue," and there is mention in the Norse Didrik saga of a "player" who sang, plucked the harp strings, and played the fiddle. In

[1] Stadfeldt, Randers, p. 88.

a church in Upland there is a picture of a fool singing to the accompaniment of a zither he is playing. Archbishop Johannes Magni (ob. 1544) relates that heroic ballads were sung to the music of pipes.[1] It is scarcely probable that the "player" took any part in the dancing; at least it would depend on the esteem in which he was held. Peder Laale, however, has the proverb: "The player dances willingly for pay." Very possibly the capers of the juggler were what he had in mind here.

From all this evidence it appears that the ballad, when not danced to, could be accompanied by stringed instruments, as was indeed the custom in other lands. In witness of this run the following stanzas from "Hagen's Dance" (No. 465):

Then awoke the Danish queen,
As in her tower she lay:
"Which one of my maidens
On the harp doth play?"

"There is no one of your maidens
That on the harp doth play;
It is the hero Hagen
Who sings so gay."

II. How the Ballad and the Dance began

I have striven to detail thus explicitly the old style of dancing and the use of the ballad in the dance, because I shall constantly need to refer to these features in the investigations that follow. And here I shall dispose of a single question at once.

[1] Axel Olrik, in Mindre Afhandlinger, published by the Philol.-Histor. Samfund, pp. 74 ff., 265 ff.; Schück, Svensk Literaturhistoria, pp. 111 ff.

How did the dance begin? In Ditmarsh, according to Neocorus, it was started by a leader of the song, who stepped out in front of the others, holding a drinking cup in his hand. After he had sung a verse, all those assembled repeated it. He then sang another, which was likewise repeated. At this point another sprang forward, who as leader assumed charge of the dance. Taking his hat in his hand, he danced sedately around the room, at the same time urging the others to join in and arrange themselves in line. The leader kept time with the song, and the other dancers kept time with the leader. The latter was thus enabled to direct as many as two hundred dancers.

Manifestly the same thing is set forth in our popular ballads:

> "Who is yon knight that leads the dance,
> And louder than all the song he chants?"

The leader of the dance must carry a drinking cup, a beaker, or a glass in his hand. This feature still survives in those localities where the "Schnada-hüpfl" is danced; and in old German accounts we often read of how the "foredancer" would dance around with a bowl or cup on his head.[1] (The leader of the dance—or "foredancer"—is the one who begins the dance and exhorts the others to take part; he is also the one who later directs it.) We have something similar to this in the North. At a betrothal in Christiania in 1637, it is said that the parish priest, Master Kjeld Stub, "danced in public with a glass in his hand and led the dance"; but the burgomaster, Laurids Ruus, jumping up from his seat, picked out a partner and, holding a glass in his hand, ran against

[1] Böhme, Tanz, p. 27.

Master Kjeld in such a way as to obstruct and break up the dance. On the fifteenth of May of the same year a royal mandate was issued to the bishops in which the priests were admonished to lead a more Christian life, and to abstain from drunkenness and, among other things, "from dancing with a glass in the hand and such worldly indecencies."[1]

Let us now see whether our ballads do not make some reference to the beginning of the dance. It must be borne in mind that our popular ballads are not lyrical in nature, nor do they voice the usual expressions of the singer's emotions. This subject I shall discuss more fully later on; here I venture to assume the general character of the ballads to be already known: namely, that they contain, not an expression of lyrical, subjective feeling, but merely an epical narration of events. Nevertheless we find as a general rule in the first stanza of a ballad a lyrical outburst; as, for instance, in "The Forced Consent" (No. 75):

B 1. Have mercy, O Lord, our grief is deep,
And sorrow reigns in our breast;
He who bears a secret sorrow,
His heart is ill at rest.
Have mercy, O Lord, our grief is deep.

2. Winters fully five Sir Peter
Proud Mettelille did woo;
But ever she put off her answer,
Though yearly he did sue.
Have mercy, O Lord, our grief is deep.

[1] *Theologisk Tidsskrift*, published by Caspari and several others, II, 463; Ketilson, Forordninger for Island, II, 414.

As we see here, the narrative is not taken up until the second stanza, or even until the third, as in "King Didrik in Birtingsland" (No. 8):

1. The king rules over the castle tower,
   And lords it over land,
   And many a gallant champion leads
   All armed and sword in hand.
   While the king rules over the castle tower.

2. Then let the peasant till his farm,
   His horse the trooper guide,
   The king of Denmark, he alone,
   O'er fort and tower preside.
   While the king rules over the castle tower.

3. King Didrik sits in Brattingsbord,
   Looks over land and sea;
   "I know not one in all this world
   Dares match himself with me."

(From Prior's "Danish Ballads.")

In this ballad the story begins with the third stanza and has nothing to do with the king of Denmark; on the contrary, it deals with Didrik and other champions. These preliminary stanzas constitute an introduction which strikes the keynote, and at the same time, in both of the examples quoted above, give rise to the refrain.[1] One more case may be cited from "The Valraven" (No. 60):

The raven wings his flight by night,
He dares not stir by day;
Ill luck befalls the wretched wight
When good luck says him nay.
The raven wings his flight by night.

[1] Scattered throughout his work, as well as in the preface to Part III, will be found Grundtvig's opinions on the subject of ballad burdens.

The maiden stands on her tower high
And gazes o'er land and sea;
She sees the wild Valraven winging
His way o'er mountain-side and lea.
The raven wings his flight by night.

Here again it is manifest that the first stanza is lyrical in feeling and gives shape to the refrain.

But there is still more to be gathered from ballad refrains. The ballad of "King Birger's Sister Bengta" (No. 155) begins:

I dare not ride by the light of day;
I suffer grief and pain for a maiden proud and gay,
They know my war array.

It was young Sir Laurids,
Had plighted his vows to his love so dear;
She spent her days in a cloister cell,
And heavy sorrow lay him near.
They know my war array.

In the first stanza it is "I" that speaks, who must be identical with Sir Laurids, the knight that dares not ride out by day because he is pursued and his shield too well known. But in the remainder of the ballad the "I" has completely disappeared, and the story is related in the customary third person. Furthermore it will be noted that the first stanza or refrain has an entirely different meter from that of the ballad proper. This has often escaped the notice of old collectors and editors, who, considering the verse to be defective, have made alterations in it. Accordingly Peder Syv has dressed up the foregoing lines into the following beautiful version!

I will not ride by day
Through field and through forest;
I suffer for a proud young maiden
Both grief and pain the sorest.

As another example may be cited the following from "Proud Signild and Queen Sophie" (No. 129):

1. The lyke-wake holds to-night,
He wakes whoever will;
Proud Signelil wakes alone out in the forest green.

2. Proud Signelil hasted to her mother and spake:
—*He wakes whoever will*—
"May I to-night attend the wake?"
—*Proud Signelil wakes alone out in the forest green.*

From "King Hakon's Death" (No. 142):

It now has come
What long ago was foretold
Of Hakon, the holy king;
Norway a captive he holds.

From "Marsk Stig's Daughter" (No. 146):

The king sits in Kollen,
—*Hey! the rose and sweet flowers!*
The king's two daughters away were stolen.
—*Nor spake they a word of their native towers.*

The eldest took the youngest by the hand,
And so they journeyed to King Sifrid's land.

Stanza one of "The Betrothed in the Grave" (No. 90) supplies an introduction if not a refrain:

1. Three maidens sat in their bower,
Two were plaiting gold;
The third bewailed her lover dead,
Lay buried beneath the mould.
For she had plighted her vows to the knight.

2. It was the rich Sir Aage,
He rode by the salt sea strand;
He wooed and won young Elselille,
The fairest may in the land.
For she had plighted her vows to the knight.

Here the first stanza has nothing whatever to do with the narrative, which is taken up at the second; it is simply an introduction which at the outset pictures the sorrowing maiden who was affianced to the rich young knight.

We could point out this circumstance in a score of ballads.[1] It is true that this is a small number among so many hundreds. But we may rest assured that many ballads originally possessed such a stanza, which in the course of time has gone astray because one no longer understood that it was a part of the ballad, or which has undergone alteration to fit the usual verse form. In every case this opening stanza indicates clearly how the ballad used to be rendered. Between the introductory and the following stanzas there exists a marked contrast, which appears externally in the different rhythm of the two parts, and internally in the different nature of the subject matter. The introductory stanza is often lyrical or general in content and suggests the mood; the main body of the ballad is narrative. If the first stanza thus differs from those that follow, on the other hand, it stands in the closest relation to the refrain of the ballad; it even gives up one of its lines to the latter, or may be evolved therefrom. The song or the dance begins in this fashion: the singer steps forth, holding some silver vessel in his hand; he strikes up the tune and bids the others to participate,

[1] Nos. 8, 32, 60, 67, 75, 83, 129, 132, 138, 155, 196, 202, 249, 261, and several unpublished ballads.

the proceeding reminding us somewhat of the well-known first thirty-five bars of Weber's "Invitation to the Dance." The mood and tune which he has set afloat, and which is naturally identical with that of the ballad proper, is maintained throughout by means of the constantly repeated refrain.

In case a ballad contains no such introductory verse, it invariably begins with the refrain. It is not likely that the singer took up at once the narrative. This we can infer from the fact that the oldest manuscript copy of any heroic ballad in our possession — "The Knight transformed into a Hart" (No. 67) — begins as follows:

I spent the live-long night dreaming of a maiden.
It was Sir Peter,
He bade his retainers run:
"Could ye to proud Ose-lille
And get me speech right soon?"
I spent the live-long night dreaming of a maiden.

There is found also another ballad copy (Unpublished No. 156) which has the refrain placed at the beginning:

I know a maiden in our land, she never leaves my fancy.

In the music to the Faroese "Song of Sigurd" (Lyngbye's "Færöiske Quæder"), the refrain is likewise found at the beginning, a feature that is in accord with the practice of the islanders of always singing the refrain first, for it determined the tempo of the dance. The circumstance that nearly all ballad versions place the refrain after the first stanza or at the end of the ballad arises from the fact that here in every case was its proper place.[1]

[1] Cf. also Grundtvig's statement to P. G. Thorsen, Om Runernes Brug til Skrift udenfor det monumentale, p. 53.

CHAPTER III

THE *I*

Are the popular ballads lyrical? That these songs do not voice the emotions of the poet himself admits of no question; on the other hand, it can hardly be denied that they are expressive to the highest degree of the inner, emotional life. A consideration of their subject matter makes evident that the ballads are nothing more than tales which recount incident and action, either past or present. A consideration of their spirit, however, reveals to us that it is not mere accident which omits all mention of the poet's name and forces the singer to remain in the background. And however much the ballad may deal with strength and heroic deed, with faith and love, it never refers to these attributes and virtues as ideas and conceptions, but it always bodies forth such abstractions in the plastic figures of the actors. Accordingly all subjectivity is eliminated, the objectivity of the narrative forbids an alliance with the thoughts and impulses of the poet himself. Emotion never gets the upper hand of narration; the poet is not given to restless moods, nor does he linger over his own sorrows. The imagination of the audience is concerned with action — and yet the ballad always awakens a peculiar feeling, a distinctive mood. This was precisely the intention of the narrative. But it brings this about so unobtrusively that we fail to note the design, and consequently we are aware of no discord. Thus far the lyric and the epic blend together in the ballad; and even a didactic, a corrective, an admonitory tone may insensibly find its way into the ballad's epic mode of narration. No matter how great the variety, how numerous the moods and tones, the chords and harmonies that characterize our ballads, individually they bear no impress of any one poet. The artist is here responsible for nothing. It is as if emotion had not yet learned to express itself without the aid of narration. Only at a later date did the lyric element diffuse itself through the ballads. In accordance with the demands of the prevailing taste, lyrical variations were woven into certain ballads as ornaments; they were even shifted from ballad to ballad. Gradually there arose erotic, satiric, didactic, and allegorical ballads, — but at this point we are wholly within the period of the Reformation, the period of the Renaissance in the North.

The distinctive qualities of our ballads can be thrown into clearer relief if we institute a comparison with the medieval folk songs of Germany. In going through one of the many collections of these songs, we shall meet with such a love song as the following, which is older than 1400:

> All mein Gedenken, die ich han,
> die sind bei Dir,
> Du auserwählter einger Trost
> bleib stets bei mir. . . .

or this one, which antedates 1500:

> Ach hertzigs Hertz,
> mein Schmertz
> erkennen thu!
> Ich hab kein Ruh
> nach Dir steht mein Verlangen. . . .

On the whole, some of the most beautiful flowers of German folk poetry of the Middle Ages are to be found in these love songs. The following charming little verse came into being as early as the twelfth century:[1]

> Du bist min, ich bin din,
> des soltu gewis sin.
> Du bist beslozzen
> in minen herzen;
> verloren ist das sluzzelin:
> du muost immer dar inne sin.

There likewise belongs to this period a great variety of *Tagelieder*, in which lovers give utterance to their grief at having to part when day breaks upon them; also *Wächterlieder*, of similar nature, in which the watchman, seeing daylight at hand, warns the lovers that it is time to part:

> Wohlauf, Wohlauf, mit lauter Stimm
> thut uns der Wächter singen.

These *Tagelieder* were probably original with the Minnesingers; but by the thirteenth century they had made their way into the ranks of the populace, where they became the property of all classes and passed from hand to hand. Furthermore we find songs dealing with nature, such as the following *dance* at the appearance of the first violet, which is from the fourteenth or the fifteenth century:

> Der Meye, der Meye
> bringt uns der Blümlein viel. . . .

and the following, which antedates 1467:

> Es ist ein Schnee gefallen,
> und es ist doch nit Zeit,
> man wirft mich mit dem Ballen,
> der Weg ist mir verschneit.

[1] Gödeke, Grundrisz z. Geschichte d. d. Dichtung, 2d ed., I, 48.

Other songs that are met with are farewell songs, wanderers' songs, riddle songs, wager songs, wishing songs, lansquenet, knight, and soldier songs, vocation songs, such as the fliting song between a nobleman and a peasant (thirteenth century), a student song from 1454:

> ich weisz ein frisch Geschlechte,
> das sind die Burschenknechte (*Burs*, i.e. college)
> ihr Orden steht also:
> sie leben ohne Sorge
> den Abend und den Morgen
> sie sind gar stätclich froh. . . .

and finally spiritual songs and historical ballads.[1]

For parallels to the greater part of what is cited above one will search in vain our great store of ballad poetry of the Middle Ages. For us lyric poetry in its entirety was perfected abroad; at least no evidence to the contrary has come down to us. On the other hand, we possess an extensive collection of songs concerning heroes, or, more properly, "heroic ballads," while Germany can lay claim to very few. Nor can the latter country point to any comprehensive body of songs dealing with magic, or to any wide range of love ballads.[2] The North has long been the

[1] During the war which has been waged in Germany the past few years over the oldest popular poetry and its relation to "die höfische Dichtung" (which had its origin in the twelfth century), it has been admitted by all that there existed previous to the Minnesingers a folk poetry with a subjective, lyrical stamp. On the other hand, it is not generally agreed whether this folk poetry had a very great acceptation, and the question has arisen, Did this folk poetry furnish a model for the Minnesongs, or did the latter evolve directly from the folk poetry? See *Zeit. f. d. Altertum*, XXVII, 343 ff., XXIX, 121 ff., XXXIV, 146 ff.; *Zeit. f. d. Philologie*, XIX, 440 ff.; *Germania*, XXXIV, 1 ff.

[2] Talvj (Mrs. Robinson), Charakteristik der Volkslieder, pp. 389 ff.; Böhme, Altdeutsches Liederbuch, pp. xxviii ff.

home, as it were, of a serious, gloomy, often demoniacal, species of poetry, which refused to be deposed by the culture of the South or by the spirit of Christianity. Notwithstanding the large number of popular songs of a ballad or romantic nature that is native to Germany, Goethe was not wrong in his observation that this kind of poetry would not have flourished with his German forefathers.[1]

In the Danish ballads we find more or less prominent an erotic element, a moral questioning, a sentiment for nature; but in an objective sense something always happens, action is always present. With the riddle songs of Germany mentioned above, we might well compare what is of a similar nature in the Icelandic riddle poems "Vafþrudnismál," "Alvíssmál," "Fjölsvinnsmál," and Hervor's and Heidrek's sagas. In the ballad of "Svend Vonved" (No. 18) we see also a series of riddles propounded and solved; but, mind you, as a component part of the action. Though a large number of historical ballads have grown up on German soil, yet they all date from the conclusion of the Middle Ages. They differ from the Danish historical ballads, which are also considerable in number — over threescore — and, in addition, of the highest worth, in that they are more political, or inclined to talk politics, and hence composed from a definite standpoint and with a definite, practical end in view. It is also apparent that the subjective element is a prominent feature of the German ballads. Moreover, whereas the latter are short, very frequently being an outburst of only a couple of stanzas, or, at the most, of five or six, our ballads are long, seldom numbering fewer than twenty stanzas, and often many

[1] Böhme, Liederbuch, pp. xxviii ff.

more. And finally, whereas the German ballads generally sing of "ein Fräulein," "ein Jünglein," our ballads almost invariably attach specific names to the personages, such as "Little Kirstin," "Proud Elselil," "The Lady Mettelil," "Sir Ove," "Sir Peter," "Sir Lauge Stisön," etc.

How near we came to having erotic lyric poetry may be seen from the following poem, which dates from the Middle Ages.[1]

> Love's true worth with song and mirth
> I shall never cease to honor;
> A flower I know well whose name I'll ne'er tell,
> But praise I shall heap upon her.
> Of all others she beareth the prize,
> Prudent, faithful, virtuous, wise,
> And loyal beyond them all.
> As the stars all pale in the light of the sun,
> So pale before this peerless one
> Women from thorp and hall.
> Heia, heia,
> Would that she gave me a call.

Although the subject of this poem is not of earthly origin, although the maiden is not a mortal maiden, but the Virgin Mary, yet we should not hesitate to regard such a mode of expression as belonging to lyrics of love. Still a comparison between this poem and the manner of erotic expression to be found in our ballads cannot help but be instructive as showing how the more conscious and learned poet (in this case the monk Peder Reff Little) strikes a tone that is several octaves higher than that of the popular ballads, and adorns his execution with shakes and runs that are quite foreign to the naïve utterance of the simple ballad.

[1] Brandt and Helveg, Den danske Psalmedigtning, I, x.

With a few exceptions, the characteristics of the Danish ballads as sketched above hold good also of the other Scandinavian lands. With respect to Sweden, however, I may add that not only is her store of ballad material much less comprehensive than ours, but also that as early as the fifteenth century there began to appear both a more artificial kind of poetry, which could be ascribed to definite authors (for example, Bishop Thomas), and a ballad poetry that was political and satirical.[1]

Leaving the subject of general characteristics, we shall now seek to determine just how far the ballads are impersonal, just how far the poet and singer remain concealed.

I. A Ballad will I sing to you

Every one knows how the modern street songs begin with a verse which resembles very closely that which we meet with in ballad No. 86:

> A ballad will I sing to you,
> Which many a time I have sung,
> All how the lovely Lady Margaret
> Was loved by Sir Flores Bendiktsön.

Every one surely knows also that this is not the way our ballads usually begin. In this particular ballad of "Flores and Margaret," the above verse is found in a number of versions; but this ballad belongs to the so-called ballads of romance, "which give us a picture, not of the actual life of the Middle Ages, but of the taste." They could better be designated as echoes of the romances of chivalry. That

[1] Hyltén-Cavallius and G. Stephens, Sveriges historiska och politiska visor; H. Schück, Svensk Literaturhistoria, pp. 119 ff.

they date from a late period scarcely needs proof. I shall later touch more intimately upon their characteristics.

The same introductory verse appears in several copies of "The Cloister Robbery" (No. 476):

1. A ballad will I sing to you,
   Come listen to my song,
   All how the young Sir Morten
   A lovely maiden won.

2. Sir Morten wooed the maiden Lisbeth,
   Virtuous she was and fair;
   Much it vexed the knight's friends
   That she lacked riches rare.

In conformity with the general practice of ballad introductions, the oldest copy of the ballad begins with the second of the above stanzas. Accordingly the first stanza should be omitted on account of both its extreme plainness and the absence of traditional warrant.

We meet this verse again in a ballad whose age is known, namely, No. 172, "King Christian of Denmark in Sweden" (1520), which is preserved in a manuscript of 1550:

1. Come listen to my song,
   A ballad will I sing to you
   Of King Christian, the high-born prince,
   To whom all honor is due.

2. There one wrote MD (i.e. 1500)
   And also the eighteenth year,
   At Helsingborg in Skaane the king
   He bade his folk appear.

23. Attend to me yet awhile
    And hear what it is about;
    Good Friday they did them all to Upland,
    There a marvellous play fell out.

30. Praised be God, our Father in Heaven,
The Danish men the glory have won!
God give us rest in Heaven at last,
With Him to dwell forever at one.

Such stanzas as the above are downright jarring on the ear, so striking is their departure from the usual ballad style. All this harangue, this learning, this direct appeal to the audience is utterly foreign to the style of other ballads. Such stanzas are therefore extremely significant for showing how people composed about 1520, and how they did not compose in the Middle Ages. This species of introductory verse clearly belongs to a later date and to a pseudo-popular ballad literature.

It is invariably the case that such verses are late additions to ballads and not part and parcel of them originally. A similar verse is found in four out of the five copies of "Knud of Borg" (No. 195). The fact that it is not found in the Norse version led Landstad to remark that its presence in the Danish versions indicated "its recent origin." It turns up again in one of the five Icelandic versions, and also in ballad No. 212 (Abr.); but in the latter instance it is wanting in the oldest text and also in the Icelandic form.

Accordingly we may safely affirm that no genuine popular ballad begins with the announcement that the singer will now sing a ballad. Long ago an excellent critic made a similar observation in connection with the Swedish ballads. Talvj (pseudonym of Mrs. Robinson) stated that, as far as she knew, not a single Swedish, and only two Danish, ballads began in the manner popular with singers: "Ich will euch eine Weise singen," or

"Kommt all' im Kreis und hört mir zu," etc., as do so many English and German ballads.[1]

In this connection the concluding stanza and its peculiarity may be discussed. "Sir Stig's Wedding" (No. 76 B) has this ending:

> Safe and sound from hurt and harm,
> Sir Stig sleeps nightly on Regisse's arm.
>
> Stig Lilles' ballad is now at an end:
> May God in Heaven His grace us send!

It should be borne in mind that the first of the two stanzas just quoted forms the conclusion of a large number of our ballads. On the other hand, it is plain that the second is sheer fabrication; it occurs only in texts B and F, texts that were not recorded until 1600. In some of the other versions, which belong in part to manuscripts older than 1600, this last stanza is wanting. "Sir Bugge's Death" (No. 158) reads in conclusion:

> D 35. He ruled in Hald a year or so,
> More than this I cannot say.

This clumsy verse appears in only one of the four texts, and this text belongs neither to Karen Brahe's Folio Manuscript of 1550 nor to Sten Miller's manuscript of 1555. Text B of "King Birger's Sister Bengta" (No. 155) has this ending:

> 46. A ballad of these two
> I shall no longer sing,
> I trust they are at rest in Heaven
> And dwell with Heaven's King.

[1] Talvj, Versuch einer geschichtlichen Charakteristik der Volkslieder germanischer Nationen, p. 340.

This text is "an uncalled-for revision of a genuine copy," whereas "only A can lay claim to being genuine"; in A we do not find this stanza. All in all, these concluding stanzas of so unpoetic a character point to a late period.

To return to the subject of ballad openings. There are a number of ballads which would seem to introduce the *I* of the singer into the ballad somewhat indirectly. One will perceive, however, that this is merely a question of the same conditions which I have mentioned in connection with the refrain. In a remarkably guileless manner both the singer and the audience are ushered into the middle of events by a stanza such as the following from "German Gladensvend" (No. 33 B,C):

> 1. Our king and his young queen
> They sailed them over the sea,
> They found their ship held fast in the waves,
> And no breeze to set them free.

Here, however, the *our* is perhaps an interloper; a text equally old and another somewhat younger have "The king and queen of Denmark."

Again we read in "Find Lille" (No. 123):

> 3. He summons the king and all his men:
> Our fair young queen shall follow them.

Since this verse is found only in Magdalena Barnewitz's manuscript of 1650, and is, in addition, borrowed from "Sir Stig's Wedding" (No. 76):

> A 48. He summons the king and all his men:
> The Danish queen home must follow them,

its testimony is of little worth. In "The Knight transformed into a Bird" (No. 68) the first verse runs:

> There lives a maiden in our land
> Denies the suit of every man.

So in versions B and C, which belong to manuscripts of 1650 and after; whereas the other five versions, among them A of 1550, do away with *our*. In "Proud Elin's Revenge" (No. 209), from Karen Brahe's Folio Manuscript, is met this opening stanza:

1. It was the bold Sir Renold,
   Rode by the salt sea strand,
   He wooed Sir Bunde's daughter,
   The fairest in the land.

2. He wooed Sir Bunde's daughter,
   He led her home:
   The king and our archbishop
   With them did come.

This *our* seems to have intruded itself a number of times into late forms of ballads; its presence may be explained, however, by the desire of the singer to plunge his audience into the thick of events right at the beginning of the ballad. This is further borne out by the fact that in certain ballads we find the refrain closely bound up with the opening stanza. Compare the beginning of "Olaf and Asser White" (No. 202):

There stands without our castle-gate
Many a noble knight;
There are two maidens fair within,
Of love they think but light.

Sir Olaf and Sir Asser White
They bade their pages run:
"Do ye to those maidens fair,
And get us speech right soon."
There are two maidens fair within.

The refrain grows out of the first of these two stanzas.

Equally significant are the opening stanzas in version C (Karen Brahe's Folio Manuscript) of "The Forced Consent" (No. 75):

1. I heard a knight in my lady's bower,
   And they were seated at play,
   Of gold the table and red gold the dice,
   And he wooed the maiden gay.
No one can with her compare.

2. "Hear my suit my lady fair,
   Nor grace from me withhold;
   And you shall wear the scarlet fine
   And shoes of the ruddy gold."
No one can with her compare.

Thus it is reasonably certain that such an opening is merely an overture, an introduction to the tale which assures the audience, as it were, that he who sings and relates was an eye-witness of the event. Another form of ballad structure opens up with the refrain:

B 1. Have mercy, O Lord, our grief is deep
   And sorrow reigns in our breast;
   He who bears a secret sorrow,
   His heart is ill at rest.
Have mercy, O Lord, our grief is deep.

The examples cited above by no means conflict, as will be evident, with my former assertion that the personality of the singer never fills the foreground of the ballad; I have shown above that it also counts for nothing in this respect when the singer steps out in front and, with cup raised aloft, leads the song and dance. And it is in the same light that we are to regard his appearance here in the first stanza.

Meanwhile it will prove instructive to note the length to which the introductory portions of ballads attain. The "Combat with the Worm" (No. 24) begins as follows:

1. When that I was a little boy
   Herding the cattle and sheep;
   I found a little spotted snake
   Gliding through the grasses deep.
   And she bore the prize from all.

2. I lifted up the spotted snake,
   And wrapped it in a mantle around;
   To Helsing's daughter at Lundegaard
   I made a gift of what I found.

3. "A thousand thanks, my bonny boy,
   A thousand thanks for the gift you gave;
   I 'll ne'er forget what I owe to you
   If e'er a boon you crave."

4. She fed the snake the winter through
   And winters fully three, etc.

Only at this point begins the tale of the snake and the maiden; the peasant lad disappears completely from view. The snake grows up into a loathsome monster, which keeps the maiden a prisoner. Her father promises that he who slays the monster shall have his daughter to wife. The first to attempt the feat, Sivard Ingvordsön, fails outright. Then Peder Riboltsön presents himself, and, protected by a bull's hide smeared with tar, succeeds in killing the snake and winning the maiden.

Similar in nature are the introductory portions of several ballads in which the singer intimates that his song and story are based on experience, or in which he practically inquires whether they have heard the same story. To this class belong those ballads in which the singer affirms (as in No. 22), "It 's talked of far and near" that such and such a thing has happened; or, as in "King Hakon's Death" (No. 142), "It now has come what long ago was foretold." Then the narrative proper is taken up. Here we must also assign "Niels Paaskesön and Lave Brok" (No. 164), which besings an event dating from 1468. Before relating how Lave Brok slew Niels Paaskesön, the singer sets forth how the Paaskesöns, a merchant family in Randers, built such a dwelling that the castles of the nobility were all dwarfed in comparison.

1. The Paaskesöns have built a house
In the middle of Randers' street;
In all my days so high a house
My eyes did never meet.
Paaskesöns' house tops the castles.

2. One finds within this same house
Stories fifteen in all;
The knobs are of the red, red gold,
They shine o'er croft and wall.

3. One finds within this same house
Fifteen doors, stout and strong;
Never yet saw I such a house
In all my life so long.

4. One finds within this same house
Both mead and cider good;
One finds within this same house
Five winters' fill of food.

5. It was Niels Paaskesön,
He strides down Randers' street, etc.

Herewith the story runs on in the usual narrative style.

II. Monologue within the Ballad

Several of our ballads present further peculiarities. As every one knows, the style of narrative usually in vogue with the ballad is akin to that of the epic; that is, the singer stands in an impersonal relation to the events of his story, intruding neither himself nor his own conclusions into his verse. This last consideration affects also the actors in the ballad, who, to a large extent, are made to speak only so far as their speeches forward the requisite dramatic effect. But it sometimes happens that that portion which in one ballad is told in the third person, in another is put into the mouth of some speaker, who at a certain point appears upon the scene. "The picture which the one ballad unrolls before us in its entirety," says Grundtvig, "is, in the second instance, thrust back to form the background. In the second picture, then, the spirited life and stir of the background is thrown into strong relief by the extreme simplicity and repose of the foreground. At the same time, the latter forms a substantial complement to the action itself" (Grundtvig, II, 390; V, 289). "Ribolt and Guldborg" (No. 82) tells how Ribolt, having carried off his truelove Guldborg, is overtaken by her father and brothers; he fights manfully with them until Guldborg, against his injunction not to speak his name ("name him to death"), calls out: "Ribolt, spare my youngest brother!" Upon this he loses his strength and receives a deadly wound. Guldborg herself dies shortly afterwards. "Hildebrand and Hilde" (No. 83) relates how Hilde sewed her seam so recklessly that it attracted the notice of the queen, who was led to ask where her thoughts were. Thus she learned of Hilde's sorrow. It had happened with Hilde as with Guldborg; she had called to Hildebrand to spare at least her youngest brother. After his death she had been sold by her parents. Then the ballad goes on to say:

> The queen then spake in changed tone,
> And fast the tears her cheek ran down:
>
> "Now that thy sad tale is done,
> Thy lord was Hildebrand, my own dear son."
>
> Scarce had Hildelil told her tale,
> When at the foot of the queen she fell.
>
> The queen in her heart was sad and wae,
> Dead in her arms proud Hildelil lay.

In the above ballad the story is set in a frame, which serves to isolate the narrator from his audience, despite the fact that a large part of the ballad is told in the first person.

The same conditions are met with in "The Maiden transformed into a Wolf" (No. 55) and in "The Maiden transformed into a Hind" (No. 58). The latter tells in the third person how Sir Peder kills a hart; when he is about to flay it, he finds his sister within the skin, who relates to him how her wicked stepmother had changed her successively into a pair of scissors, a sword, a hare, and a hind. Sir Peder cuts his little finger and gives her blood to drink, whereby she is retransformed into a beautiful maiden. In revenge they cast the stepmother into a spiked barrel. The same story is found in "The Maiden transformed into a Wolf" (No. 55), where the maiden herself relates how she, in the shape of a wolf, has torn her stepmother to pieces. In the end she enters a cloister. As the third set of parallels may be mentioned "The Bold Sir Nilaus' Reward" (No. 270) and "Redselille and Medelvold" (No. 271) in conjunction with "The Son's Sorrow" (No. 272). The first two recount the fortunes of a maiden who has been abducted. In the journey through the woods she is overtaken by the pangs of childbirth. She dies while her lover is in search of water. When he finds her dead, he slays himself. The third text puts the story into the mouth of the lover himself — a manifest absurdity, especially when it appears that he sings in conclusion:

> A 21. I set my sword against a stone,
> Off the point my heart's blood ran down.

This verse is impossible. The Icelandic, Norse, and Swedish versions represent the lover as narrating the story to one of his parents, as, for instance, in the following Norse:

> Up and spake his father then:
> "Why sittest thou so still and wan?
>
> "Your noble brethren leap and run,
> But ever thou sittest still and wan."
>
> "I served a count for meat and fee,
> And he had daughters three," etc.
>
> When he had told his tale so sad,
> In his father's arms he fell down dead.

An exactly parallel situation is found in a fourth Danish ballad, "The Companion's Grief" (No. 273), in which it is a comrade who asks his fellow if he is borne down by a secret sorrow. The latter then details the causes of his melancholy and dies immediately.

The result of this investigation brings out that a couple of ballads are characterized by monologue spoken by the chief personage, and furthermore that these ballads are supplemented by others, which incase the monologue in a setting of narration, thus allowing the third person to appear at the beginning and at the end of the ballad. Here again we seem to be reminded that narration in the first person is not in favor with ballad style, that it is even looked upon as foreign, and that, when it is used in isolated cases, it is made a part of the story itself.

We can note exactly similar characteristics in Old Norse poetry. As an exception to the general run of the "Elder Edda" may be named the second "Lay of Gudrun," in which Gudrun herself tells her experiences. Now this lay could be easily transposed, by scarcely more than changing *I* to *she*, into a form analogous to the other lays, since the monologue of Gudrun contains in direct discourse not only her own words, but also the words of those with whom she speaks. As was pointed out by Grundtvig, the original form of this lay was doubtless that of an impersonal narrative recited by the poet. Those who came upon the stage spoke in their own persons. The lays resembling most closely the structure of this lay are two from a later period — "Oddrúnargrátr" and "Guðrúnarhvöt"; but here we have in the introduction the situation and the occasion of the retrospective monologue, which then follows as the main body of the recital. And in this monologue none of the characters speak in their own persons. Narrative in the first person does not seem to have become prevalent until later.[1]

[1] Svend Grundtvig, Udsigt over den nordiske Oldtids heroiske Digtning, pp. 79 ff.

III. The Change of Narrator in the Ballad

A number of ballads present the curious feature of changing the person of the narrator. "True as Gold" (No. 254), for instance, begins with:

> A I. Early in the morning the knight rides out
> To chase the roe and the deer;
> I found a maid on the mountain-side,
> My service I offered to her.

Hereupon the *I* disappears, leaving behind only the knight and the maiden. In B and C we have the stanza:

> I rode me out in the morning early
> To chase the roe and the deer;
> I found a maiden under a linden,
> My service I offered to her.

In the stanza that follows the recital deals only with the young man and the maiden. As will be shown later, the ballad is borrowed from abroad; but in the four German and the one Netherland parallels which Grundtvig cites, the narrative is told entirely in the third person.

"The Maiden transformed into a Bird" (No. 56) is an account of how a maiden was metamorphosed by her wicked stepmother, first into a hind, and then into a hawk, and her attendant maids into wolves. Her lover is on the point of attempting her capture, when he is told that he cannot hope to insnare the hawk unless he offers as a bait the flesh of a domesticated animal. He thereupon cuts a slice from his own breast and gives it to the hawk, which at once assumes the form of a most beautiful girl. In the first eight stanzas of the ballad it is the girl herself who speaks; but from this point on to the end the recital is concerned only with the girl and the hawk.

1. When that I was a little boy,
   My mother fell sick and died;
   My father rode out o'er the land,
   Brought home another bride.

8. My love he serves at the court of the king, etc.

15. The youth he cut a slice from his breast
    And hung it high on the linden tree;
    Full glad was she, for sore was her need,
    And flapped her wings right lustily.

23. The youth has now got his reward,
    Safely has he won from harm;
    At night he sleeps full joyously
    Within his truelove's arms.

This singularity manifests itself in several texts with the following arrangement: A stanzas 1–8 *I*, 9–23 *she;* B 1–8 *I*, 9–24 *she;* C 1 *I* (but the *I* of the singer, not of the maiden), the remainder in the third person; D third person throughout except in 2; E 1 *I* (of the young man), 2–8 *he;* F 1–16 *I* (of the maiden), 17–18 *she.*

"The Maiden's Morning Dream" (No. 239) tells the story of a girl who is treated rather harshly by her maternal aunt. She dreams that she is a duck in the pond of the Wendish king; when pressed to sell her dream she refuses. Immediately the Wendish king appears on the scene and demands her in marriage; this is consummated, despite the efforts of her aunt to prevent it. Three good texts start out with the narration in the first person (A 1–4, B 1–3, D 1, 2) and then change to the third person, which carries it on.

"Folke Algotsön" (No. 180) relates how a young man carries out the request of his truelove to arrive on the scene in time to prevent her marriage to another. At the proper moment thirty youths clad in mail appear on the spot and carry off the bride. The different copies of this ballad present the greatest variations: B 1, 26–29 third person, 4–25 *I*; G 1–3, 9–16 third person, 4–8 *I*; H (from 1650) 1–3 third, 4–12 *I*; I and K also fluctuate; and D (from Peder Syv) has in the beginning (1–4) and the conclusion (23, 24) the first person, and in the intervening stanzas (5–22) the third. In an unpublished ballad (No. 46) we likewise find an *I*, which gradually gives way to *he*. Another unpublished ballad (No. 299) offers us two old forms, one of which uses the third person throughout; the other uses the first up to the middle of the ballad, where it changes over to that of the maiden, who, by the way, comes to her death.

The inference that ballads so constructed would not admit of singing is untenable in the light of the similarity presented by ballads collected in our own day by the schoolmaster Kristensen. For instance, in "The Faithless Bride" (Kristensen, I, No. 78; II, No. 54) we find *I* in the first part, but in the last stanza *he*. In "The Meeting in the Wood" (Kristensen, I, No. 79; Grundtvig, No. 284) the first few stanzas are told in the words of the actors themselves, whereas the remainder is related in the third person. In "The Poacher" (Kristensen, II, No. 6) *I* runs through all the twenty-two stanzas except the fifteenth; in this instance, however, the alteration might well be due to a lapse of memory, which so often has disfigured the original aspect of a ballad.

In reply to the question, Which of the two forms is the older,—narration or monologue,—only one answer is possible. The simple recital of events that have befallen others appears to be far more natural than a monologue, which is open to many objections. In addition to the fact that they contain the speeches of all the actors, the ballads are otherwise highly dramatic in structure. Although, as a rule, it is not said who is speaking, yet it is never a matter of doubt. Now, if he who is the main character in the ballad is at the same time the narrator, and if he has occasion to speak with any one of the other characters, it will be difficult to make his replies appear as such,—namely, to make them stand out distinct from his narrative,— unless he uses the rather unfortunate "I said." In other words, the dramatic force of the ballad is ruined and the impression confused by such a multitude of *I*'s. Moreover monologue is absurd when a tragic end awaits the singer, since it is manifestly impossible for a person to tell the story of his own death. Accordingly the stanza cited above in "The Son's Sorrow" (No. 272) is sheer nonsense. Such a novel style of storytelling as is met with in the "Rimed Chronicle," in which each king relates how he died and was buried, does not lend itself to imitation in a song which has a musical delivery.

But first and foremost must be taken into consideration man's natural timidity about laying bare his whole history to the general multitude, especially where, as in the ballads, it is a case of exposing his innermost feelings. When Ingemann decided to write his experiences, he sought a mode of expression that would permit him to stand objectively apart from his life and to look back upon his career as though it were terminated. This "insulating stool," which, by permitting him to overlook his past, would vouchsafe him freedom and spare him confessional obligations, he discovered at last, he writes, "approximately by just using *he* for *I* in writing about himself."

If this is true of a literary artist in a thoroughly cultured period, how must it be with an unsophisticated singer appearing before an artless folk? Even if the balladist, unlike Ingemann, does not precisely relate his own experiences, yet he knows full well that he whom these things did befall would have been reluctant enough to speak without the aid of this "insulating stool."

"The simple man," says a German writer, "who is wholly possessed by an emotion that demands expression lacks the courage to body it forth in its naked reality; he is ashamed to appear as suffering from the force of his own emotions. Therefore he conceals it under the form of a simile or picture, or assuming the character of a dispassionate narrator he employs an epic situation to give vent to the feelings under which he labors."[1] It is precisely on this basis that the epic-lyric romances have become the most accepted form for all folk poetry, and this is most eminently true of our Danish ballads. Whenever these deviate from that form, whenever the *I* becomes predominant, we have every reason to believe such cases to be exceptions. We can well understand the need, which might easily have arisen even when the *I*-form of narration was used, of concealing the face, as it were, by letting what was told take the shape of a story foisted upon some one else and not as the experiences of the narrator, — who would now be in the position to stand by as an auditor.

[1] Berger, in *Zeit. f. d. Philologie*, XIX, 443.

In the same manner we may explain those ballads in which *I* gradually and unobtrusively goes over into *he*. In certain ballads the *I* that is found in the introductory stanza, where the singer himself speaks, or where he stands in some definite relation to the action, has, to be sure, spread improperly throughout the entire ballad. But this does not account for all the cases where there is an interchange of the first and third persons. Nor can it be assigned to chance or to mistakes in writing the ballad down, for we see the same thing obstinately persisting in the songs of the peasants to-day. Hence there seems to be no other alternative possible than to regard it as a peculiarity inherent in popular poetry and in artless methods of singing. Children and negro servants exhibit a similar inclination to substitute their own names for *I*.[1] The folk singer never obtrudes himself, and, during the progress of the ballad, he always remains an outsider. And it is well to notice that the shifting of persons in the ballad is always from the first to the third, never from the third to the first. If this exchange rested upon mere caprice or upon a faulty memory, the reverse phenomenon would certainly have taken place. This, however, we never find.

IV. *I* THROUGHOUT THE ENTIRE BALLAD

It is manifest from the above discussion that one will have to search a long time before he finds a ballad in which the singer is completely merged into the chief character. The question naturally arises, If no ballads exist in which the poet has composed according to the art of song

[1] Cf. also Jakob Grimm, Kleinere Schriften, III, 241 ff.; Burdach, in *Zeit. f. d. Altertum*, XXVII, 351.

affected by modern lyrics, what has become of him? The answer does not admit of detail, since the number of such ballads is very small, and since they all virtually lead to the same conclusions that have been already reached.

As the first of these can be cited "Hedeby's Ghost" (No. 91), which begins as follows:

1. I rode abroad till eventide,
I tethered my steed by my side.

2. I laid my head on the bent so brown,
And longed right sorely for slumber sound.

3. The sleep that first did seal my eyes,
Before my view a corpse did rise.

4. "If you are a man of my race,
You shall set to rights my case."

The dead man goes on to relate how his wife encompassed his death, how she lives with his squire as a mistress, and how she humiliates his children. Here the ballad ends, being only a fragment. Several versions from other lands, however, have preserved the conclusion. The Norse text, for instance, which Bugge heard sung in Telemark ("Old Norse Popular Ballads," No. 15), begins with *I*, to whom the ghost appears and relates his melancholy tale; this *I* is changed at the end of the ballad to Herrepær, who wreaks vengeance on Lady Ingeborg.

1. I walked abroad late at night, etc.

8. An angry man waxed Herrepær,
And from the wood the corpse he bore.

9. Herrepær cast the corpse to the floor
Pale, then black, was Ingeborg's color.

13. They buried her alive under a stone.

With this the ballad concludes. The dead man was avenged and the wife punished. The Norse version has lost its significance for our purpose, however, for it will be noted that it employs the old, familiar device of starting out with *I*, which toward the end gives way to Herrepær. The Swedish, German, and Slavic versions, moreover, tell the story in the third person. The source of the Danish version, which is found only in Vedel's collection, is not known to us.

Peculiarly unique is the highly subjective little ballad of "The Young Man's Complaint" (No. 53). *I* was banished by my stepmother during my father's absence from home; in the valley lived a huge serpent, of which *I* was much afraid; *I* saw two red roses, but they were uprooted by the serpent; in a green meadow *I* saw a maiden preparing a young man's bed; under the coverlet *I* found my brother with my truelove; *I* went away, and on a green stretch of land *I* came upon a roebuck playing with a roe; since the death of my father and mother (but note that the father was still alive in the first stanza) *I* have not a single true friend left; "the more I mourn, the less relief I find." Neither Northern nor foreign parallels exist to throw light upon this curious ballad. It tells of many different things and throws out occasional hints and allegorical suggestions; but these are only half intelligible. Its main drift is apparently to voice the lowest depths of pessimism, a feature often met with in ballads dating from the conclusion of the sixteenth century (see below). The oldest manuscript in which it is found belongs to the age of Frederick II.

In the manuscript of Anna Basse's (c. 1600), but in no other place, is found a ballad (Unpublished No. 134) which tells how *I* arrived at a castle, where *I* was well received by two maidens and put to bed; one of them lay down by my side. The remarkable thing about this meager, worthless fragment is that the majority of its verses are repeated in a ballad from Arwidsson's collection (No. 147), which has to do with a mountain maid whose singing makes the streams to stop and listen. This Swedish version belongs to the class of fairy hillock ballads, and accordingly ends with the well-known verse, that if the cock had not flapped his wings, the young man would not have escaped from the hill. I shall revert to the fairy hillock ballads shortly.

"The Nightingale" (No. 57) — "I know well where a castle stands" — is, as Grundtvig pointed out, entirely wanting in popular elements. That it belongs to the seventeenth or eighteenth century will be shown later. Another ballad (Unpublished No. 171) — "I dreamed at night as I lay in sleep," — which has affinities with a lyric of love, is a translation of a German ballad — "Mir träumte in einer Nacht gar spät."

Schoolmaster Kristensen has discovered in Jutland a ballad which contains rules that are to be observed by young men when courting (Kristensen, II, No. 27):

> 1. I rede you, young men, come learn of me
> What to do in the bower of a fair lady.

Hereupon follows a deal of good advice. In Anna Urop's "Book of Ballads," from 1610, there is found a similar ballad with directions for the conduct of young men; as, for example,

> Clasp her fingers gently, draw boldly near;
> If thou knowest how to love, she will hold thee dear.

According to this old ballad, it is the young man who goes to his foster-mother and asks her to advise him how to win a maiden. In a Swedish, and also in a Norse, version, the mother gives the advice to the son as he is about to set out for the wedding feast. Here we see again how the ballad will not allow direct speech to run through the whole. None of these forms can be traced farther back than 1610, and their whole character, marked as it is by wide departure from popular ballad style, indicates that the ballad itself is not much older. Furthermore some of its versions are borrowed directly from German ballads.

A noteworthy exception comes to light in "The Elfen Hill" (No. 46) — "I laid me down on an elfen hill." Here we have before us virtually a subjective, lyrical ballad. Of action there is very little. A youth, enchanted with the dancing of an elf maid, is on the point of being lured into the interior of the hill, when, fortunately, the flapping of the cock's wings announcing the approach of day warns the maiden that she must flee. Text A alone contains the additional features of the youth's recognizing his sister in the elf maid, and of her counsel not to drink the draft which the girls offer to him, but to let it run down his breast. In this text, however, as in all the others, the main point is the presentation of a scene showing the effect of the song on nature, on the streams, the fishes, and the birds. This capital ballad, it seems to me, must assuredly be referred to a late period, certainly as late as the beginning of the sixteenth century, both because of the forms of speech used, and because of the stress laid upon the lyrical element, together with an absence of epical content. In any case, it constitutes an exception to the general run of ballads.

It remains to note a couple more of ballads which use *I* throughout; the first, a rather extravagant production, is "The Maiden's Punishment"[1] (No. 464), and the second "The Cloister Maiden" (No. 20 in Grundtvig's "Heroic Ballads," 1867). In this last ballad a maiden sings of how she was betrayed by her lover, and how she desires to take the veil.

9. I 'll now seek out some cloister lone,
And serve the Virgin meek;
Never again will I trust a young man,
Though he burn to a fiery gleed.

10. The first step you step that cloister within,
You meet three bad dishes;
The first is Hunger, the second Thirst,
The third is Wakeful Nights.

11. Oh! and if the cloister were burned,
And all the nuns were dead,
And that I had a faithful friend
Who would me clothe and feed.

12. Now I am like the silly man
Who built his house on the ice;
The ice gave way, and the house sank down,
Sorrow has made him wise.

13. Now I am like the lonely tree
That stands on the plain so wide;
Far from shelter, far from town,
Where the wind sweeps from every side.

[1] A maiden has taken refuge with a young man; she is driven away by his relatives; she wanders about as a beggar until the plague visits the land, when all her relatives die, leaving her rich; she then accepts the youth who was her lover, and who had given her bread and water when she was in poverty.

14. Now I am like the little bird
Which flies o'er the plain so wide;
Try where it may, it finds no spot
Where it and its nest may abide.

Grundtvig has already remarked that this lament cannot be old: "It is perhaps no older than the fifteenth century." It would be more correct to assign it to the first half of the sixteenth. There is altogether too much art displayed in its parallelism. Stanzas 5 and 6 are parallel; also 7, 8, and 9; also 12, 13, and 14. The similitude in stanza 10 of the "three bad dishes" smacks too much of a taste that belongs to the world of culture, and is entirely foreign to ballad style. On the whole, its accumulation of images and its use of proverbs agree but little with the language of popular ballads. This point will be discussed at more length later on. All in all, the form of the ballad seems to have been affected by subsequent accretions. It begins with the singer proposing to enter the cloister, but it ends with her being already an inmate, who wishes that it would burn down. Quite otherwise runs the Swedish version (Arwidsson No. 123), which consists of only five stanzas. In stanza 4 we find the line, "They led her into the cloister," etc. Here, then, we notice that the first person is not employed throughout. When we take into further consideration the fact that this same subject is treated very vigorously in a German ballad, we seem to have sufficient ground for regarding this ballad as heterogeneous and, at any rate, recent.

Thus I have gone through all the modes in which the *I* manifests itself in the ballads. I have shown to what extent the balladist remains incognito, and how little it is known that some ballads are monologues which are spoken by the chief characters, and that others are given up to subjective, lyrical expression. The two ballads that partake of this latter nature bear every token of belonging to the sixteenth century, and not to the Middle Ages. As a rule, the *I* and the pure lyrical element appear in the first stanza and in the refrain; the remaining portion of the ballad is always taken up with objective, epical narrative.

How little known it is that the above is the main tendency of ballads is strikingly borne out by the following instance. On the basis of two ballad lines, which are preserved in a runic manuscript of Skaane laws (c. 1300), the learned Professor L. Fr. Läffler has recently composed a little song of five stanzas, "just as he thought the ballad would have continued it." [1]

> I dreamed a dream late last night,
> Of silk and the velvet fine.
> He has won to his prize at last,
> This gallant knight of mine.
> *But where — Oh! where will he find rest?*
>
> He bore me away from the cloister wall,
> And set me on his charger brown.
> And so with pomp and prancing steed
> We rode into the town.
> *But where — Oh! where will he find rest?*

The wedding passes off safely and merrily, and she sleeps in her lord's arms.

> I awoke and still in my cloister bed
> I lay, cold and alone.
> Vanished were all my garments gay,
> The bridal feast was gone.
> *But where — Oh! where shall I find rest?*

[1] Nyare bidrag till Kännedom om de svenska landsmålen och svenskt folklif, Vol. VI; see Minor Articles, p. cl.

Granted that it be very pretty indeed, yet Professor Läffler has wholly missed the mark. Not only do the complaints of nuns dissatisfied with their chosen lot belong entirely to the close of the Middle Ages or to the period of the Reformation, but also the *I*-form, as has been pointed out, is practically unknown to our ballads of the Middle Ages. Above all, the poet failed to perceive that the two extant lines constitute an introduction, in which the *I*, in accordance with the old laws of poetry, has the right to appear; and that it should vanish at once after having struck the key-note and possibly indicated the refrain. It is therefore utterly beside the mark to surmise how the ballad may have run. Thus much is certain, however, it was not a lyrical, erotic lament, but an epical ballad whose story was told in the third person.

V. This I say to you in Sooth

Hitherto I have avoided mentioning one form of *I*, namely, that verse which we meet a hundred times: "This I say to you in sooth." We are fully aware by this time how seldom the *I* of the poet makes its appearance in the ballads, even if the *I* of the actor now and then is found. The poet can intrude himself only in the introductory stanza, and in the line just referred to, which greets us with such extraordinary frequency that it has come to be regarded as a characteristic of ballad form. Keeping in mind the fact that the *I*, as we have seen, is all but constantly held in leash, could we entertain the supposition that its continual appearance in the ballads resulted from the need which the *I* felt of expressing itself? Or could it not rather be a line which, not the poet, but he who in later times sang or noted down the ballad used whenever his memory failed him?

We meet with this line even in the first ballad of Grundtvig's collection — "Thor of Havsgaard" (No. 1), which is handed down from antiquity in two old manuscripts, A together with Vedel B. In A we find the line three times:

> A 14. Then they brought the young bride forth,
> They brought her into the bridal court;
> This I say to you in sooth:
> No gold was grudged the players' sport.
>
> 20. Eight there were of warriors
> They carried the hammer on a tree;
> This I say to you in sooth:
> They laid it over the bride's knee.
>
> 21. It was then the young bride
> Took the hammer in her hand;
> This I say to you in sooth:
> She tossed it lightly as a wand.

Its very position here in the middle of the ballad goes to prove that it is a corruption, for certainly one would expect a heightening of expression or an unexpected turn in the thought to justify the use of the assertion that the balladist is telling the truth. There is nothing wonderful, however, in a warrior's placing a hammer on the bride's knee. Vedel, therefore, in his rendering, which is based on the two manuscripts, has corrected the line to:

> They laid it then so artfully
> Right over the bride's knee.

The same general criticism holds true of line four in stanza 14 — "No gold was grudged the players," — which appears constantly in the ballads, and which was never omitted by the "players" when they performed for money; probably it was often introduced as a suggestive reminder to the audience. The insertion in this stanza, as well as that of the other line, seems wholly mechanical; apparently the reciter had forgotten the two genuine lines. The text of the same ballad which Kristensen noted down in Jutland not long ago has the following stanzas corresponding to stanzas 20 and 21 above:

22. Twelve there were of warriors
To lift the hammer at all;
But eighteen there were of warriors
Bore it into the hall.

23. Eighteen there were of warriors
Bore it into the hall;
But it was the stout young bride
Raised it with her fingers small.

From this stanza then, it would seem possible to construct a more correct stanza than stanza 20 of Grundtvig's version; as, for example:

Twelve there were of warriors
Carried the hammer on a tree;
Eighteen there were of warriors
Laid it over the bride's knee.

Furthermore it may be noted that the modern text mentioned above contains in none of its twenty-five stanzas the line, "This I say to you in sooth"; nor does the Swedish text, which is preserved in two manuscripts of the seventeenth century. It can safely be affirmed that this line is not a part of the original ballad, and that accordingly it should be omitted.

Let us pass on to "Sivard Snarensvend" (No. 2), where the same peculiarity repeats itself. In A we find the line twice, but not at all in B. The story is concerned with Sivard's wonderful horse Skimling, or Gram:

A 9. It was Sivard Snarensvend,
He clapped his spurs to his steed;
It gave three bounds out o'er the field,
And they served him not at need.

10. He gave three bounds out o'er the field,
And they served him not at need;
This I say to you in sooth:
He sweated drops of blood.

Every one must feel that this commonplace, tedious verse, with its endless repetitions, can be neither original nor correct. In B the corresponding stanza, though not perfectly clear, is at least complete and is free from that line:

B 7. Gram he led out to the heath,
It served him not at need;
Sorely wounded he sat in the saddle,
He sweated the blood so red.

Further on in A runs a stanza as follows:

A 15. It was Sivard Snarensvend,
He clapped his spurs to his horse;
This I say to you in sooth:
He leaped into the castle court.

Here are the first two lines of B 11:

Gram took the bit between his teeth
And sprang o'er the castle wall.

Perhaps it is not unreasonable therefore to conjecture the last two lines of A 15 to have run so:

Gram took the bit between his teeth
And leaped into the castle court.

These characteristic lines occur again in a Jutland version of the ballad taken down by Kristensen (Grundtvig, IV, 583):

D 13. It was Sivard's gallant steed,
In his teeth he champed the bit;
Fifteen fathoms he plunged o'er the wall,
So both their lives they quit.

In "The Lombards" (No. 21) occurs the stanza:

A 10. When they reached the open sea,
Joyful grew each eye and heart;
This I say to you in sooth:
Of fame and wealth they had their part.

How flat and insipid this verse sounds! And when we compare it with the last two lines of the other two texts, which are preserved in old manuscripts:

B 12. When they came to the foreign shore,
They won both wealth and fame.

C 11. When they fared them through the land,
They won them many victories,

we cannot entertain the slightest doubt that the line in question is mere padding used to fill out a defective memory.

In "Queen Dagmar's Ballad" (No. 135) we read:

A 6. St. Mary's book she then took up,
She read it the while she might;
This I say to you in sooth:
The salt tear blinded her sight.

The copy of this ballad noted down in recent times (Kristensen, I, No. 56) has a line which may well have stood here:

9. She took up the Bible and the holy book,
And read all that she might;
And every line she read therein,
The salt tear blinded her sight.

Grundtvig is of the opinion that this latter text has its original in Vedel's "Book of a Hundred Ballads"; but Vedel's text wants this third line, which, however, reads as naturally as if it were native to the ballad. Thus this ballad goes to show that whenever the above notorious line creeps in, the expression becomes enfeebled and puerile; whereas we should expect, according to the context of such an affirmation, — that is, from what is foreshadowed, — a heightening of expression.

Furthermore, in all these ballads cited there is room nowhere for an *I*, whether it be in the introduction or in the conclusion; the narrative runs along entirely in the objective third person. Only in that one line an *I* suddenly obtrudes itself. Is not this fact significant, and does not such an interpolation clash with all good rules of artistic composition?

Let us look at it from another point of view. Here is a good, complete stanza from "German Gladensvend" (No. 33), which is found with some variations in four of the five texts of the ballad:

B 11. It was German Gladensvend,
He rode by the salt sea strand;
He wooed the maiden Adelude,
The fairest in the land.

Note how this stanza can be diluted. In the remaining version (A 14) we find the last two lines replaced by:

This I say to you in sooth:
He wooed so fair a maid.

Curiously enough, Grundtvig, who, on the whole, has not been sensible of the peculiarity of this line, has refused to adopt it in his popular edition of the ballads. And which of the two following forms is correct?

B 24, C 27, E 22. She then took out her golden comb
And combed his yellow hair;
With every lock she stroke,
Let fall a bitter tear,

or as in the last two lines of D 20?

This I say to you in sooth:
Let fall a bitter tear.

In this instance Grundtvig has not sanctioned the line. In both cases, however, there seems to be no doubt that it is an illegitimate verse which has displaced the genuine verse.

Another objection that follows in the wake of this verse is that it is never found twice in the same place in any two versions of the same ballad. For example, in "Peder Gudmandsön and the Dwarfs" (No. 35), Grundtvig, who first regarded A as the best text, has later adopted the view that B "gives us everything that belongs to genuine old tradition, whereas A is a later, arbitrary expansion of this framework" (IV, 790). In this Grundtvig is wholly right. Now in B we meet the stanza:

3. "Right welcome, Peder Gudmandsön,
Right welcome are you here;
This I say to you in sooth:
You shall drink the Yule with dwarfs this year."

Although this line, since it is spoken here by a character other than the hero, does not wholly conflict with ballad style, yet beyond all question it ought to be omitted. In the corresponding stanza of A the line is wanting, but its place is taken by an intolerable prolixity:

> 6. Right welcome, Sir Peder Gudmandsön,
> Right welcome are you here;
> We 'll pour for you the mead so brown
> And the blood-red wine so clear.
>
> 7. We 'll pour for you the mead so brown
> And the blood-red wine so clear;
> By my faith, Peder Gudmandsön,
> You shall drink apart with dwarfs this year.

In addition A contains the following meretricious set of verses:

> 19. It was early in the morning,
> As soon as day was come;
> It was Sir Peder Gudmandsön
> Was fain to be up and gone.
>
> 20. It was Sir Peder Gudmandsön,
> Was fain to be up and gone;
> This I say to you in sooth:
> Of help was there none.
>
> 21. This I say to you in sooth:
> It brought him grief and woe,
> Since that (sic!) the elf-man's daughter
> Was loath to let him go.
>
> 25. She yielded to his wish at last,
> He must away from the hill;
> This I say to you in sooth:
> With her it never went well.

The amount of padding used in this ballad illustrates how memory is accustomed to stuff and patch its gaps. It is also significant that *gange* (go) occurs as a riming word in stanzas 19 and 20; *fromme* (benefit, to go well with one) in 16, 20, 24, 25; *komme* (come) in 13, 16, 17, 24, 25, 26. The stanza last enumerated Grundtvig considers to be "a late fabrication." The fact that it is found in such bad company is in itself a sufficient indication of its worth.

"The Elfen Hill" (No. 46) is related entirely in the first person; hence the line in question does not clash with the style. Nevertheless, even in this case, its genuineness is open to doubt. In "Queen Sophie's Ballad-Book" and in several other manuscripts, we find the following stanza:

> B 3. "Wake up, wake up, my bonny boy!
> Come dance with us right featly;
> My maiden shall sing a song for you,
> And Oh! but she sings sweetly."
>
> 4. The maiden then began her song,
> Fairest was she under the sun;
> The bustling stream it ceased to flow
> So fast was wont to run.

There is no call for regarding an interpolation necessary between these two stanzas; this would result rather in weakening the dramatic force. Yet in A appears a stanza explaining that a stool was first handed to the maiden to sit upon while she was singing:

> A 5. They brought a stool of the burnished gold,
> A seat for the elfen maid;
> This I say to you in sooth:
> The game for me was badly played.

This stanza is inserted between the two cited above. It is found only in Sten Bille's manuscript; neither text B nor any of the modern copies recognize it. To acquiesce in its usurpation would be an unparalleled instance of good nature.

In the diffuse, spun-out romances of the Middle Ages, in which length and rime are aimed at, the above line, together with "What more can I say?" leads an acceptable existence. Compare, for example, verses 250, 269, 365, 477, 1375 in the romance of "Persenober and Constantianobis." In these romances the *I* of the singer constantly forces itself upon our notice. It has gained a place in the ballads as a result of the frequent use of the ballad in the dance, and of the unique mode of preservation by tradition instead of by writing. But since it originally had no place in the ballad, it should be banished entirely. I shall illuminate this point from another direction.

Although repetition is somewhat characteristic of ballad style, as I shall make clear later, yet, in many places, repetitions have crept in that were not part of the original ballad. In the Faroese ballad of "Regin the Smith" are met the stanzas:

> 74. The sword's pieces Sigurd struck
> With mighty blow across the knee;
> Then shook with fear Regin the Smith
> Just like a lily leaf.
>
> 75. The sword's pieces Sigurd took
> And laid them in his hand;
> Then shook with fear Regin the Smith
> Just like a lily wand.

The communicator of this ballad, Pastor Lyngbye, remarks that the last stanza repeats with only slight variations the substance of the preceding. "I have omitted many such verses, which were patently variations; yet I have allowed several to stand as specimens, for this repetition is somewhat peculiar to old Faroese poetry (it is found sometimes in the old Danish heroic ballads), and at times is necessary; inasmuch as the songs were not preserved in writing, this repetition afforded the leader of the song a breathing-spell, during which he could recall to mind what was to follow" ("Færöiske Quæder," pp. 74 ff).

As we can readily see, the same observation applies equally well to our Danish ballads. Among others, the stanzas cited above from "Peder Gudmandsön" could serve as examples. Now if it were the case that a singer was obliged to compose a new stanza alongside of the old with but trifling changes, here was a line — "This I say to you in sooth" — all ready to his hand as material toward such a stanza. It is now plainly conceivable how such a stanza as the second of the following, from "Marsk Stig" (No. 145), has originated:

B 24. It was Eric the king
Gazed out his window high;
"Yonder I see Sir Marsti
Come riding his steed so gray.

25. "Yonder I see Sir Marsti
At the gate he stands to view;
This I say to you in sooth:
He glistens like the dove so blue."

None of the other texts have a stanza corresponding to this last. The repetition in this case is not only superfluous, but is also monotonous and wearisome. The stanza contains nothing new; it is merely a dilution of the preceding. It belongs solely to that style of verse which exists only for the convenience of the singer; and it would never have been acknowledged by the original balladist as his own.

I shall illustrate by one more example how this superfluous verse arose. In "Marsk Stig" (No. 145) we have:

F 7. It was Ranild Jenssön,
He hewed both beam and board;
This I say to you in sooth:
He proved a traitor to his lord.

8. They have stricken him in to his shoulder-bone,
It stood out beyond his neck;
This I say to you in sooth:
It was a traitor's trick.

9. They have stricken him in to his shoulder,
And out his left side too;
"Now have we done a deed to-day
All Denmark will sorely rue."

Not only the diffuseness, but also the quadruple rime (*Balk*, *Skalk*, *Hals*, *Falsk*), clearly show that here lie before us an addition and an expansion; the mortising line moreover is forced into service twice. The text most closely linked with F, namely G, runs as follows:

5. They have stricken their lord through the heart,
And out his left side too;
"Now have we done to-day a deed
All Denmark shall rue."

6. It was then that Ranild
So fierce did hew and slay;
Upon the floor their king lay dead,
For he got no help that day.

He who sang these lines had a good memory, he had no need of padding; he knew that the beauty of the text was not to be measured by the number of words. And every one will find, by testing for himself, that the line which asserts the truth of the singer's statements frequently makes its appearance in company with verse repetition and with lines whose riming words have been used before.

In conclusion I shall discuss an illuminating feature connected with the influence exercised on the original form of the ballad by the mode of delivery. I refer to the fashion of singing their runic songs in vogue with the Finns. These are commonly executed by two singers, of whom only one is properly the performer, the other acting merely as an echo, as an assistant or supporter. The two join hands and sit facing each other. Number one then chants a line. By the time he has reached the last stave his assistant has grasped what is to come and thereupon sings the same thing in concert with him. Now the second singer repeats the whole line by himself in a slightly varied pitch of voice, and usually with some little addition, such as "truly," "rightly," "indeed," "I say," "it was said," "in truth," etc. The last word of the line is sung anew in unison, after which the first man sings the second line of the poem. The second singer joins in on the last word and then repeats the line. Meanwhile the first man has had time to recall what is to follow. After the pair have sung the concluding word of the line as a duet, number one takes up the third line. And so on to the end.[1] Here is appended a specimen of such a poem in order to make clear how this performance looks. I omit, however, one of the duets, which, at any rate, is not always found, and have distinguished by different type the part sung by the fore-singer from the part sung by his comrade.

[1] Gustaf Retzius, Finska Kranier jämte några natur- och literaturstudier, pp. 132 ff.

Old, confident { Wäinamöinen / *Wäinamöinen* }

Old, confident Wäinamöinen

Drew the sharp steel from the { scabbard / *scabbard* }

Drew so surely the sharp steel from the scabbard

Thrust the sword deep into the { water / *water* }

Thrust, I say, the sword deep into the water

Struck up from under the side of the { vessel / *vessel* }

Struck up, in truth, from under the side of the vessel

Into the great pike's { shoulder / *shoulder* }

Into the great pike's shoulder

Against the cruel water-dog's { backbone / *backbone* }

Against the cruel water-dog's backbone

Old, confident { Wäinamöinen / *Wäinamöinen* }

Old, confident Wäinamöinen

Sought to draw the fish to the { surface / *surface* }

Sought, in fact, to draw the fish to the surface

Lifted the pike out of the { water / *water* }

Lifted, they say, the pike out of the water

The pike burst into two { pieces / *pieces* }

The pike, indeed, burst into two pieces

The tail sank and went to the { bottom / *bottom* }

The tail sank, I say, and went to the bottom

Only the upper half fell into the { vessel / *vessel* }

Only the upper half fell into the vessel.

If one should here set down the version sung by the comrade as the correct text of the poem, he would sin grievously against the poet. The same holds good of our Danish ballads; namely, that the line "This I say to you in sooth" and many other repetitions are additions, a little dressed up, which arose from the manner of performing the ballad. They have nothing at all to do with the original ballad, and, for the reading of the ballad to-day, they work only for confusion.

Thus, I believe, I have thrown considerable light on the worth and significance of this well-known line. It is to be hoped that in the future efforts will be made to extirpate this weed which has grown up in the garden of our popular ballads.

CHAPTER IV

THE REFRAIN

The refrain is a distinctive characteristic of the Scandinavian ballads and gives rise to a discussion of a varied nature. As is well known, it is most frequently found at the end of each stanza; but double, and even triple, refrains are not uncommon. The first part of such a many-jointed refrain can be interpolated in a two-line stanza after the first line, and in a four-line stanza after the second line, the second and third parts after the fourth line. The refrain is by no means unrhythmical, but its rhythm is not that of the ballad proper; on the whole, it can show the widest variation. Time with its gnawing tooth has worked nearly as much destruction on the refrains of our ballads as on the texts themselves. Many refrains have become meaningless; by daily repetition their form has been marred and their substance rendered uncertain. Finally many ballads have lost their original refrains and have been forced to borrow others, in many cases getting hold of one which did not fit. At length they have ended up with the modern nonsensical refrains, *nonnenino*, *didaderit*, and the like.[1]

[1] Note by translator: Instances of similar breakdowns of refrains into meaningless syllables will readily come to the minds of English readers, such as, for example, the "Downe a downe, hay down, hay down . . . with a downe derrie, derrie, derrie, downe, downe," of the ballad of "The Three Ravens."

I. Nature of the Refrain

Though our refrains are diversified and multifarious, yet they can be grouped into certain leading divisions.[1] In the refrain the ballad may all but announce its title; it may set forth its principal event or its chief personage and his attributes; or it may specify the nature of the treatment to be meted out to him whom the ballad would especially emphasize:

No. 30. Holger Dansk has overthrown Burmand.
No. 92. Dead rides Sir Morten of Fuglsang.
No. 135. In Ringsted there dwells Queen Dagmar.
No. 145. My noble lord, that young Sir Marsti!

As it appears, this is particularly true of the historical ballads. But the refrain may likewise endeavor to accentuate the dominant mood, the ground tone of the subject matter that is to prevail:

No. 83. Sorrow is heavy when one must bear it alone.
No. 145. And we are driven from Denmark.
No. 146. And wide they roamed through the world.

More frequently, however, a joyous ring greets the listener's ear, such as is found, for example, in the references to the season of the year:

No. 45. While (*men*)[2] the linden grows leafy.
No. 125. As far as the leaves are green.

[1] Cf. N. M. Petersen, Den danske Literaturs Historie, 2d ed., II, 157; Rosenberg, Nordboernes Aandsliv, II, 524.

[2] *Men* (but) possibly means here *medens* (while); yet, since this *men* occurs so frequently, I shall call attention to the fact that "the peasants in Jutland usually begin their conversation with this conjunction" (Lyngbye, Færöiske Quæder, p. 577). Cf. Feiberg, Ordbog over jyske Almuesmaal, *men*. Ballad No. 298 L begins so: "But (*men*) there dwells a rich lady south of the river."

No. 184. The woods are wondrous green —
In the growing summer time.
No. 186. So early in summer.
No. 199. It is so fair in summer.
No. 201. There stands a noble linden in the count's garden.
No. 252. All through the winter so cold —
Await us, fair ladies, all through the summer
No. 273. Both winter and summer time.
No. 234. The leaves spring forth so green.
No. 297. Why dawns not the day, I wonder.

In the case of the double refrain one can sometimes distinguish two chords in vibration:

No. 116. On grassy mountain-sides —
The king of Sweden's crown he seeks to avenge (or, with the crown).
No. 186. There fall so fair a frost —
So merrily goes the dance.
No. 189. Forget me not!
She stepped so stately.
No. 210. While the summer grows —
I cannot sleep for my longing.

Many ballads furthermore take into account the singer's environment. Attention has been called several times already to the mention of dancing; references are also made to riding and rowing:

No. 124. All ye row off!
No. 140. Betake yourself to your oar.
No. 460. To the north —
And now lay all these oars beside the ship.
No. 244. (Norwegian). Row off, noble men!
To the maiden.
No. 399. Row out from shore, ye speak with so fair a one!
No. 16. Long before the dawn we come far over the moorland.
No. 84. Beneath so green a linden —
Ye ride so wary through the woods with her.

No. 141. Ye do not ride!
No. 134. Ride to the maiden's bower, comrade mine!

The word which we meet with most frequently in the refrains is certainly "maiden." Still it would be a mistake to infer on that score that those who sang were invariably young men; there are ballads which allow the maiden herself to speak in the refrain:

No. 20. Whether you win me or so fair a one.
No. 121. Would I were as fair as Tovelille was!

And indeed, according to the story related by the ballad, it is the maiden who very often leads off the singing. In one instance it would seem as though the balladist stood in a definite relation to the chief character of the ballad, namely, "Marsk Stig" (No. 145): "My noble lord, that young Sir Marsti!" I have pointed out before that similarly in the first stanza the singer at times considers himself to be present or to be taking part in the action.

That which we never find in our genuinely popular ballads, on the contrary, is those exclamations which occur so generally in the German ballads and which appear in late Danish copies, where they must have displaced, within the last two hundred years, the good, old refrains: namely, interjections such as *Haa! Haa!* or *Eja!* which are usually accompanied by a repetition of the last line. In "Redselille and Medelvold" (No. 271), for instance, from a broadside of about 1770, we find the refrain "Haa, haa, haa!" with a repetition of the last line. Such an exclamation might have exceptionally slipped into a ballad which could be traced back to an old manuscript, but rather under the guise of a preliminary chant at the beginning of the ballad, and later before each stanza. Similarly we find "Saa vel hei" (much the same as "hey noninony") as some such fore-song introducing each stanza in two ballads from Karen Brahe's Folio Manuscript (No. 25 and Unpublished No. 119) and also in a ballad from Anna Basse's manuscript (No. 373; cf. Grundtvig, I, 351). A German dance "Hoppeldei" and a related "Heierlei," in which the cry *heiahei!* was used, are known to have existed.[1] The South German poet Nithart (ob. 1220) sings in one place:

> die sah ich den heijerleis
> schone springen,

and in another place:

> dennoch haben s' einen sit':
> swer dem reigen volget mit,
> der muosz schrîen heia hei! unt hei!

It is my opinion that here we are to seek for the source of the exclamations in the Danish ballads. Since these ballads have in addition a regular refrain at the end of each stanza, it is manifest that here we have to deal with something out of the ordinary. On the other hand, such a cry can have a place in the refrain itself:

No. 37. Eia! Oh, sorrow, how heavy art thou!

All the refrains have this in common: they voice the mood. Even though they deal with a purely matter-of-fact situation, they can still indicate the fundamental tone; or they may engross the reader's attention in a way that is explicable only at the close of the ballad. But the same

[1] Weinhold, Die deutschen Frauen, p. 373; Böhme, Tanz, I, 35; Von der Hagen, Minnesinger, III, 189, 283.

feeling may be roused by a variety of refrains, and the same fundamental mood may serve as the basis or the object of many ballads; hence it follows that a ballad may well have several refrains, and that the refrains may easily be shifted from one ballad to another. At the same time the refrain often possesses a cohering quality; it contains, to use the words of Wilhelm Grimm, "many a time the basis upon which the whole circumstance rests, it explains the connection, and again rings out as a voice of destiny." It creates a certain repose. While the body of the text forges ahead in its epical progress, the refrain remains stationary and reflective.[1] It gives the listener time to apprehend the narrative; it rounds off every stanza to a whole; it provides the fore-singer with an opportunity to recall what is to follow. It is the custom in the Faroes, when the fore-singer cannot recollect the verse, for the participants to repeat the refrain until the missing lines come back to him, and in the Finnish runic song, as has been shown above, every single line is repeated in order to give the fore-singer time to recall those succeeding.

Geijer has been inclined to deny that the refrain was delivered by the chorus. But in support of such a theory there is plenty of testimony. There is a verse from an old German poet which runs:

> ein maget in süezer wîse
> diu sanc vor, die andern sungen alle nâch.[2]

Both in Germany and in Scotland the chorus seems to have sung the refrain.[3] In Iceland, according to an old

[1] Peder Grönland, in *Allgem. musikal. Zeitung*, 1816, No. 35.
[2] Böhme, Tanz, I, 27.
[3] Talvj, Charakteristik der Volkslieder, p. 336.

account,[1] the chorus sang responsively to the fore-singer: first one took up the song, with two or more others repeating the same after him, while the remainder danced to the rhythm; the hemistich was repeated in unison by the general body. In the Faroes all, as a rule, took part in singing the ballad, and all, without exception, joined in the refrain.[2]

On the other hand, Geijer is right in his conclusion that the refrain is essentially a subjective element. It has been the main task of several of the above investigations to show with what extraordinary nicety the ballads have drawn the limits and bounds between the narrator and his story. As a result the poet has been denied all opportunity of inserting remarks and arguments of his own. It is only in the refrain that he finds such an opportunity; there it is that the mood expresses itself; and there it is, as is indicated by their responses, that the listeners are recognized as participants. It is precisely this participation of the singers and dancers in the lyrical utterance that works for the finest totality of the ballad and the refrain. Thus the refrain is preëminently a component part of the ballad; æsthetically it is fully justified, but when read it becomes,

[1] Crymogæa, per Arngrimum Jonam, p. 57: staticulos voco saltationem ad statos musicos contentus; quae carmen vel cantilenam, quasi praeceptum saltandi adhibet: praecinit autem unus: duo pluresve paulo subcinunt: reliqui ad numerum seu rythmum saltant. Orbis saltatorius viris et faeminis alternatim incedentibus constabat et quodamodo intersectis et divisis (in the margin: wikivake) . . . hic singuli ordine cantilenam aliquam cantant per certas pausas, dimidiis versibus (qui a choro reliquo una voce canendo repetuntur) constantes: ad finem singulorum versuum, principio vel fine primi versus reduplicatione quadam (aliquando etiam sine ea) intercalato.

[2] Lyngbye, in *Magazin f. Reiseiagttagelser*, I, 216.

on account of its constant repetition, very monotonous, and in consequence it has been shortened in the texts, or else omitted, except in the first and last stanzas. It is only when it is sung, when it is elevated by the melody; only when another, in addition to the fore-singer, helps to deliver it, with the remainder joining in, and when the dance is combined with it, that it fully comes into its own. "The sentimental or, as it might be called, the egoistic song, in which the poet or singer is alone with himself, as it were, is not known to the old North, for here the individual never wanted for comrades and witnesses." [1]

The refrain assumes a somewhat different character when it undergoes alteration in its text, namely, when individual words or phrases are changed with every stanza in order to bring it into a definite relation with the context of the stanza. That is scarcely in accordance with the good old ballad style. The result is that the singer has no chance to rest, for he must ever be reminding his company of what they shall sing. This constant adjustment to every stanza easily goes over into something trivial or attenuated. In such a case the refrain becomes a definite part of the text, whereas it almost invariably forms a contrast. That the variable refrain can be used with great success for comic purposes is brilliantly demonstrated by Baggesen's familiar song of "Sir Ro and Sir Rap"; but this instance serves also to disprove the supposition that the variable refrain permits of a general usage in the ballads. And in a lengthy ballad, whatever the contents may be, the variable refrain will become downright intolerable. Even if we imagined ourselves to be present at the singing of a

[1] Peder Grönland, in *Allgem. musikal. Zeitung*, 1816, column 597.

song that altered its refrain with every stanza, we should not find the æsthetic result satisfactory. The great dearth of ballads that possess such a refrain indicates also that here lies before us an abnormal case.

The truth of the above statements is borne out by a consideration of every one of these ballads. In "Young Ranild" (No. 28), a ballad of thirty stanzas, we find a continual change:

1. Had I been so wise! said Ranild.
2. I am not greatly afraid! said Ranild.
3. It grieves me sore! said Ranild.
4. So would I like to do! said Ranild.

It is evident here that the fore-singer must also sing the refrain, since his company could not be expected to remember what fitted in with each individual stanza. On the whole, the variable refrain seems better adapted to a ballad that is to be written down than to one that owes its preservation to memory. Although "Young Ranild" may be an old ballad, yet it makes use of a number of modern expressions; it is found only in a single manuscript, that of Anna Basse's, of about 1600.

Another ballad, "Gralver the King's Son" (No. 29), preserved in nine texts, of which four belong in manuscript to the time of Frederick II, evinces great pains and ingenuity in adapting the refrain by slight changes to every stanza. But in text B, which is preserved in a manuscript from the time of Christian III, the refrain runs constantly, "Because of her proud Signild beneath Stjernfeld"; likewise two of Schoolmaster Kristensen's newly recorded copies have a constant refrain, "There lies a worm before Isereland upon the flood." To this corresponds the unchanging refrain found in two Norwegian copies, "Because there lies a worm upon the flood." Grundtvig says that this refrain must certainly be an old one in the ballad here in Denmark. Thus all warrant for the variable refrain disappears.

In texts A (64 stanzas!) and B of "Rane Jonsen's Marriage" (No. 48) there is also a variable refrain; but Vedel, who seems to have used only B, prints the ballad with a constant refrain: "I have often been told — Although I am banished from friends and comrades." The same refrain is also found in No. 128 C (manuscript of 1555).

In "The Mermaid's Prophecy" (No. 42), on the other hand, Vedel has given a variable refrain, despite the fact that his source ("though possibly it was not his only one"), namely, the only copy preserved, has the constant double refrain: "The mermaid dances upon Tillie — For she had obtained her will." Kristensen's copies from modern times also make use of the variable refrain (I, No. 55; II, No. 82), but since their only source, as Grundtvig declares, is Vedel's "Book of a Hundred Ballads," they do not count for much. A corresponding Swedish ballad (Geijer and Afzelius, No. 94) does not employ the variable refrain.

The two copies of "Daniel Bosön" (No. 421) which were recorded in olden times have a constant refrain, while the six from modern times show a variable one. The Norwegian form of "Dalebu Jonsen" cannot be considered as belonging to the class of ballads with variable refrains, although its refrain, "Dost know Dalebu Jonsen?" is changed in the sixteenth and last stanza to "Now dost know Dalebu Jonsen?" (Landstad, No. 24). In like manner the Swedish form (Arwidsson No. 18) has, "But he was one! — For he was one."

Finally we can cite the well known ballad of "Sir Lave and Sir Jon" (No. 390) with the trebled refrain, the middle one of which is variable:

> You are well prepared,
> I ride too, said Jon.
> Tie up the helmet of gold and follow Sir Jon!

The same is true of Kristensen, I, No. 62; II, No. 86. In manuscript this ballad goes no farther back than to the middle of the seventeenth century.

These investigations seem to lead to the conclusion that at the most only a few old ballads preserved in old manuscripts use the variable refrain. The latter was in accord, on the other hand, with the taste of the times in the sixteenth and seventeenth centuries, when people having grown tired of much that belonged to the older form of the ballad desired a change; at the same time, it is true, some of the most characteristic features of the old ballads were thus discarded.

The refrain is also known in other lands. In fact, it is found in folk poetry the world over. In the refrain the instinct for beauty finds one of its favorite modes of expression, namely, the sense of rhythmic recurrence, the parallelism.[1] But I doubt if the refrain has anywhere been felt to be so integral a part of the ballads as in the Scandinavian, and especially the Danish, ballads.[2] It follows also from the epic nature of our folk poetry that a far greater opportunity here offers itself for the contrast which a lyric

[1] Talvj, Charakteristik der Volkslieder, p. 135.
[2] Cf. also Rosenberg, Nordboernes Aandsliv, II, 531.

refrain presents. The refrain is found in Germany, too, but particularly in narrative ballads, and by no means so generally as in Denmark. Many of the German refrains are doubtless lost, but in a number of ballads they were wanting originally.

I shall now call attention to how peculiarly the refrain and the text proper can be interwoven in the Danish ballads. In "Memering" (No. 14), for example:

1. Memering was the smallest man
   That ever was born in King Karl's land.
      My fairest maidens.
      The smallest man
   That ever was born in King Karl's land.

2. Even before he saw the light,
   His clothes already for him were dight.
      My fairest maidens.
      He saw the light,
   His clothes already for him were dight.

3. Even before he had formed his gait,
   He bore the armor's weight.
      My fairest maidens.

A ballad that progresses in this fashion is liable to prove, when read, tiresome and difficult; when sung, however, it becomes all the more alive, since the refrain is taken up by the chorus. But the question involuntarily arises, Did the fore-singer join in also with the repeated lines of the stanza? It might seem plausible to wish for a variation here. If so, this would be secured provided there were two fore-singers, the one supporting the other by repeating half of what the first sang, and thereby leading the narrative one verse forward. The chorus meanwhile would constantly be chiming in as the third participant in the execution of the ballad. I am not the first to voice this theory; it has already been advanced by Peder Grönland.[1] But this interruption and repetition are found in many ballads, such as, for example, "Hildebrand and Hilde" (No. 83):

1. Proud Hildelil sits in her bower sewing,
For the Danish queen a cap she is making.
Sorrow is heavy when one must bear it alone.
Sewing,
For the Danish queen a cap she is making.

2. She sews with gold so red
What calls for silken thread.
Sorrow is heavy when one must bear it alone.

In some copies of this ballad this repetition is not found; in its place stands a double refrain.

Is it known that there were two fore-singers? Yes, to be sure. We read in Köster's account of Ditmarsh that the fore-singer "either sings alone or else chooses another, who also can sing the song, in order that he may have assistance and relief."[2] In Iceland, likewise, we see that the song was divided up between a fore-singer and others, who sing in response. How closely the fore-singer and his assistant are linked together in the Finnish folk poetry has already been pointed out.

But there are undoubtedly many ways in which a song could assert itself that are now not at all, or only in part, intelligible from the appearance which the ballad makes

[1] *Allgem. musikal. Zeitung*, 1816, column 598.

[2] De Vorsinger, de wol alleine edder ok wol einen tho sick nimbt, de den Gesang mit singen kan, dat he ehne entlichtere unnd helpe, steidt unnd hefft ein Drinkgeschir in der Handt. Dahlmann's edition of Johann Adolfi's (called Neocorus) "Chronik des Landes Dithmarschen," I, 178.

on paper. I shall merely point out how marvelously the song and its refrain must have dovetailed when the two fore-singers led off the singing; as, for example, in "Marsk Stig's Daughters" (No. 146):

FIRST SINGER

Marsti had two daughters fair,
And bitter fate fell to their share.
The eldest took the youngest by the hand,

CHORUS

And wide they roam through the world.

SECOND SINGER

The eldest took the youngest by the hand,
And so they journeyed to King Malfred's land.
King Malfred home from the meeting rode.

CHORUS

And wide they roam through the world.

FIRST SINGER

King Malfred home from the meeting rode;
Before him Marsti's daughters stood:
"What are these women that I see here?"

CHORUS

And wide they roam through the world.

Since we have ground for believing that the delivery of the ballad was made as lively and dramatic as possible, and since we know from the account just given[1] that in Iceland the stanza was divided into halves, I do not think I am wrong in assuming that the ballad was sung in the manner detailed above.

[1] See p. 87, note 1.

Finally it would be perfectly reasonable to conclude that the ballads in which the two refrains have a wholly different trend were sung each by its own circle; as, for example,

MAIDENS. Forget me not!
189 YOUNG MEN. She stepped so stately!
KNIGHTS. Here stand the Duke's own men.
115 LADIES. They come not yet.
MAIDENS. Step boldly up, young knight!
244 YOUNG MEN. Honor the maidens in the dance!

We might also conceive of a portion of the refrain as devolving upon the singer's assistant, and the remaining portion upon the chorus; as, for example, in No. 278:

FIRST SINGER

Sir Peter mounts and rides away.

SECOND SINGER

While the cuckoo calls.

FIRST SINGER

He meets a woman who greets him good day.

SECOND SINGER

Upon the balcony walls.

CHORUS

In the tower Malfred is weeping.
In the grove she is sorrowing.

II. BALLADS WITHOUT REFRAINS

Should the refrain be regarded as an essential constituent of our ballads? It can by no means be denied that there are ballads which lack refrains. Geijer has answered the question thus: that as a rule refrains go with a ballad, but that they cannot be regarded as a necessary adjunct to the ballads. Nevertheless it may very confidently be asserted as a fundamental principle that the popular ballad is invariably attended by a refrain, and that every ballad which is not has either worn it out in the course of time, or else is assuredly not a genuine popular ballad. It is precisely because this characteristic is so marked that further investigations on this point are necessary.

In Grundtvig's collection (completed by Axel Olrik) there are four hundred and eighty published ballads, and about forty more are known to me from his collected writings or from other sources. Among these half a thousand ballads there are found about a score which have no refrain. These consequently form positive exceptions and are in no position to affect the general rule. Since the ballads were not recorded in writing until long after their genesis, it is indeed very possible, not to say highly probable, that the ballads mentioned have lost something they possessed originally, especially as it is often forced upon our attention that, while the refrains are missing in several versions of a recorded ballad, they are present in other forms of the same ballad.

But let us turn to the above-mentioned score of ballads to see whether the majority of them do not present some additional peculiarities. Among these I find, for example, "The Murdered Housewife" (No. 110), which was recorded in 1845; "Child Jacob" (No. 253), whose earliest date of communication is 1840 (and one of the texts has a refrain yet); "The Meeting in the Woods" (No. 284), recorded in 1868; "Sir Sallemand" (Abr. No. 153), a prosaic, sentimental, romantic ballad, which ends so:

> Never was told a tale of greater love,
> Since the days of Tristram and his lady Isold.

In addition may be cited an artistic, six-line song (Unpublished No. 292) and the ballad "The Dialogue of Two Maidens" (Unpublished No. 291), which is translated from a German ballad, "Es waren einmal zwei Gespielen." The absence of refrains in these ballads manifestly does not affect our consideration of the question, What were the ballads of the Middle Ages like?

Another example of this group is "Agnete and the Merman" (No. 38), which can show in the way of a refrain only a tiresome *Haa ja!* together with a repetition of the last line of its two-line stanza:

> Agnete walks on Highland bridge,
> There mounts a merman to the top of the sea,
> — Haa ja! —
> There mounts a merman to the top of the sea.

Grundtvig has been slow in arriving at a clear decision over this ballad. Although he was obliged to admit in the second volume of his work that it had wandered up into this country "only a few hundred years ago," yet he retracted this statement immediately afterwards; but in his fourth volume he repeated that "at a comparatively late period it had emigrated from Germany into Denmark, although it is impossible to state more explicitly the time and the way" (II, 39, 661; IV, 812). The possibility of an earlier immigration Grundtvig would meanwhile reluctantly abandon, and accordingly he included the ballad of "Agnete" in his works "Heroic Ballads and Folk Songs of the Middle Ages" (1867, No. 9) and "The Popular Ballads of Denmark" (1882, II, No. 6). Here again I shall confidently assert that if one would really know what the poetry of the Middle Ages was like, he must reject everything obscure and ambiguous and, above all, everything which lacks the remotest proof to substantiate its claim to so great an age. And this applies most peculiarly to the ballad of "Agnete." It can be traced back no farther than to a printed broadside belonging to the close of the eighteenth century; moreover it contains not a single word, not a turn of phrase, not a glint of anything which would suggest antiquity.[1] It is impossible to believe otherwise than that the connection with the popular poetry of the outside world, which we know existed in the Middle Ages, should have persisted in the following centuries; and in such a manner the ballad of "Agnete," like many others, was attracted to this country.

This situation fits in admirably with what Grundtvig himself has noted; namely, that in contrast with those Norse ballads which treat of a similar subject (Nos. 37, 39, and 40) this ballad exhibits certain distinguishing marks that point to Germany. "First, the name *Agnete* appears in the German versions as Agnete, Agnese, Angnina, Annerle, Hannale; second, the mention of Engelland (she is the daughter of the king of England), her enticement down to the bottom of the ocean, the sea, or the flood, in contrast with her enticement into the mountain; the

[1] The kinship between the ballad of "Agnete" and Ewald's "Little Gunver" is rather distant. Ewald meant, if anything, to imitate the popular ballad in general, wherefore he also provides his song with a refrain. For the rest he might well have become acquainted with the ballad of "Agnete" in the course of his roving life in foreign lands, and even if he had known it in a Danish form, we could still maintain that he had led us back no farther than to the middle of the eighteenth century.

sound of bells and the going to church; — all these traits distinguish the borrowed ballad from the older Norse ballad, with which it has in modern tradition blended itself." To this I can add that precisely such an exclamation as that *Haa ja!* is just as general in German ballads as it is rare or rather wholly unknown in Danish. In his popular edition of the ballads, Grundtvig has given the double refrain "The birds sing . . . Beautiful Agnete!" one of the refrains with which it is sung at present; but that this is not good ballad style, nor in the least degree smacking of the Middle Ages, scarcely needs to be asserted. None of the old refrains are written or sung in such a dreamy mood. This ballad has therefore not the least claim to consideration when the discussion concerns the poetry of the Middle Ages.

There exist, in addition, several religious ballads which lack refrains; such as, for example, "The Boyhood of Jesus, Stephan, and Herod" (No. 96). The ballad was communicated in a work by Erik Pontoppidan, which appeared in 1736. It begins as follows:

> A maiden pure is born to earth,
> The rose among all women;
> She is the fairest the world has seen,
> And she is called the Empress of heaven.

No less modern than this verse are the remaining verses. Over half of the eleven stanzas employ terminal rimes in all four lines, a feature wholly foreign to the ballads of the Middle Ages. Since Grundtvig groups this ballad with the Stephan ballads of the Middle Ages, attention must be called to the fact that only the three following stanzas out of the eleven have to do with Stephan, and that not even the most discriminating critic will be able to recognize in them the style of the Middle Ages:

6. Saint Stephan he led the colts to drink,
   All by the starry glimmer;
   "For surely now the prophet is born
   Who shall save all sinners!"

7. King Herod made him answer thereto:
   "I do not believe this story:
   Save that the roast cock on the table will crow
   And flap his wings so sturdy!"

8. The cock he flapped his wings and crowed,
   Our Lord his natal hour:
   King Herod fell down from his royal throne,
   And swooned for very sorrow.

As early as 1695 this last verse was referred to by Peder Syv as belonging to a ballad on Christ's boyhood; there are found also Swedish and Faroese ballads on Stephan, but none older than the Danish. When one assumes these ballads to be relics from our Catholic days, he fails to take into account the fact that their form by no means points so far back, and also the ready possibility that many foreign Catholic ballads were later conveyed into Denmark orally. Several investigators have interpreted Saint Stephan's patronage of horses as an offshoot of Frey's relation to that animal and to horse-racing at Yuletide; but however one explains that question, the solution cannot affect the interpretation of the ballad, which has merely appropriated the popular belief. And even if one may be wholly disinclined to share the doubts here expressed, he can place no reliance on the absence of a refrain in the Danish ballad as proof of anything, for that seems to be due to pure accident; a refrain is present in both the Faroese and the Swedish versions.

A refrain is also wanting in "Grimild's Revenge" (No. 5). This ballad presents a most curious situation, and this I shall dwell upon at some length, since in many ways its striking colors illuminate and clarify, by way of contrast, what is genuinely Danish and old in Denmark. It treats of the destruction of the Nibelungs and relates how Grimhild, in order to avenge the murder of her husband, Sigfred, sends an invitation to such famous heroes as Hero Hagen and Folkver Spillemand. Hagen has been disquieted by a dream, which he gets a mermaid to read for him; upon her finding it to portend evil, he slays her. He likewise slays a ferryman who refused to row him, and thereupon he ferries himself across to Grimhild's land. When they arrive there they are seized by the followers of Grimhild's consort, King Kanselin, but Folkver, snatching up a steel bar, slaughters a great number of his foes. The king himself receives a severe wound, and Folkver dies.

I entertain no doubt that Professor Sophus Bugge has pointed out the right source of this ballad. Professor Gustav Storm would maintain, on the basis of certain peculiarities in narration, that it had borrowed its substance from the Swedish "Didrik Saga" or "Didrik Chronicle," which dates from the years 1420–1450, and not from German sources. Several details, however, should be credited to the German "Heldenbuch" (printed 1477), which the author of the ballad probably did not use directly; it was more natural to assume that the manuscript of the "Didrik Chronicle" which he used contained also this borrowing from the "Heldenbuch." Storm differs in his interpretation from Döring, whose line of proof attempts to show that the chief sources were the Norse "Thidrik Saga" (of 1250) and the "Nibelungenlied." In opposition to these views, Grundtvig points out that the ballad must be regarded as a reshaping of a Low German ballad, which in turn stood closely related to the "Nibelungenlied"; on the other hand, there is no evidence of any particular connection with the Norse or the Swedish "Didrik Saga." Moreover the Swedish "Chronicle" was not very generally known, and the widely spread Didrik traditions could not have sprung from it.[1]

Bugge's arguments seem to me to be incontestable. In content the ballad clearly approximates most closely to the sources he has named, and the linguistic evidence certainly points toward a Low German form. In the following discussion I shall have occasion to repeat the greater part of Bugge's proofs; what I shall bring forward must be looked upon rather as a continuation of Bugge's line of argument. But at the same time I arrive at another conclusion; namely, first that the ballad ought not to be regarded as a popular ballad, and next that it belongs to a very late period, a period much more recent than that to which Gustav Storm assigns it.

Bugge calls attention to the remarkable expression,

A 2. There was many a hero
Who should part with (*fordoie*) his young life.

7. Am I in the heathen land
To part (*fordoje*) with my young life.

9. You are parted (*fordoit*) with your young life.

[1] Bugge in Grundtvig's Folkeviser, IV, 595 ff.; Storm, Sagnkredsene om Karl den Store," pp. 197 ff.; Döring in Höpfner u. Zacher, *Zeit. f. d. Phil.*, II, 274.

Beyond a doubt *fordöje* wás used in old Danish in the sense of "to waste," "to squander"; but there was scarcely ever a time when it could mean "to lose one's life." Hence it must be regarded as a rendering of Low German *vordoden,* "to slay"; *sik vordôn,* "to commit suicide," in modern Dutch *zijn kind verdoen,* "to kill his child."

In A 4 we read:

> Frem da gick hun Buodel
> Hellet Hagens moder:
> "Mig töcte, de fogle
> alle döde vaar."
>
> Forth then stepped Buodel,
> The Hero Hagen's mother;
> "The birds, it seemed to me,
> All were dead."

Here are wanting both rime and assonance, whereas in the model upon which the ballad was formed, — the "Nibelungenlied" (Lachmann's edition), — both, as Bugge points out, are present:

> 1449. Mir ist getroumet hînte
> von engestlicher nôt
> wie allez dasz gefügele
> in disme lande wære tôt.

In verse 17,

> Saa kast hand det blodige hoffuit,
> han kaste hende udi sund,
> saa kaste hand kropen effter
> han bad, de skulde findes ved grund.
>
> He cast away the bloody head,
> He cast it far into the sound,
> So cast he then the body after,
> And bade at the bottom they both be found,

we find the same rimes as in the "Nibelungenlied":

> 1502. Er sluoc im ab daz houbet
> unde warf ez an den grunt:
> diu mære wurden schiere
> den Burgonden kunt.

Compare, in addition, the following lines:

> B 25. That heard Falcko Spillemandt,
> And over the table he sprang (*han snart offuer borden spranck*)

with "Nibelungenlied," 1903:

> von dem tische spranc.

In B 22 *slag* (blow) does not rime with *laa* (lay), but the corresponding German words, *slag* and *lag*, rime well enough.

It may safely be granted that Bugge has made no mistake in the line of argument he has chosen to follow. At the same time, according to my belief, it leads us much farther.

When Hagen steps ashore he finds a *marraminde* (mermaid) asleep upon the bank. The language of the Middle Ages offers us no clew to this word, although Anders Vedel uses it to suit himself in his version of the ballad on the Danish "Series of Kings" (No. 115, B 19). In version B of our ballad we read:

> 6. sig mig det, god maræ,
> mon du est en kunstig quinde:
> skal jeg paa det hedenske landt
> forlade unge liiff min.
>
> Tell me this, good *maræ*,
> An thou be a canny woman:
> Am I in the heathen land
> To quit my young life?

Grundtvig ingeniously suggests that here we should read: *god marœmon* (mermaid) *Du est*, etc., and that *mon* is probably Old Norse *man* (girl), whence *mareminde* (mermaid), which corresponds to the German *mereminne*. But *man* in the sense of girl is utterly unknown to the Danish, and hence it will not do to relate the word in any way to the Norse form. He who noted down the ballad heard sung the German *mereminne*, or some word formed upon it, which he did not understand, and for that reason he split the word, as it stands above. In the other transcript (A 6) stands *mare-mynd*, which is prudently glossed *haff frue* (the usual Danish for "mermaid"). As for the rest, how far it is good Danish to say *forlade mit unge Liv* (quit my young life) must be passed by; Kalkar's Dictionary gives no parallel to this. In Low German the expression is *dat levent vorlisen* (*ich verliese mînen lîp* is also a standing formula with the German minnesingers).

Hagen addresses the mermaid so:

> 7. Wake up, wake up, my mermaid,
> Pretty *lande-viff!*

Bugge remarks, "*lande-viff* I am not acquainted with; *vande-viff* (water-wife) would give us a quite unknown expression for 'mermaid.'" It seems to me that we need only to look to the Low German *lantwîf*, which signifies a "countrywoman," "a girl native to the country" (Flensborg, "Stadsret," §11: "quænæs lanzman til by eldær lanzquinnæ giftæs til by: gyft sick eyn lantman edder lantvrowe in de stat" [that is, if a country man marries into the city or a country woman marries into the city]).

Hagen thereupon rides *saa friskelig* (so heartily) (stanza 11) into the heathen land, and later we meet the expression *tre saa friske helt* (three such hearty heroes) (stanzas 24, 37). There is no doubt that by this is meant "intrepid," "bold"; but when it is objected that the ballad "King Didrik and the Lion" (No. 9, B 2) has *den friske Löve* (the bold lion), we may reply that the word is rarely found in our older tongue, while, on the contrary, it is peculiar to the heroic language of Germany. In the unintelligible stanza 15,

> Jeg kommer aldrig i den stad
> jeg tager ey for hender nöd,
>
> "I never come to such a state
> I suffer aught for her sake,"

(meaning, no doubt, "I am never so situated as to have need of") we seem to note the presence of the German *not hebben* (with the genitive), "to have need of something."

> 18. When they came into the sound,
> A storm rose up *til haan* (against them).

Bugge compares with this the Old Norse *til handa;* it is true that Old Danish offers examples of the use of *til hand*, but in Icelandic and in Danish (see Kalkar's Dictionary) *til hand* most frequently means "in favor of," "in support of," whereas a storm suggests precisely the opposite. It is but natural to call to mind the German *to hant*, the usual German expression for "at once," "immediately."

With stanza 20,

> The man that next stepped after him,
> It was Falquor Spilmand,

can be compared "Nibelungenlied," 1416,

> dô kom der küene Volkêr
> ein edel spilman.

Here it must be remembered, however, that *Spilmand* is not an Old Danish word and never appears in the ballads; on the contrary, we have "Folkvar Spillemand" in Nos. 7 and 8.

> 23. Den ene hand förde en hög,
> er det sinner skjold;
> den anden hand förde en feddel,
> en hertugs sön saa bold.
>
> The one he bears a hawk,
> It is (on) his shield;
> The other he bears a fiddle,
> A brave duke's son it wields.

The second line assuredly can only mean: *ist es seiner schild* (a hawk was pictured on his shield), and, as far as fiddles are concerned, they are never found in the ballads. The popular book "Lucidarius" mentions "the finest fiddle that one may hear"; otherwise "fiddle" is first spoken of in the sixteenth century (see Kalkar's Dictionary under *Fidle*).[1]

> 25. "Let them now all come in,
> Except Hero Hagen."
>
> 27. "We shall hold a *rend* (race) to-day
> With Hero Hagen (*met Helle Hagen*)."

Bugge remarks that here we must read "Hagen" with the accent on the last syllable. If we change the word to *Hagenen* (nominative *Hagene*), as it is generally

[1] In Thomas Gheysmer's "Chronicle," the man who sang before Erik Eiegod is called "citharedus vel fiellator," since apparently a foreign expression was used. The same holds true of the "Rimed Chronicle," which tells that King Erik brought a "Spelman" with him from Rome. Cf. A. Olrik in "Mindre Afhandlinger," ed. by the phil.-hist. Samfund, p. 265.

found in the German text, we shall have made good the missing syllable. When finally we run across stanzas 32, 33,

> In nomine domini, said Hero Hagen,
> Now goes my fiddle well,

we learn what never before was heard of or known; namely, that Latin was spoken in a popular ballad!

As for text B, Bugge has compared stanza 20,

> Her maa ingen suerde
> paa dett slott nu drage,
>
> "Here must be no sword
> Within the castle worn,"

with "Nibelungenlied," 1683,

> man sol deheiniu wâfen
> tragen in den sal.

One will notice here how slavishly and laboriously the Danish text follows the German, and how the verb and the word it governs fail to stand in the same line — a style foreign to ballads.

By this time, surely, the character of the ballad must, on the whole, have been sufficiently indicated. To press the conclusion home I shall call attention to the following lines and to the remarks subjoined thereto:

> A 7. Skal jeg til den hedenske land
> fordoye mit unge liff?
>
> "Am I in the heathen land
> To part with my young life?"

This must be, *to dem lande*.

> A 8. Thou art a knave so bold.

But is a knave (*Knægt*) mentioned anywhere else in the ballads, and is the word used to designate a warrior? I recall having met with it in only one place, namely, in Vedel's version of the ballad "Queen Margrete":

No. 159. 2. King Albret with his knights and knaves (*Rytter oc Knecte*)
And they would go to Skaane;

where, however, all the older texts from various manuscripts testify against Vedel: "King Albret and his good courtiers (*Hofmænd*)." None of the citations in Kalkar's Dictionary are older than the sixteenth century, with the exception of a reference in an Inventory of Agerhus Castle from 1487, which says: "1 Knecktpill with 6 Dozen" (*Danske Magazin*, 3d Series, II, 14). Such stanzas as the following have miscarried remarkably in their transit to Denmark:

A 9. Du haffuer paa dit eget land
Saa meget gods saa fri.

10. Det vaar söllige marre-mind
och der han hoffdet aff hug.

16. Det vor den sellige ferri-mand,
der hand hoffden fra hug.

25. Ud stander frue Kremold
I siner skind grön.

A 9. You have at home in your own country
Castles and lands so free.

10. It was the silly mermaid
Her head he there struck off.

16. It was the silly ferryman,
And off his head he struck.

25. Forth stands Lady Kremold
Arrayed in green fur.

In conclusion there are found everywhere inversions and absurd, annoying repetitions; such as, for instance, in stanza 17: "so cast... he cast... so cast... he bade."

The result of the above investigations may be summed up thus: Here lies before us a translation, often meaningless, of a Low German ballad, characterized by faulty meter and faulty Danish. That should by no means be regarded as a Danish form which has been patterned after a German model, itself an import into Denmark. The ballad is frankly a translation, made particularly by the pen, a translation that could never have resulted in a singable ballad. This view is strikingly confirmed by various conditions. Because of its form and meter this ballad stands unique among all other ballads. Both versions A and B are written in eight-line stanzas, and their division by Grundtvig into four-line stanzas (like that of Vedel's earlier) is wholly arbitrary. Several of the stanzas have now and then a couple of lines too many. Moreover the rhythm is incontestably foreign to that of the average popular ballad; it is based on a meter that is ordinarily never found in Denmark, namely, that of the "Nibelungen" stanza (more of this later). Then, too, the absence of a refrain points to the conclusion that the ballad was never intended for singing. Of not the least significance is the fact that the ballad is preserved in only one manuscript, namely, Svaning's, and then in the composite, final section of the manuscript, where it appears in two different places. Hence this ballad, in all probability, never boasted of a wide circulation; it progressed no farther than a single manor, where some German servant made it known to the housewife, who wrote it down twice. Or more likely, the

German's fellow-servants attempted to give the ballad a Danish dress, which, however, did not fit well; this would account for the two copies of it.

There is not the slightest ground for assuming that a Danish ballad with so meaningless a verse, with so faulty and unintelligible a language, with so unsingable a form, would have been taken up by popular tradition. It has been preserved by the pen and is quite late, certainly as late as the sixteenth century.

Clearly, notwithstanding, this ballad has a certain amount of interest. It manifests to us the vital energy of the "Grimhild Saga," and instructs us concerning an unknown German poem; through its wholly incongruous character it enables us to understand the remainder of our ballads. But its worth lies, not in its holding up to view a sample of ballad style prevailing in the Middle Ages, but in its furnishing a contrast to such a style.

With respect to the ballad of "The Nightingale" (No. 57), Grundtvig has gradually come to the right conclusion. In the second volume of his work he had already pointed out its close relation to foreign versions; the following comparison will show what a family resemblance exists between it and a Netherlandish ballad:

1. I know well where a castle stands,
And it is bedecked so richly
With silver and the red, red gold,
With carved stones walled rarely.

1. Daer staet een clooster in oostenrijc,
Het is so wel ghecieret
Met silver ende rooden gout,
Met grauwen steen doormoeret.

6. Art thou a wild bird alone in the world
   And no man doth know thee;
   Hunger will nip thee, and cold and snow
   That falls on thy way so lonely.

6. Sidi een clein wilt voghelken stout,
   Can u gheen man bedwinghen,
   So dwinghet u die haghel, die coude snee
   Die loovers vander linden.

Still these strophes are not entirely conclusive, since they belong to a kind of unsettled lyrical verse which recurs in various Swedish and German ballads. But the entire atmosphere of the ballad is foreign.

In the Danish ballad the nightingale tells the knight that she is a young girl who has been metamorphosed by her stepmother. She is captured by the knight and imprisoned in a cage. She then undergoes various transformations, ending up in the shape of a serpent; when the knight cuts the serpent with his knife, it turns into a maiden, the daughter of an Egyptian king. Although the corresponding foreign ballads tell no such story of enchantment and disenchantment, yet Grundtvig entertains no doubt that the ballad originates in a foreign type, "its rich lyricism and its land of Egypt invest it with a decisively foreign appearance"; yet he adds, "to regard one of them (the Danish or the Swedish text) as a matter-of-fact translation made by the pen from another language is forbidden by nothing more than the defective rime of the text, for this bears earmarks of having been taken up by popular tradition before it came into print." Later Grundtvig has been more clearly impressed with the ballad's "lack of genuine popular foundation," and with the fact "that from the first it has worn an untraditional guise with, in part, a more artistic (though certainly not a prettier) form than belongs to the genuine popular ballad. It once had complete rime, whereas now it lacks even the ordinary half-rime" (III, 833). Grundtvig has also pointed out that no Danish tradition appears independently of the broadside in which it first came out. Since this ballad is dated from the time of Frederic IV, having been "printed in the year," say somewhere previous to 1721, it seems to me to be a simple matter to name the ballad rightly. It is not a popular ballad, but it is a street song, translated from the German by some poet of Holberg's day.

A ballad which Grundtvig has treated with great fullness is "Fair Anna" (No. 258); it takes up forty pages of his text and is accompanied by a general synopsis. Beyond a doubt it has figured as the most popular ballad of the past few centuries. It tells of an abducted king's daughter, who had been bought by a knight and kept as his mistress, becoming by him the mother of seven sons. The knight concludes later to take another woman as his wife. When the concubine offers wine to the bride, the latter looks curiously at the sorrowing woman and asks her name. Thus she discovers that Fair Anna is her husband's mistress, and even learns that she is her own sister. She then withdraws, and Anna becomes the lawful wife. The ballad, which is found in two of our oldest manuscripts, — Sten Bille's and Karen Brahe's (c. 1550), — resembles very closely, as Grundtvig has pointed out, a German and a Netherlandish ballad. If we now examine text A, we shall find the following striking conditions:

1. Der red en Mur ad stellen ud;

that is to say, there rode a Moor out for to steal.

> 2. Fair Anneck is she called.

This German form of the name is found throughout the entire ballad.

> 17. I give to her my new mills all
> That lie on the plains so wide;
> And they grind out the cinnamon meal,
> And nothing else besides.

> 30. She let fall many bitter tears
> Down into the cup they sank.

See the Netherlandish form (Grundtvig, App. 3, V, 17):

> zii liet er alzoo menigen traan
> al in de gouden wijnschaal zinken.

> 38. Had I now a lansquenet good
> Of honor and of price,
> Who would follow me all through the land
> Like as a faithful wife.

> 19, 23. Fair Anneck, my *frynd-ynne* (a female friend).

These specimens indicate sufficiently well that here we have to do with a German importation; for our ballads indeed never deal with Moors, cinnamon, or lansquenets — who first arose in Germany at the conclusion of the fifteenth century. The language is superlatively un-Danish. *Frynt*, for *Ven* (friend), unquestionably found its way into Denmark during the sixteenth century, but scarcely earlier. No instance of it prior to this time is recorded in Kalkar, and hardly ever is it met with in the ballads. In Langebek's Quarto Manuscript of the time of Frederic II, is found the phrase (No. 254 B) "With great *frynt-lighed* (friendship) she received him"; the other two manuscripts of B, and also the other texts, have "With great *tucht* (propriety)."

The other two texts of "Fair Anna" belonging to the sixteenth century exhibit German forms of words to a less degree:

> B 27. Take with thee thy *kamer-viff* (lady of honor, German *kammerweib*),

but such a mode of address and such a splitting up of the speech as follows, though common to all the forms of this ballad, whether of our time or of that of the earliest recorded copy, is unknown to our other ballads:

> B 4. Fair Anne is to his mother gone;
> "Mother!" said she, "lady!
> Will you ask your own dear son
> If me he will promise to marry?"
>
> 12. Her lord is to Fair Anne gone;
> "Anne, my trust, my treasure!
> What gifts do you intend for my noble bride,
> Will surely give her pleasure?"
>
> 13. "Gifts enow I 'll give to her,
> My king!" said she, "my master!
> I 'll give to her my seven bold sons,
> Of whom I am the mother."
>
> 14. "That is not a generous gift,
> Anne, my trust, my treasure!
> Other gifts you must give to her,
> If you hold dear my pleasure."
>
> 15. "Then I 'll give her gifts enow,
> My king!" said she, "my master!
> I 'll give to her your own dear self,
> And I live alone hereafter."

This mode of address, together with the attempt to employ two titles on either side, runs throughout the whole ballad. For counterparts to this usage our other ballads yield nothing; besides it conflicts with all ballad style to introduce "said she" in the middle of a verse-line and in direct discourse. Foreign texts, on the contrary, furnish parallels to this practice: "och moeder, zeide ze, landsvrouwe!" or "koning Alewijn, zeide ze, heere!"

Whatever else comes to light in the Danish texts of this ballad, thus much is certain: none of them represent the genuine style of the Danish popular ballad; some of them are German in language, and version A exhibits marks of the translation, which add in no way to its æsthetic value. Grundtvig declares that the ballad "could scarcely be dated back farther than about 1400." The facts, however, stand as follows: The ballad was written down in Denmark in 1550, and even at that time it bore most distinctly telltale marks of its homeland; so overwhelmingly present are these that the language is meaningless. Hence it failed to get its German accent rubbed off; if we then concede that it was translated into Danish during the sixteenth century, we surely give to the ballad all its due. It does no more than indicate the nature of the taste obtaining in the sixteenth century; it has nothing to do with the fifteenth century or with the Middle Ages. It presents an incongruous appearance in the company of our other ballads. If the art of song-writing had been known here in Denmark in the fifteenth century, it certainly would have exerted a lasting and unmistakable influence on Danish song-writing.

In "True as Gold" (No. 254) we have likewise a foreign ballad in Danish guise. A young man meets a maiden, who is listening to the song of a bird, and proffers his love to her; but she replies that she already has a good friend.

He then removes his hat from his head and discloses himself as her lover. The foreign and somewhat learned tone is repeated in practically all of the texts. Such verses as these, for example, run through nearly all versions:

A 3. I listen to peace and the song of birds
In this the summer's verdure.

10. The birds they sang in a shady dale,
The nightingales in song were wooing;
They both were afraid of calumny's tale,
Which ever is joy's undoing.

C 10. The birds did sing within the dale,
Lady Nightingale in song was wooing.

Compare Grundtvig, App. 3, V, 1:

Darauf da sitzt Frau Nachtigall,
Das kleine Waldvögelein vor dem Wald.

The ballad has near relatives in a number of lands, and its whole bearing shows its remoteness from the general popular style. The popular ballad falls short of such properly constructed verse. Especially open to suspicion is the precision of such lines as "I hold a youth so dear in my heart," "With all decorum (*Tugt*) she received him then." (Bb has here "With great friendliness [*Fryndtlighed*] she received him then.") Our ballads are not at all given to speaking of so abstract a thing as calumny, which is joy's undoing (more of this later); they do not treat of a youth and a maiden, but of Sir Oluf and Young Else. Hence one is no more surprised to find that a refrain is wanting than he is to find that texts A, B, and C begin the narrative in the *I*-form (though they conclude in the third person), for both of these features are characteristic of the German ballad.

"Little Karen" (No. 101) is built upon the old legend of St. Catherine, whom the emperor attempts to make his mistress. She firmly defends her virtue, and as a result she is cast into the tower, there to suffer the painful tortures of being broken upon the wheel and stuck full of spikes. The ballad exists here in the North only in modern copies; yet Peder Syv mentions a "St. Karen's ballad." On the other hand, there is found a series of German ballads on St. Catherine, one of which is so nearly akin to a Swedish ballad as to suggest that the ballad was translated either from the German into the Swedish or from the Swedish into the German. Grundtvig considers the original to have been Swedish, whereas Bergström and Höijer[1] take the opposite view. Six out of the seven Danish versions have no refrains and go to the other extreme in a repetition of the first or of both lines in a stanza. The seventh form has the refrain "Yes, it is you I was engaged to in my youth," which is also found in version M of "Ribold and Guldborg" (No. 82). It is certainly difficult to make good the assumption that this ballad can be assigned to the Middle Ages; we have far greater reason, or even right, to regard it as having been imported from Germany into Denmark in the seventeenth century. Why, indeed, should the importation have been impossible at this period? At a very recent date, as Bugge has pointed out, the ballad has strayed from Sweden into Eastdale in Norway, and an almost perfect Danish form has forced its way even up to Telemark (II, 546, III, 895). As a final proof of its modern character let me call attention to its

[1] E. G. Geijer och A. A. Afzelius, Svenska Folkvisor; new, much enlarged edition, ed. by R. Bergström and L. Höijer, 1880.

meter, which is altogether different from that of all other ballads; this feature will be dwelt upon more precisely in the following chapter.

"The Bald Monk" (No. 15) sings of one of those intrepid monastic characters which were not infrequently the subject of song and popular tradition in the later periods of the Middle Ages. Twelve warriors lie in ambush before the cloister gate and kill the oxen and cows of the monks. Upon this the bald monk snatches up a heavy ax, and, engaging in combat with them, slays them all. Seized by a sort of Berserker fury the monk rushes out into the woods, where he meets a *trold*, whom he puts to such hard straits that the *trold* in order to persuade his foe to leave off must surrender to him a large amount of gold and silver. On his return home to the monastery the monk continues his violent behavior, mistreating his brother monks and striking out one of the abbot's eyes. The monks therefore conclude to choose him for their abbot.

Some of the verses must have been badly remembered; as, for example:

> 7. de skreff krensen (Kredsen) paa den iord,
> de quad huer-ander en vise;
> det vil jeg for sanden sige:
> det vaar saa beesk en lise.
>
> They wrote a circle upon the ground
> They sang each one a ballad;
> This I say to you in sooth:
> It was relief so wretched.

In others German words appear:

> 9. He fain then would be walking (*spatzere*).

Stanza 13 has: "He struck the monk on the tonsure (*plade*)," where *plade* is the German word *Platte*, that is, "tonsure."

Only one version of the ballad is extant, and that belongs to a broadside of the seventeenth century. Although the printed ballad in this case is virtually of the Middle Ages, we have no reason to assume that the ballad originally lacked a refrain merely because one is not found in the broadside.

In "Henry of Brunswick" (No. 114) Henry has gone away to fight the heathen; he bade his wife to wait for him seven years and not to put a hare in the bear's den. Henry is taken prisoner by the heathen and is compelled to draw the harrow and the plow. One day he sees a lion and a serpent fighting together; he assists the lion, who thereupon follows him about as faithfully as though he were his hound. He sits down upon a stone and falls asleep. Then an angel appears and leads him seven hundred miles to Brunswick, where he arrives just as his wife is about to marry another. The following verses will, I believe, sufficiently indicate the character of this ballad:

A 1. The Duke of Brunsvig,
hvor finder man ien iginn nu slig! [1]
A 11. Du læg aldrig Hare in Björnens Leie.
12. Fangen blev Hertugen, det var værre.
18. Saa underlig Ting emthyrit ham.
25. Saa underlig Ting wyndthyres han.
28. Du sætte Dig neder og hvile Dig,
men jeg vil bede min Skaber for Dig.

[1] Cf. "Persenober," stanza 4 (Brandt, II, 35): "man finder ikke nu mange slig" (one finds not now many such).

1. The Duke of Brunswick,
Where will one find again now such!
11. Never lay a hare in the bear's den.
12. A captive was the Duke, that was true.
18. So wonderful a thing befell him.
25. So wonderful a thing he had to endure.
28. Now sit you down and rest you,
But I shall pray my Maker for you.

If it were really true that the language of the old ballads knew a verb *emthyre*, "to experience," "to endure," such a word would have been found in daily use, for so largely is the language of our ballads a part of common speech; but this is not the case. Just as little do the ballads speak of "my Maker," and just as little do they speak, on the whole, in the language of this ballad. It presents essentially nothing more than the character of a rimed tale.

Two forms of the ballad, A and B, are found; but B, according to Grundtvig, bears throughout "the stamp of an untraditional revision"; "it seems to be an arbitrary revision, for which A has furnished the basis, but for which, in addition, was used another genuine copy, which is not now known." A is found in Karen Brahe's Folio Manuscript and in two other manuscripts, which had a common source, but the first-named manuscript, according to Grundtvig, furnishes the oldest and best text. The text is written, however, in six-line stanzas, of which the first and second lines are a repetition of the last line and a half of the preceding stanza; the third and fourth lines rime together, likewise the fifth and sixth. B has four-line stanzas with the first and second lines riming, and the third and fourth; the repetition, however, is absent (though it may have been present originally). Hence only

Ab and Ac have the general two-line stanza, of which one and a half lines are repeated; but it is extremely doubtful whether this form is not a reworking and an expansion of the heterogeneous form, by which it was forced more into the general style of the popular ballad.

"St. George and the Dragon" (No. 103) is a rather dull and unpoetic composition; its three Swedish forms have the following introductory stanza:

> Praised be the Virgin Mary
> And her well-blessed Son!
> A ballad will I sing to you,
> It was made on the knight St. Orrian.

"Beyond a doubt such a stanza was present in our ballad too," says Grundtvig. If this be the case, the romances and the religious poetry of the monasteries come into close touch with each other. In the Battle of Brunkebjerg (1471) the Swedes are said to have sung the ballad of "St. George." Possibly that is the one which has been preserved; though it is hard to understand how the ballad could serve as a war ballad. At any rate it dates from the late Middle Ages, and it properly belongs to the romances.

The historical ballad "The Defeat in Ditmarsh" (No. 170) (1500 A.D.) is, as Grundtvig says, "composed in an entirely new style,—the allegorical," and it "has a verse-form differing from that of every other old popular ballad. Nevertheless it is neither an art form, nor even a rimed chronicle, but a genuinely popular ballad; it was the property of the people and remained so down to the time when half a century later it was put to paper. All three versions are much distorted, first by oral tradition, and second by the pen." Of the ballad's æsthetic worth I shall not speak here. Thus much, at all events, is certain: the ballad with its stanzas in from three to five lines, with its whole vacillating, enigmatical, and allegorical character, is such a departure from the hundreds of other ballads that it cannot enter into any discussion of the general structure of the popular ballad. The closing lines of version B, "this says the boy who accompanied the host," remind one of the German historical ballads, in which the conclusion often states that the ballad was sung "von einem, der auch dabei gewesen."

There are found a few other ballads which lack refrains; but these are cases where the refrain has been lost. The most noteworthy of these is "Niels Ebbesön" (No. 156), a genuine popular ballad; in none of its five forms nor in Vedel's text is there any refrain. The ballad must consequently be regarded as a peculiar exception. Yet there is no doubt that only by an untoward chance was it robbed of what it originally possessed.

The results of the foregoing detailed investigations may be summed up thus. There are extant only a very few ballads which possess no refrains, and in the majority of these cases the absence of this feature should certainly be charged to an accidental loss attendant upon the course of time. With a few of these exceptions, the lack of a refrain is peculiarly significant, in that a close examination makes them stand forth as ballads that do not belong to the Middle Ages, or, at any rate, to Danish popular poetry. Several of them were imported into Denmark during either the last two hundred years or the sixteenth and seventeenth centuries; others are downright translations, bearing both in their language and in their form marks of their original nature and birthplace; others again can be looked at only as pseudo-popular ballads, since they appear neither to have been sung nor to have been constructed for being sung, but simply and solely to have been written. As a consequence they are met with in only one manuscript.

In the next chapter, when we come to discuss the genuine ballad style and genuine ballad tone, and to investigate what is unique in the contents and spirit of the ballads, we shall meet with these same ballads again. If one should be of the opinion that a sentence of "guilty" ought hardly to be passed upon all the ballads just analyzed above (though certainly they must be classed as suspects), still it will cause no surprise, at any rate, to find again later on the same ballads in the felon's dock prosecuted for other offenses.

CHAPTER V

RIME, RHYTHM, AND MELODY

My investigations in this chapter will cover the outer form and appearance of the ballads. The metrical structure of the ballads, however, I shall not discuss in any great detail. That has already been done very competently by Ernst von der Recke and by Carl Rosenberg. I dare not lay claim to any special knowledge in that field, nor can I bring to bear any new observations. But precisely because Von der Recke's researches lead to several of the same conclusions at which I have arrived independently, I shall give a brief account of the ballad meter.

Using the terms proper to the metrical art of the classics, we may describe the basic form of the ballads to be iambic dimeter, with a strophe of two or four lines. It is seldom, however, that we find the iambic measure intact; its place may be taken by the anapæst, and the dancing step of the choriambus — a single arsis followed by an anapæst — is often heard. On the whole, great freedom prevails. I have had to search for several days to find so regular a verse as this:

No. 114 (B 51),

> Du rag mit Skjæg, Du to mit Haar!
> saa maa Du se mit dybe Saar.
>
> "You shave my beard, you wash my hair,
> So you may see my wounds laid bare."

No. 31 (A 16),

> End haver jeg an danske Hest,
> er födt i Sæbylund;
> hver Sinde han til Möllen gaar,
> da bær han femten Pund.
>
> "And I have yet a Danish horse
> Was born in Sæbylund;
> And ev'ry time he goes to mill
> Bears fifteen hundred pounds."

Hence it is purely by reconstruction that we meet the iambic dimeter as a basic form. In view of the great freedom in which the rhythm moves, it may well be regarded as a fixed rule that each verse-line consists of four (or three) accented syllables, with one or several unaccented syllables in between each pair of accents.

The two-line strophe, which is perhaps the oldest, holds its own throughout the entire Middle Ages down to their conclusion and into the sixteenth century. But the language meanwhile had undergone a change which must have exercised an influence on the verse measure; the terminations disappeared, being supplanted by prepositions; the unaccented particles became numerous, and the articles assumed prominence.[1] This evolution forced out the old metrical system, making way gradually for a broader rhythm, which created a place for extra syllables in the verse. Thus the two-line strophe took on an expanded form.

Ernst von der Recke has illustrated the change in the ballad structure by a comparison of the following verses:

[1] Rosenberg in *Nordisk Tidsskrift*, issued by the Letterstedtska Föreningen, 1883, p. 294.

Icelandic: Förste Terning paa Tavlbord randt,
Svenden tabte, Jomfruen vandt.

Norse: Förste Guldterning paa Tavlebord randt,
Ungersvend tabte, skjön Jomfru hun vandt.

Danish (E): Den förste Gang Guldterning over Tavlebordet randt,
den Baadsmand han tabte og Jomfruen vandt.

Danish (C): Den förste Gang Guldterning
over Tavlebordet randt,
den liden Baadsmand tabte,
og den skjön Jomfru vandt.

Icelandic: The first dice over the checkerboard ran,
The youth he lost, the maiden won.

Norse: The first gold dice over the checkerboard ran,
The young man lost, the fair maid she won.

Danish (E): The first time the gold dice over the checkerboard ran,
The boatman he lost and the maiden won.

Danish (C): The first time the gold dice
Over the checkerboard ran,
The little boatman lost
And the fair maid she won.

We can thus readily see how the number of accents has increased and how the rhythmical movement has changed. The dimeter has been expanded by means of small additions, exchange of words, and embellishments, first in the direction of the anapæst, and next in that of the pæon, until the pæon (◡ ◡ ◡ —) breaks over into two pure iambics (◡ — ◡ —). We then fall back upon the old fundamental iambic foot, but with a doubled number of arses, for an accent has stepped in between the accents originally contiguous.[1] This accounts for the appearance, among other things, of the so-called Little Karen strophe:

> Og hör Du, liden Karen, og vil Du være min,
> syv silkestukne Kjoler dem vil jeg give Dig.
>
> "And hear thou, little Karen, and if thou wilt be mine,
> Seven silk-embroidered dresses I promise will be thine."

This strophe has reproduced some of the peculiarities of the Nibelungen verse (which I shall presently discuss), namely, the use of a pause after the third foot (Kar-en, Kjo-ler), and its dipodic structure. These two styles of verse, however, are not wholly identical.[2]

Here I wish to call attention to the unique situation in which we again meet this ballad of Little Karen (No. 101). In the preceding chapter I pointed out that, on other grounds, it is a late ballad, which was brought over into Denmark from Germany in the course of the seventeenth century (p. 118); now, on metrical grounds, it proves to be a foreign import. Several of the ballads recently found in Jutland appear to have adopted the same metrical system as that of the Little Karen ballad. The late Swedish ballads especially have made general use of it, and to a certain extent that language is better adapted to such a system, since Swedish words often have a secondary accent where the Danish have a wholly unaccented syllable (Dan. *hellige*, Sw. *heliga*), which could easily become weak after a pause (Dan. *og alle de Guds Engle*, Sw. *och alla små Gudsenglar*).[3]

[1] Recke, Principerne for den danske Verskunst, I, 101; Recke, Dansk Verslære, § 93.

[2] For a more detailed treatment, see Rosenberg, in *Nordisk Tidsskrift*, 1883, p. 502.

[3] Rosenberg, in *Nordisk Tidsskrift*, p. 501.

In addition to the ordinary two-line and four-line strophes, we find in some ballads a very peculiar metrical system. In "Sivard and Brynild" (No. 3), for instance, we have:

1. Sivard han haver en Fole,
   den er saa spag.
Han tog stolt Brynild af Glarbjerget
   om lysen Dag.

3. Stolten Brynild og stolten Signild,
   de Jomfruer to,
de gaar dennem til Strande,
   deres Silke at to.

1. Sivard he has a filly,
   A gentle wight.
He bore proud Brynild away from Glarbjerg
   In broad daylight.

3. The proud Brynild and the proud Signild,
   The maidens twain,
They went down to the seashore
   Their silks to clean.

Likewise in "The Betrothed in the Grave" (No. 90):

"Du stat op, stolten Elselille,
   luk op din Dör!
jeg kan saa vel Jesu Navn nævne
   som jeg kunde för."

Op staar stolten Elselille
   med Taare paa Kind:
saa lukker hun den döde Mand
   i Buret ind.

"Get up, get up, proud Elselille,
   Open the door!
I can name the name of Jesus as well
   As I could before."

Up then rose proud Elselille
  With tearful face;
She let the dead man then enter
  Into the place.

In version B of this ballad the meter has already begun to disintegrate. A similar phenomenon is apparent in a number of ballads, in which the old rhythm, such as that above, can but faintly be made out through its disguise. This meter is not found in many ballads; the few that may be named are: "Proud Elin's Revenge" (No. 209), "Peder and Duke Henry" (No. 334), "Hagen's Dance" (No. 465; see above, p. 12), Unpublished No. 42, and Kristensen, I, No. 65; II, Nos. 11, 27.

I have no doubt that this rhythm is old. Rosenberg surmises that the following stanza from an Icelandic satirical ballad (1221 A.D., "Sturlunga Saga," VII, c. 44) once possessed the same meter:

Loptr er í eyjum	Lopt er paa Öerne,
bítr lunda-bein;	gnaver Ben af Lunde (Fugl);
Sæmundr er á heidum,	Sæmund er paa Hederne,
etr berin ein.	spiser ikkun Bær.

Lopt is on the islands,
He gnaws the legs of puffins;
Sæmund is on the moorlands,
He lives on berries alone.

It seems to me, however, that an accent ought to fall on *bítr* and *etr* combined with a weak secondary accent; in other words, the second and fourth lines contain three beats. This indeed is confirmed by one of the manuscripts, in which the fourth line runs: "ok etr berin ein." Hence the above can scarcely be regarded as the parent of this ballad measure.

The most peculiar feature of this rhythm is that the first and third lines form a decided contrast to the second and fourth. While the first line goes dancing upon the tiptoes, the second marches along beating time; one feels, as it were, the heavy tread. I shall touch again upon this feature when I come to speak of the melodies.

The metrical system discussed above is far removed from that of the Nibelungen verse. The latter is well known in the poetry of Denmark. It consists of eight lines, of which the second and the fourth, and the sixth and the eighth, rime in pairs and, as a rule, have masculine endings; whereas the other lines, likewise riming in pairs, have feminine endings, with a characteristic pause at the end of the first, third, fifth, and seventh lines; or, to speak more technically, in place of the fourth arsis in an imperfect iambic tetrameter line stands a pause, which makes up a component part of the rhythm itself. This is the most obvious token of this kind of verse.[1] The genuine old Nibelungen verse has, in addition, the peculiarity of an extra arsis in the eighth line; that is, four complete accents make up the eighth line.

This last characteristic has slipped out of the verse of our modern poets who have composed in this kind of meter, and the strophe has, on the whole, suffered some small modifications. To recall the rhythm to mind I subjoin as a specimen a stanza from Öhlenschläger's "Helge":

Da sagde Konning Helge:
af tvende haarde Kaar
det blideste vi vælge,
som Helten vel anstaar.

[1] Recke, Verskunst, I, 178 ff., II, 68 ff.; Verslære, chap. viii.

Jeg seiled over Vandet
med Kæmper og med Mod,
men jeg vil skaane Landet,
og jeg vil spare Blod.

Then spoke the good king Helge:
" Of two conditions hard
Why let us choose the lesser,
Befits both knight and lord.
I sail far o'er the water,
With men of fearless mood,
To lands I shall give quarter,
And shall also spare blood."

At first sight one might be tempted to scan this form as being made up of iambic lines of six feet with an anapæst in the fourth foot. But then one would miss precisely what is most characteristic of this verse, namely, the accent which falls in between the third and fourth arses (Hel-ge). Here one must imagine the arsis which the ear demands as being replaced by a pause.

The Nibelungen strophe can undergo a series of modifications without the groundwork of its form being in any way disturbed. The second syllable of the thesis can be dispensed with (*Des antwurte Sîvrit*) ; the pause can be shoved forward, two thesis syllables in two adjoining feet can be omitted (*Wol ûf, sprach Sîvrit*), and so forth. The metrical system is extraordinarily rich, capable of being expanded and contracted with wonderfully expressive variations, and with a wealth of forms surpassing all other systems.[1] According to Recke's computation 50,000 millions of combinations can appear in the eight-line strophe ;

[1] Recke, Verskunst, II, 68 ff.

but in spite of the multiplicity of variations, the verse still holds its own character unimpaired.

Not the slightest trace of this meter is to be found in our popular ballads, although, to be sure, the two rhythms have at times been likened with one another, especially since the theory has originated that herein is to be found the source of the Little Karen strophe. The features which differentiate the two meters so sharply are the absence in the ballad both of the above-mentioned pause and of the four accented syllables in the last line of the stanza, and the failure to exhibit a double arsis, which the elision of the syllables of the thesis should create. An exception is exemplified in one ballad, namely, "Grimild's Revenge" (No. 5). Grundtvig has remarked the kinship existing between this ballad and the "Nibelungenlied"; he has set up in parallel columns verses from the German poem and from the ballad of "Grimild" in order to establish the likeness, but without going so far as to pass judgment upon the rhythm of this ballad. Both Rosenberg and Recke have meanwhile shown adequately that the meter of this ballad is wholly out of keeping with that of the other Danish ballads, and, on the other hand, have pointed out its correspondence with that of the Nibelungen verse. A comparison will easily make this apparent:

Dô wuohs in Niderlanden	Det var Fru Kremold,
eins rîchen küneges kint,	hun lod Mjöden blende:
des vater der hiez Sigemunt,	det var saa mangen fri Helled,
sin muoter Sigelint,	hun Buden efter sende:
in einer richen bürge,	"Du bed dennem komme til Orlog,
wîten wol bekant,	Du bed dennem komme til Krig!
nidene bî dem Rîne:	der skal saa mangen fri Helled
diu was ze Sántén genant.	forlade sit unge Liv!"

In sînen besten zîten,	Det var Helled Hagens Moder,
bî sînen jungen tagen,	hun drömte saa underlige,
man möhte michel wunder	at den gode Fole styrte,
von Sivrîde sagen.	som han skulde hen ride:
waz êren an im wüchse	"Den Dröm, han haver at sæde,
und wie schöne was sîn lîp.	kjære Sönne min!
sît heten in ze minne	Vogte Dig alt fuld saare vel,
diu vil wätlîchen wîp.	Din Söster forraader Dig!"

"It was Dame Kremold,
She set the mead a-brewing;
There was many a bold hero
Her summons would be rueing:
'Go bid them come to battle,
Go bid them come to fight!
There is so many a young hero
Is doomed to lose his life!'"

"It was Hero Hagen's mother,
She dreamed so uncannily,
That the good filly stumbled
He was to ride away:
'The dream it will be fateful,
My son, so dear to me!
Guard thyself, I warn thee well,
Thy sister is false to thee!'"

In the words *Orlog*, *Moder*, *styrte*, *sæde*, one can readily notice the pauses spoken of above; the elided theses appear most characteristically in: "Det var Fru Kremold, hun lod Mjöden, . . . 'Du bed dennem,'" etc. Accordingly there is no question that in this one ballad, out of the whole store of ballads, we meet with the Nibelungen verse. Here I have additional proof to bear out my assertion, which I have maintained on many other grounds, that this ballad should by no means be regarded as a popular ballad. It is not a reworking or a reshaping of a German ballad; it is a translation of a foreign text.

I shall now make some comments on the origin of the strophe of the popular ballads. Several critics — for example, N. M. Petersen, Grundtvig, and Rosenberg — have expressed the belief that the two-line strophe must be the oldest. Rosenberg has proposed further the theory that the four-line strophe has developed from the two-line strophe by absorbing the two refrains (the *Indstev* and the *Efterstev*[1]) and making them a component part of the text. Ernst von der Recke has rejected, on good grounds, it seems to me, such an assumption. He calls attention to the facts that in an overwhelming number of cases in which this double refrain occurs, the first refrain is short, the second long, — as, for example, "Med Raade — Kong Valdemar han lover dem baade," — and that, in metrical respects, this type is more perfect than that of two equally long lines, since the *Indstev* clearly discovers itself to be a *Bistev* (secondary refrain) and the *Efterstev*, a *Hovedstev* (principal refrain).[2] Hence the ordinary form of the refrain does not lead to the supposition that the two refrains formed a transition to the four-line stanza.

For a connecting link one must rather by far look to the ballad form where the first and second refrains rimed together. But this type is comparatively rare. Rosenberg has cited as an example of a transitional form "The Mermaid's Prophecy" (No. 42), where the first refrain runs constantly, "Den Havfrue danser paa Tillie," while the

[1] Note by translator: The *Indstev* comes after the first line, and the *Efterstev* after the second line, of a two-line strophe.

[2] Recke, Verskunst, I, 114 ff.

last refrain varies: "For hun skal fremme min Villie," "Nu haver jeg fremmet Din Villie," "Da fremmed hun ikke min Villie," etc., thus to a certain extent becoming a part of the strophe. This example does not seem to be happily chosen, since Vedel alone has given this variable refrain. The old text in Svaning's manuscript, which was Vedel's source, shows without variation: "For [once *men*] hun haver [havde] fremme hendes Villie." Finally the variable refrains are, on the whole, as was pointed out above, such a late product and so incongruous with the entire essence of the ballad that they surely could not have exercised such an influence on the basic form of the ballads.

I do not believe that we are in any position to point to any transition between the two-line and the four-line stanzas, and I am far rather inclined therefore to agree with Ernst von der Recke, who advances the theory that the four-line stanzas of the Heroic Ballads made their way up into Denmark from Germany along with the subject matter, which in general, to be sure, has been brought to us from the South. For confirmation of this one needs but to call to mind all that has been advanced concerning the traditions dealing with Dietrich of Bern.

According to N. M. Petersen, the two-line stanza of the Heroic Ballad had its origin in the old Norse *Kviðuhátt* (name of an Icelandic verse). Hence such a stanza as this (from the "Völuspá")

Önd þau ne áttu	Spirit they had not,
óð þau ne höfðu	And mind they had not,
lá né læti	Blood nor voice
né litu góða	Nor fair appearance.[1]

[1] Taken from "The Elder Edda," by Olive Bray, p. 283.—Translator.

should be reconstructed so that the first and second lines would form the first line of the two-line stanza of the Heroic Ballad, the other two its second. Rosenberg subscribes to this theory, which he finds strengthened by the appearance presented by some of the earliest recorded ballad stanzas. To this end he cites a fragment of a ballad met with in a runic manuscript of about 1300: "Drömde mik en dröm i nat um silki ok ærlik pæl [pæl — some costly stuff]" (I dreamed a dream late last night of silk and the velvet fine), and another fragment discovered in an old Swedish manuscript of 1420–1450:[1]

Redhu kompana redhobona (Fællerne rede redebonne)
iwer thiockka skogha
oc gildo met synd
venisto jomfrw.

The company rode ready
Through thick forests
And beguiled into sin
The fairest maiden.

Here where the verse contains alliteration, the resemblance ought presumably to be striking. Rosenberg then compares the verses in this manner:

lá né læti	drömde mik	redhu kompana
né litu góða	en dröm i nat	redhobona

Meanwhile Rosenberg himself has set forth an objection to this theory.[2] He remarks that in the Kviðuhátt every accent is equally strong, whereas in the line "Drömde mik en dröm i nat," the second and fourth accents are weaker than the first and third. And this is precisely the

[1] Fornsvenskt Legendarium, p. 877.
[2] Nordboernes Aandsliv, II, 412.

case with all ballads; or, in other words, the ballad verse has a far more nimble and rapid movement than has the Kviðuhátt. Rosenberg brings to light still another point which might induce one to look upon the Kviðuhátt as the source of the two-line strophe; namely, that in our ballads a pause is perceptible (Dronning Dagmar ligger — i Ribe syg, "Queen Dagmar lay — in Ribe sick"). This incision in the line is, as he presumes, general and seems to point to a keen desire on the part of him who first invented such a verse to hear each portion of the verse by itself. Or, in other words, in that place where the two short lines of the Kviðuhátt have grown together, a scar is noticeable. Recke has satisfactorily established, however, that no such pause is found in the verse-line; if such had been present, one would never have been permitted to set polysyllables with two accents exactly across the alleged gap (Det maa nu hver Danekvinde vide, "That now may each Danish woman know"), as often happens to be the case.[1]

As an additional objection to the theory of descent from the Kviðuhátt Rosenberg himself urges that it is inexplicable why only half of the Kviðuhátt strophe should be used to form the ballad verse; whereas the last four short lines ought to have formed two more ballad lines. Furthermore the remaining ornamentations of the ballad rhythm differ wholly from those of the Kviðuhátt. In the measure of the latter, end-rime is never found, but alliteration appears; and Rosenberg admits that in the ballads the alliteration is "never sought for as a regular embellishment." I shall point out below that alliteration plays no part whatever in the ballads. Finally the refrain is an

[1] Recke, Verskunst, I, 109 ff.

indispensable part of the ballad. For the rest I shall merely remark, with reference to the old ballad verses cited above in parallel form, that there exists some difficulty in using them as examples, because they are the opening verses, which very often possess a firmer structure than does the body of the text, and besides are composed in a meter that varies from that of the stanzas following. On the whole, it is best to leave alone the question, How did the meter of our ballads arise? There is only one thing, I believe, which can be asserted in all reason, and that is that we gain nothing, but rather involve ourselves in confusion and obscurity, by taking the verse laws of old Icelandic prosody as a starting point for comparisons. It holds good here, as in so many other instances, with respect to the form and subject matter of the ballads, that one arrives at a far more correct judgment if he bears in mind the great distance and the glaring differences between the ballads and the poetry of antiquity.

We shall next consider the rime. The ballads have syllabic rime; that is, the final vowel sounds of the accented syllables in the riming words accord. The ballads, however, do not require perfect rime (consonantal); that is, a rime in which all the letters following the vowels accented are in agreement. If we examine a ballad like "German Gladensvend" (No. 33), we shall find, in addition to rimes like *Hand — kan*, *smaa — slaa*, *Ö — Mö*, rimes such as *Stavn — kan*, *sammel — Vand*, *Strand — Barn*, *hvide — given*, *Vinge — paa Kinde*, *Rhin — Tid*, which can be denominated assonantal rimes; that is, rimes in which the consonants following after the same vowel are different. In this same ballad, however, we meet with rimes in which the vowels are different, such as *fem — kom*, *fem — Sön*, *Hand — hjem;* that is, the so-called consonantal assonance, in which the similarity of sounds and the euphony are brought into agreement by the consonants.

It would seem then that the poets of the Middle Ages were far more lax in their rimes than are the poets of modern times. Our day has the great advantage, however, of possessing a language that is rich and various in a wholly different way; and, in addition, many rimes which were then not allowable or usable are now regarded as good and permissible. I shall call attention to a fact which every one who knows anything of the language of the popular ballad will confirm; namely, that diphthongs were never employed, except very reluctantly, as riming vowels; hence there would not be found such rimes as *Vei — ei*, *Feide — Leide*, *havde — lagde* (in No. 196, recorded in 1650, stanza 13 has *Ravn — Navn*). If one did use a diphthong in one of the riming words, he never made it rime completely with the second riming word. Of precisely such a nature are the rimes in "German Gladensvend" — *Stavn — kan;* and in the rimes *Stavn — Havn*, which appear in one stanza, we have a mistake for *Hav* (*ud af den vilde Hav*, "out of the wild sea"). Such rimes as *undre — dundre*, *vandre — andre* we shall search the ballads for in vain. Whereas such rimes as *Bjerg — Dværg*, *Konster — Blomster*, *Borrig — Sorrig* swarm in the poetical romances, their presence in the ballads was not permitted. Least of all will one come across such rimes as *ringende — klingende*. This points to a self-imposed restraint, and leads to the conclusion that everything which could smack of jingle was avoided.

Furthermore let us investigate whether, besides end-rime, the ballads employed alliteration. By alliteration, consonantal rime, alliterative verse, is meant that two words following in close succession have the same consonant or consonants at the beginning, immediately preceding the vowels (*Skam og Skjændsel, Spot og Spe, fra Top til Taa*), together with the condition that these occur in the most important syllables.[1] In the introductory stanza to "Sune Folkesön" (No. 138) we have "strongly alliterative verse," as Grundtvig calls it:

A 1. Nu ligger de Helte veien
saa vidt over Sveriges Land:
det voldte Hr. Sune Falkursen,
voldtog den Lillievand.

Now lie the heroes fallen
O'er Sweden far and wide;
That was the fault of Sune Falkursen,
Beguiled a lily maid.

The same holds good also of the corresponding stanza in the Swedish ballad:

De hjelther de ligge slagne
så vitt om Sveriges landh,
alt sedan Hr. Sone Folvarson
borttog det lillievand.

The heroes they lie slaughtered
O'er Sweden far and wide,
All since Sir Sone Folvarson
Rode off with a lily maid.

As for the Danish verse, I shall merely remark that the singer, if he had been truly artistic, would have used a

[1] Recke, Verslære, p. 192.

new alliterative letter in the last two lines; and, as for the Swedish verse, that only the third line contains genuine alliteration; that is, an alliteration in which all the consonants preceding the accented vowel agree.

That alliteration is found in our ballads is commonly regarded as an accepted fact. Even Rask made mention of it in the introduction to his Anglo-Saxon grammar (p. 28). Many people, especially philologists, have later remarked it or have gleefully pointed it out, even though they possibly confessed that it was not used as a regular embellishment. Against this supposition, however, one voice has been raised in loud protest, that of Ernst von der Recke, and his fine, poetical ear ought indeed in such a question to count for more than the eyesight of philologists, deceived as it is with the aspect of words. We shall now demonstrate that alliteration is by no means any more prevalent in our ballads than it is in any euphonious poem, that it was never employed consciously by the balladists, and that he labors under a misapprehension who either believes that he has frequently observed it or believes that he can produce an older and more correct version — one which once had alliteration, but which now has broken down under the tooth of time.

The poets of that day felt no less than do the poets of to-day the unconscious value of alliteration in giving the verse cadence and ring; but they never adopted it deliberately, unless exceptionally for a special purpose. They did not place the alliterative letter in the weightiest syllables nor in the accented syllables, and it is only when the alliterative letter and the accent fall together that there can be talk of alliteration. One will perceive this more clearly by running through the examples cited. Concerning text A of "Young Sir Thor and Lady Thore" (No. 72), for instance, Bugge says that it "sounds ancient and sonorous and vigorous; alliteration occurs very frequently." Let us append here the following stanzas as a specimen of this long ballad (III, 843), in which this ornament supposedly manifests itself. The knight's daughter comes to her father and says:

A 40. *L*over I mig til Tavlbord at gaa,
den *l*ange Dag maa mig forgaa.

41. Den Ridder *l*ærte sin Datter
den *l*ange Dag til Aften.

42. "En *l*iden Stund dog ikke *l*ænge;
Du vinde ikke Guld af fremmede Svende!

43. "Du *v*ogte Dig *v*el for Thor hin rige,
jeg frygter saa *v*ist, han *v*il Dig svige."

44. Bruden axler *Sk*arlagen*sk*ind;
hun gaar i Loft for unge Thor ind.

45. Jomfruen ind ad Dören *t*ren,
unge *Th*or staar hende op igjen.

46. Den förste *T*avel paa *T*avelbordet randt,
hin unge *Th*or Legen vandt.

40. Promise to sit at the chessboard with me,
To pass the tardy day away.

41. The knight he taught his young daughter
The tardy day's long measure.

42. "One little hour, but stay no longer,
And win no gold from foreign suitor!

43. "But guard thee 'gainst Sir Thor the wealthy,
I fear the game will go for thee badly."

44. The bride flung on her robes so red,
And aloft to meet young Thor she sped.

45. The maid stepped in the open door,
Then stood up to meet her young Sir Thor.

46. The first move on the chessboard done,
The young Sir Thor the match had won.

In these stanzas I have pointed out all the places where alliteration shows the slightest trace of having been used; but it is manifest to all how weak and tame, how flat and meager all that alliteration sounds, simply because the alliterative syllables are, for one thing, only half such, and, for another, are found in weakly accented syllables.

Highly significant are the remarks which Bugge makes concerning "The Soul at Heaven's Door" (No. 106), as well as his general conception of this ballad. The ballad runs as follows:

1. Der kom en Sjæl for Himmeriges Dör:
Herre Jesu være her inde hos os!
hun bad sig ind udi Jesu Navn.
Herre Jesu Christ, for han bær Himmeriges Krone.

2. Der udkom en Engel, for Sjælen at staa:
"Slet ingen Naade saa kan Du faa.

3. "Hvad gjorde Du om *M*andagen?
Du vilde ikke give den Hungrige *M*ad.

4. "Hvad gjorde Du om *T*irsdagen?
Du vilde ikke lædske den *t*örstige Sjæl.

5. "Hvad gjorde Du om Onsdagen?
Du vilde ikke laane den Nögne Dine Klæder.

6. "Hvad gjorde Du om Torsdagen?
Du vilde ikke laane den *H*usvilde *H*us.

7. "Hvad gjorde Du om *F*redagen?
Du vilde ikke höre den *F*attiges Bön.

8. "Hvad gjorde Du om *Lö*verdagen?
   Du vilde ikke op*l*ukke de Fangnes Dör.

9. "Hvad gjorde Du om *Sön*dagen?
   Du vilde ikke gaa til Kirken med *Bön*.

10. "Prædiken var ikke halv endt,
Herre Jesu være her inde hos os!
   förend Du gik hjem og syndede igjen."
Herre Jesu Christ, for han bær Himmeriges Krone.

1. There came a soul up to Heaven's door;
Lord Jesus be here about us!
   She prayed to get in in Jesus' name.
Lord Jesus Christ, for He bore Heaven's crown.

2. Out came an angel the soul to halt:
   "You cannot win such favor at all.

3. "What have you on Monday done?
   You would not give the hungry meat.

4. "What have you on Tuesday done?
   You would not slake the thirsty soul.

5. "What have you on Wednesday done?
   You would not loan the naked your clothes.

6. "What have you on Thursday done?
   You would not loan the homeless a house.

7. "What have you on Friday done?
   You would not hear the poor folks' prayer.

8. "What have you on Saturday done?
   You would not set open the prison door.

9. "What have you on Sunday done?
   You would not go to church with prayers.

10. "The sermon was scarcely half at an end,
Lord Jesus be here about us!
   Before you went home and sinned again."
Lord Jesus Christ, for he bore Heaven's crown.

In admitting this ballad among the old popular ballads of Denmark, for such is the title of his work, Grundtvig clearly implied that it belonged to the Middle Ages. It seems to me, however, that the question may properly be raised, What right has this song to a place among our popular ballads, and, everything considered, why should one assume that it is older than 1732, the date of its appearance in a broadside? Its only resemblance to popular ballads lies in its double refrain. But the refrain had its place in the folk poetry of the seventeenth and eighteenth centuries as well as earlier. By this time the old popular ballads with refrains had become widely spread in popular tradition, just as the refrain is yet to be found to-day; even religious songs were provided with refrains. It is extremely doubtful whether this ballad can be said to possess a meter. The rimes are not worth mentioning; in place of genuine rime the "author" of the ballad has used a sort of rime, similar to which nothing has ever been seen before or after; as, for example, *Fredagen—Fattiges Bön, Löverdagen—oplukke Dör, Söndagen—Bön,* etc. In the whole ballad there is not the slightest trace of Catholicism; hence on this ground one should not regard it as being hundreds of years old. Not the slightest trace of old linguistic forms exists to constrain us to date it back farther than 1732. Finally, as Grundtvig points out, the theme of a soul at Heaven's door has been handled a number of times in German song. Here, in other words, we have every reason for insisting on the rules observed of all other historical sources; namely, that the age of a document is first and foremost determined according to the date when it first appeared. Accordingly the ballad may be characterized as a childish, unpoetical production by some penny ballad monger and poet of Aabenraa[1] in Holberg's day.

Nevertheless Bugge says in connection with this abortion of a ballad that "it seems to be something more than an accident that alliteration is found in several stanzas where on the other hand rime is wanting," and that from this alliteration we must conclude "that alliteration was present also in stanzas 5, 6, and 9. Perhaps in stanza 6 we should read *Tag* for *Hus*, and in stanza 9 *Sang* for *Bön*. From stanza 4, moreover, we should conclude that the ballad was composed after the sound þ had disappeared from Danish; for the words *Tirsdag* and *törstig*, which here rime together, were in old Danish *Týrsdagr* and *þyrster*. The alliterating verse was therefore composed in Danish in that period when the sound þ was no longer heard" (III, 903). This theory has found another distinguished supporter in Gustav Storm, who cites this ballad as one of his proofs that alliteration and *Fornyrdalag* (a special kind of Icelandic meter) maintained themselves a long time in Denmark; the ballad "is no older than the fourteenth century, perhaps the fifteenth," "but it is apparently in a transitional stage, since it has given up *Fornyrdalag*."[2]

I can make out nothing else than that some wretched street versifier, who lived at the beginning of the eighteenth century, has led these learned gentlemen entirely astray. If it were not for the fact that we have been accustomed

[1] A street in Copenhagen where, in Holberg's day, a ballad monger lived.

[2] Storm, Sagnkredsene om Karl den Store, p. 171.

to look at the popular ballads en masse, according to a tradition that goes back to the Middle Ages, without deeming it possible for us to discriminate between the recent and the remote, the new and the old, we should never have imagined a source to be five hundred years old which bears the date 1732.

The cause of the misunderstanding meanwhile lies in the wholly inaccurate conception of the time when alliteration made its appearance in the ballads. For the facts represent the precise antithesis of what is held by many scholars. Alliteration is something recent and originated in the poetry of art. In the following arguments I shall try to make good my position.

Let us turn again to the stanza cited above from "Sune Folkesön" (No. 138):

C 1. Nu ligger de Helte veide
saa vide under Sveriges Ö:
det volder Hr. Sune Folkesön,
voldtog den væne Mö.

Now lie the heroes fallen,
On Sweden's strand so wide;
That is the fault of Sune Folkesön,
Beguiled so fair a maid.

This ballad is recorded in a score of different manuscripts and exists in half a score of different versions. Hence there is no lack of good material to use in investigating the question, Which is the best and earliest text? The earliest is found in Karen Brahe's Folio Manuscript of 1550 and in Rentzel's manuscript of Frederick II's time, as well as in several later manuscripts. It begins as follows:

B 1. Kong Magnus var Konge i Sverrig,
han havde de Döttre to;
de var dem baade liden og unge,
der dennem faldt Moder fra.
Nu ligger de Helleder veien.

King Magnus was king of Sweden,
He had two daughters born;
When they were yet both young and tiny,
Of their mother they were left forlorn.
Now lie the heroes fallen.

Here we see that the introductory verse with alliteration is altogether wanting. The version next to this one in point of time of recording is that of C, which is found in Langebek's Folio Manuscript, belonging close to 1600 and in other manuscripts. Its first verse reads as above. This same verse appears likewise in texts A, D, E, F, K, and L, that is, in manuscripts the earliest of which hark back to the period between the beginning and the middle of the seventeenth century; on the other hand, it is wanting in G, which is recorded in Countess Christiane's manuscript (1660). H, which belongs to about the same period, does not possess alliterative verse, although its last stanza runs:

H 33. Nu ligger de Hellede veied
og ind i Sverriges Rige:
bort da red Hr. Sonnildt
alt med den Jomfru saa rige.

Now lie the heroes fallen
Within the realm of Sweden;
Away then rode Sir Sonnildt
All with the rich young maiden.

Text I, of the seventeenth century, lacks this stanza altogether. The result shows therefore that in the oldest manuscripts the alliterative stanza in question is not present, and that, in several other forms of the ballad also, it is wanting.

If we examine the Swedish versions, we shall see that B (Geijer, No. 92), according to a broadside of the eighteenth century, presents an entirely different beginning and exhibits no alliteration in the first stanza. The same can be said of C. Version A (Arwidsson, No. 163), according to a manuscript of the seventeenth century, opens up, on the other hand, with the following stanza:

> De hielther de ligge slagne
> så vitt om Sveriges landh,
> alt sedan Hr. Sone Folvarson
> borttog det lillievand.
> *Der ligge de hielther slagne.* (See p. 141.)

The alliterative letter, if such can be found, is here a different one; but, in any case, only the third line has genuine, regular alliteration. It is therefore extremely doubtful whether, on the whole, this stanza will serve as proof that alliteration existed in the Middle Ages.

Another example will help to show when alliteration arose. We find in Vedel's tragical ballad of "Sir Ebbe's Daughters" (No. 194):

> 33. Hver den Svend, som rider ad gilie,
> og *B*eilen til *B*olen vil vende,
> han *v*over der*v*ed baade Liv og Gods,
> slig Forsæt tager aldrig god Ende.

> Whoever the youth rides out to a brothel,
> From wooing to whoring is descending,
> He places in peril both life and wealth,
> Such purpose comes never to good ending.

There is no question here that the stress falls upon the alliterative syllables with a clear consciousness of its significance. Peder Syv has a proverb: "Many turn wooing to whoring" (in proverbs alliteration is common). We know, however, the source of Vedel's stanza, and there the above stanza is not found; nor is it met with in any other manuscript of this text, nor in texts B and C. Therefore no doubt exists that Vedel himself is the author of the verse.

Alliteration strikes the ear just as forcibly in the following stanza from "Mettelil and Queen Sofie" (No. 130):

C 13. Ingen *F*ugl *f*löyer saa *f*ast under Sky,
som Hr. Nielus rider sin *G*anger *g*jennem By.

No fowl flies so fast above the ground,
As Sir Nielus rides his pacer past the town.

But here, too, Vedel's source is well known to us, and his stanza is, as Grundtvig points out, borrowed from version B, whose ninth stanza runs very differently:

Ingen (Fugl) flyer saa snart under Sky,
som Hr. Nicholaus rider igjennem den By,

None (fowl) flies so swiftly above the ground,
As Sir Nicholaus rides past the town;

here we have no alliteration, but rather a decided euphony, which is gained without the aid of the much prized alliteration. Furthermore let us cite a well-known stanza from "Niels Ebbesön" (No. 156), which in Vedel runs:

F 25. Herr Anders Frost, den duelig Mand,
forsvarer saa vel sin Ære;
*v*ilde han af Eder Orlov have,
hvi *v*ilde I ham det *v*ægre?

Sir Anders Frost, the gallant man,
Knows well how to defend his honor;
If he of you a furlough seeks,
Then why refuse him the furlough?

The other and older texts have:

A 20. vilde han Orlov af Eder tage,
hvi maatte han det ikke gjöre?

B 18. vil han Orlov have,
hvi monne han det ei faa?

C 17. Om en Svend vil Orlov have,
hvi maa han det ei gjöre?

A 20. Would he a furlough of you request,
Why should he then not have it?

B 18. If he a furlough will have,
Why may he then not get it?

C 17. If a youth asks for a furlough,
Why should he then not have it?

(This verse is wanting in D and E.) Here again Vedel has refined the last line in order to give it alliteration. It cannot be gainsaid that in fullness and variety of tone the old verses are just as effective.

Thus we see that it is Vedel who concocted the alliteration, but we have no reason for following the same methods, as is often done by modern editors. In "Svend Vonved" (No. 18), which tells of the wonderful hero who carries so many animals, occur the lines:

A 16. Og han havde Lossen paa sin Bag
og Björnen paa sin höire Hand.

B 22. Bassen havde han paa sin Bag
og Björn i Hænde.

C 28. Han havde Björnen paa sin Bag
og Bassi paa sin Lænde.

A 16. And he had the lynx upon his back,
And the bear in his right hand.

B 22. The boar he had upon his back,
A bear in his hand.

C 28. He had the bear upon his back,
And the boar upon his loins.

Concerning the above Bugge remarks: "This verse has no rime in any of its three forms, and I see no evidence that it ever had. On the other hand, it has alliteration, for *Bassen* in B and C is more correct than *Laassen* in A. Here therefore, in the middle of a ballad with end-rime, is left standing a verse which, in olden time, contented itself with the customary alliteration" (III, 787). As has been pointed out already, there does not exist in our ballads the slightest evidence of alliteration having been handed down from an older period, let alone its having taken the place of end-rime. Furthermore it seems to me an easy matter to find the end-rime which the verse probably had; namely,

Han havde Björnen paa höire Hænde
og Lossen paa sin Lænde.

In his version of the ballad in his "Selected Popular Ballads," Grundtvig happens upon the same idea; but since he starts from the point of view that the ballads aspired to alliteration, he writes:

22. Bassen bar han paa Lænde
og Björn i höire Hænde.

For several reasons I am inclined to believe that my attempt at reconstructing the verse comes nearer to the genuine tone of the Middle Ages.

On the whole, it is significant to observe how alliteration, in the course of time, becomes attached to verses; where one verse, for instance, originally possessed simple and natural alliteration, gradually several became infected with it. This will be evident from a comparison of the following stanzas of "King Hans' Wedding" (No. 166):

A 17. Dagen dages östen,
og Bölgen blæser blaa.

B 16. Dagen den dages östen,
og Bölgen den blæser blaa.

C 19. Bören blæser for Östen,
og Bölgeren [Bölgerne] driver paa Sand.

A 17. Day is dawning eastward,
And billows are blowing blue.

B 16. Day it is dawning eastward,
And billows they are blowing blue.

C 19. The breeze is blowing easterly,
And the billows dash on the sand.

The last version is undoubtedly the genuine one; not only is it found in the oldest manuscript (1550), — A is nearly contemporaneous, — but it also agrees far better with the context, which relates that the present time offers a favorable opportunity to return home to Denmark. The desire for alliteration, however, in A and B has given rise to a meaningless line ("Bölgen blæser blaa"). In "Svend Felding" (No. 32) is set forth exactly the same situation; namely, that they who are to fetch home the foreign princess will not wait longer, but will fare homeward:

A 16. Bören blæser saa mildelig,
og Bölger leger paa Sand.

The breeze is blowing so gently,
The billows play on the sand.

There is a ballad whose capital verses often use, among other devices, alliteration; namely, "The Trold and the House-wife" (No. 52). In one of the oldest texts we find:

B 4. Hunden gjöer i Gaarden,
og Hyrden tuder i Horn;
Hanen galer i Bænke,
som hannem gives Korn.

The hound cries in the courtyard,
The herd toots on his horn;
The cock on his perch is crowing,
When they feed him corn.

Have not these lines a splendid ring? But does it lie entirely in the fact that the ballad aimed to use alliteration? No, certainly not in this alone; rather it lies in the facts that alliteration was not allowed to dominate, that, on the whole, all the devices which go toward making a language sonorous — variation in sound and shifting cadences — have operated to this end. In these four lines not one of the total sum of vowels in the language has been forgotten. For the sake of comparison one should read how this stanza runs in a later form, which, through the fondness of the seventeenth century for having verses permeated with alliteration, allows this feature a prominent place:

C 7. Saa höit da *g*jöde den *g*ode Hund,
som Jægeren blæser i Horn:
og saa da *g*aled den *g*ode Hane,
som Bonden havde *g*ivet sin Korn.

As loud then growled the good hound,
As the hunter blows on his horn;
And so then crowed the cock so good
When the farmer had fed him his corn.

Or let us cite another verse from the ballad, such as, for example:

B 2. Han hugger neder Eg, han fælder neder Bög,
han bygger op Husen saa faste.

C 3. Han hugger Eg, han hugger dér Birk,
og Bögen monne han dér fælde.

B 2. He hews down the oak, he fells down the beech,
He builds up a house so strongly.

C 3. He hews the oak, he hews the birch,
The beech he did there harry.

B is pleasing simply because of its rhythmical vibration, its parallelism, and, at the same time, its variation; C, however, has laid a preponderating stress upon alliteration, calling therefore into requisition the birch tree, which otherwise has no place in the botany of the ballads.

Altogether I can heartily agree with the assertion of Ernst von der Recke that the ballads exhibit no trace of alliteration: "The opinion that such a trace was actually to be found has been repeated from one time to another, but it is wholly groundless."[1] Thus I have attempted to show that the supposed alliteration is in reality no such thing, and that it is not found in the oldest texts; I have also pointed out the desire of the later, artistic age to make use of this same kind of rime in the construction of verses.

To the above I shall add meanwhile one more observation. Of the marvelous stuff which makes up a verse-line —its coloring, ring, and atmosphere, that which changes prose into poetry—alliteration is and always will be a part.

[1] Recke, Verskunst, I, 112.

Even in our daily speech we cannot avoid using it; every one who says from top to toe, head over heels, fair and free, with hide and hair, every one who speaks of foul and fair, employs such rime; it comes to our hands as a natural instrument and adornment. Only when we are first made aware of this do we discover to what great extent we are inclined to its use. When Jourdain in Molière's "Le Bourgeois Gentilhomme" becomes informed of the difference between poetry and prose, he breaks out in a transport of joy: "So I have truly been talking prose for over forty years without having had the least suspicion of it." So it is with us when our attention is called to the fact that we use alliteration, and when we see how the popular ballads employ it as they do many other poetic devices.

Every language strives after euphony; likewise did our language of the Middle Ages. The modern poets also frequently use alliteration; but here again we should determine clearly whether alliteration predominates in the poet's song, whether it coincides with the verse's weightiest word and with the accent, whether it is the poet's main poetic device in addition to end-rime, or whether it is supported and shaped according to the presence of the devices which generate euphony. Among these last I must lay especial stress upon assonance, that is, agreement between the principal vowels of two words, as being of far more value than alliteration; for it gives rise to a chord, whereas alliteration often sounds only the same note an octave lower. This is frequently overlooked by our latest poets and prose writers; for, along with a very disgusting affectation, which has broken out over the country, alliteration has made its appearance in prose. Œhlenschläger and our older poets certainly did not commit such errors, and even the following well-known verses of the priest Laurids Kok (ob. 1691) can prove suggestive:

> *D*anmark, *d*eiligst *V*ang og *V*ænge,
> lukt med *B*ölgen *b*laa,
> hvor de *v*akre *v*oxne Drenge
> kan i Leding gaa
> mod de *T*ydsker, Slaver, Vender,
> hvor man dem paa *T*og hensender;
> en Ting mangler for den Have,
> *L*edet er af *L*ave.

> Denmark, fairest fields and forests,
> Hedged with billows blue,
> Where the sturdy, stalwart warriors
> On expeditions go
> Against the Wends, Slavs, and Germans,
> When one to war them summons;
> In the garden is one thing lacking,
> The gate itself is sagging.

Is not this stanza closely packed with alliteration, and yet many other factors operate with it in the most beautiful union, such as a sonorous assonance built upon all the vowels of the language, a variation in sound that causes one to pass by the alliteration and to delight only in the euphony. The statements here set forth will be borne out by a consideration of the refrain.

In the refrains the absence of rime as an ornament leads indeed to a more frequent use of alliteration. On the whole, the refrains are subject, as I shall have many occasions to point out, to other rules than to those of the stanza. I shall cite here:

No. 146. Og foer de vide om Verden.
No. 183. Se, Folen för Liget over Hede.
No. 63. Saa render han rank alt under skjönne Jomfruer.

No. 146. And wide through the world they roamed.
No. 183. See, the colt bears the corpse over the moor.
No. 63. The horse runs so brisk beneath the beautiful maidens.

In his "Selected Popular Ballads," Grundtvig offers as a refrain to No. 1:

Tor han tæmmer Fole sin i Tömme,

Thor he breaks his colt to the bridle,

but whether this refrain was in use in Denmark is open to question. Manuscripts from the seventeenth century, on the other hand, show us that in the Norse it ran: "Torekal tömmaa föelen sin med toumaa," and in the Swedish: "Thorer tämjer fåhlen sin i tömme." In Denmark the refrain ran, both early and late: "Saa vinder man Suerkin" (So wins one Suerkin, that is, the proud, haughty woman). Far more frequently than alliteration, however, we find in the refrain assonance, or agreement between the accented vowels of two words:

No. 8. Men K*on*gen raader for B*or*gen.
No. 35. Maatte jeg *en* med de *vœ*neste f*an*ge!
No. 59. Den R*os*en vilde han l*ov*e.
No. 79. Saa haver hun l*ag*t hans Hjerte udi T*vang*.
No. 80. Saa vel da for*gang*es vor *Ang*est.
No. 84. De *dans*ke Fruer udi *Dans*en.
No. 84. Det volder min egen R*os*e; min Hjerte haver ei R*o*.
No. 127. Saa let da *gan*ger der *Dan*sen.
No. 206. Der min *Fo*le render igjemmel *Sko*ve.
No. 231. Alt om en *So*mmerens *Mo*rgen.
No. 260. Denne *So*rg haver I mig *vo*ldet, Herre.
Abr. No. 146. Thi *sö*rger hun for hannem saa *lö*nlig.

No. 8. The king rules over the fortresses.
No. 35. Might I one of the loveliest capture!
No. 59. On the rose he praise would bestow.
No. 79. So has she laid his heart in chains.
No. 80. So lightly our terror has ended.
No. 84. The Danish women in the dance.
No. 84. For this I blame my rose; my heart has no repose.
No. 127. So light then goes the dance.
No. 206. There my horse runs through the forest.
No. 231. All on a summer morning.
No. 260. This sorrow have you brought to me, my lord.
Abr. No. 146. She mourns for him so sad and lonely.

Several of these rimes should perhaps be called assonances; the name is immaterial. They certainly are far more significant than alliteration. Often it is merely a certain parallelism in structure, a certain lilt in the rhythm that produces this strange, wonderfully pleasing, melodious impression; such as, for instance, may be found in the following:

No. 45. Men *Li*nden hun *lö*ves.
No. 66. Im*od* saa bl*id* en Sommer.
No. 84. Det volder mig den *e*ne, som jeg haver *A*gt paa.

No. 45. While the linden grows leafy.
No. 66. Toward so mild a summer.
No. 84. I blame for this the one for whom I have esteem.

How much greater stress is laid upon the euphony of vowels than upon the similarity of initial consonants will be brought home to us by reading a refrain such as belongs to "King Didrik and his Warriors" (No. *7*):

Der stander en B*o*rg hedder B*e*rne, han b*o*r derpaa Konning Diderik.

There stands a tower called Berne, there dwells therein King Diderik.

In several forms of the ballad (D, E, G) the refrain runs so:

Det donner under de raske Hovmænd, dér de udride,

It thunders beneath the impetuous warriors, there they ride out;

and from this Vedel has again concocted:

Det donner under Ros, de danske Hovmænd dér de udride,

It thunders under the horse, the Danish warriors there ride out.

Against this verse one can urge, among other objections, that the word *Ros* (horse) is a German word, one that is never used in our ballads. It is likewise presumable that in "Sir Bugge's Death" (No. 158) there should be a sort of alliteration in the refrain:

De fare saa fri igjennem Jylland.

They fare so free through Jutland.

This is found in the first stanza of A, but all the remaining stanzas of this text, and, in addition, B, C, and D have:

De rider saa frit gjennen Jylland.

They ride so freely through Jutland.

In "Bedeblak" (No. 63), from a manuscript of the beginning of the eighteenth century, we meet with a pretty alliteration:

Saa render han rank alt under skjönne Jomfruer.

The horse runs so brisk beneath the beautiful maidens.

Yet here again it is rather euphony of the vowels that produces a pleasing sound.

I shall now mention as characteristic of the ballads a final instance of what they strive for in this direction, and of what they do not aim at. In version A of "Malfred and Magnus" (No. 49), the refrain, which is found in many manuscripts, runs so:

> Saa *r*ask da *v*a*r* de Ædeling udi deres Brynje,
> So rash then were the nobles in their breastplates,

and in B (likewise an old manuscript):

> Saa karsk da rider de Ædeling i deres Brynje,
> So hale then ride the nobles in their breastplates.

It would be the most natural thing in the world then for the poet to strive after alliteration in molding a refrain:

> Saa rask da rider de Ædeling udi deres Brynje.
> So rash then ride the nobles in their breastplates.

But none of the versions were willing to purchase such a rime at the expense of such harmony as this: "saa rask da var," "saa karsk da rider."

Therefore it can be asserted positively that the poets of our popular ballads did not care for alliteration; they made no greater effort to secure it than they did to secure rime between the first and third lines. Herein it is evident how completely our ballads are differentiated from the poetry of antiquity, and furthermore how far removed they stand from the ballads of the Faroes and Iceland. As a typical example of a verse which is marked by a superfluity of alliteration can be cited the first stanza of the Faroese version of "Iron-Wolf" (No. 10):

> *v*ítt um *v*ölli gyltir hjálmar *s*yngja,
> *s*tíga teir á *s*inar hestar, teir springa,
> hoyrast mátti *l*angt á *l*eid, hvar teirra sporar ringja,
> *v*ítt um *v*ölli gyltir hjálmar syngja.

Far over the fields golden helmets are singing,
They up and mount their horses and away are springing,
And afar could be heard the sound of their spurs ringing,
Far over the fields golden helmets are singing.

This stanza was not recorded, however, until 1846 (V, 113). But in the Faroes and in Iceland the popular ballads were taken up, far more so than in other lands, by the priests and the cultured people, who had been immersed in the literature of antiquity, and consequently had become very familiar with it. Therefore it is not at all surprising that we should here meet with poetic devices which are never found in Denmark.

In conclusion I shall add some remarks on the melodies. The Middle Ages did not possess the major and minor scales in force to-day. In their places were used the so-called Greek, or ecclesiastical, modes; namely, the Ionian (nearly like C major), the Dorian, Phrygian, Mixolydian, and the Æolian (nearly like our A minor). In these modes there were found intervals of semitones in only two places; namely, between *e* and *f*, and *b* and *c*; hence, to use a modern illustration, only the white keys of the piano were in use; exceptionally, however, a single other note, especially *b*, appeared. Our modern scales, which arose about 1600, have a far greater range of modulations and more mobility; whereas the older were extraordinarily rich in chords, indeed far more so than the modern scales.

If now we examine Berggreen's "Folkesange og Melodier," we shall see that he has established beyond question that several of the melodies are in the Greek mode ("The Valraven," No. 28a; in the Swedish folk songs, Nos. 39, 49), but that altogether the great majority are in the major and minor scales.

That this can originally have been the case is exceedingly improbable. In the Middle Ages there existed no difference in modes between the ecclesiastical and the secular music; or, in other words, the secular songs and the folk songs were in the Greek modes. If therefore our melodies at that time had used the modern scales, we Danes must have been a couple of hundred years in advance of the rest of Europe, for it was only as the sixteenth century was passing into the seventeenth that the new modes appear, and only in the middle of the latter century that the old modes withdrew.[1]

As for the German popular melodies, it is also known that they were originally composed in the ecclesiastical modes.[2] In his "Om Kirkesangen" (pp. 45 ff., 134) the organist Thomas Laub has succeeded, by going through all the melodies preserved in Denmark, in establishing clearly that several of those printed in Berggreen do not fit in with the new modes, since they can be classed neither as major nor minor. On the contrary, they find their place in the ecclesiastical modes. Others of the melodies agree very well, it is true, with our present modes, but they fall in just as well with the old. Those melodies taken down by Schoolmaster Kristensen also point back to the old musical system. It certainly cannot be denied that it is solely the circumstance of their having been recorded at a late date and at a time when the old system was no longer well known that has carried the melodies over into the new modes.[3] This very same observation has been made by another musical authority with

[1] Böhme, Altdeutsches Liederbuch, p. lxi. [2] Ibid., pp. lix ff.
[3] Grönland, in *Allgem. musik. Zeitung*, 1816, column 613.

respect to the Swedish folk melodies.[1] It ought therefore to be the clear duty of musicians to restore, in any case, a portion of the Scandinavian melodies to their former shape.

It is an unmistakable characteristic of the music of olden times, especially of folk music, that it had no set or regular rhythm, that it did not require, as does the music of the present day, the entire piece to be written in the same kind of time. True it is that to-day we may vary the time of different portions of a composition; but, as a rule, we do not permit, for instance, in a single, continuous piece of music several parts or a short series of notes to stand in three-four time, the next in two-four time, etc. To our forefathers this did not serve in the least as a hindrance. Many melodies were, to be sure, written in a measure that was carried through unvaried; but very frequently the rhythm was changed, with the result that the melody gained a peculiar warmth and naturalness. Even in the dance, where we to-day insist on a rhythm maintained uniformly throughout, a variation was often indulged in, as, by the way, is still the practice in the dances of the German peasantry. In German dance melodies, some of which have been recorded as far back as the fourteenth century, we run across changes in the time; for example, after several measures in three-four time come several measures in four-four, whereupon the three-four time resumes.

It cannot help but be instructive to observe how the peasants still dance to-day in Oberpfalz. In addition to

[1] K. Valentin, Studien über die schwedischen Volksmelodien, pp. 22 ff., 55, 72.

the *Schleifer* (a waltz) in three-eight time, there is the *Dreher* in three-four time; the latter, however, is most commonly danced with *Eintreten*, as it is called, which obliges one to change over rapidly from one time to another. In a *Dreifach*, for instance, one sings and dances the first three measures in three-four time, three measures in two-four, four in three-four, and three in two-four. The dance is performed as follows: where the melody runs in three-eight time, the movement is about the same as in our waltz; during the two-four measures, the dancers execute certain movements which resemble those of a bear rocking; that is, they sway themselves without bending the body forward, smartly from one side to the other, standing alternately on the right foot and on the left. What distinguishes a very jaunty dancer in Oberpfalz is not any real innate grace of movement, or any great liveliness, but rather an astounding virtuosity in being able to vary the time.[1]

Our own melodies are no strangers to this variation in time. Even among Berggreen's popular ballads we find a number of melodies which exhibit several changes in the tempo; as, for example, that of No. 25b, "I know well where a castle stands." There is no doubt, however, that this change took place far oftener than we now have evidence of. Furthermore we can find in individual melodies, and in their relations to the texts, other traces of this change; and also at the present day we can sometimes hear in the songs of the peasantry the free rhythm together with the fixed tempo.[2] A question that deserves

[1] Böhme, Tanz, pp. 192 ff., 248, 254.
[2] Laub, Om Kirkesangen, pp. 64 ff., 135.

to be investigated is whether or not the variation in tempo could have been indicated in the verse measure. At any rate, there is one rhythm found in ballads that draws especial attention to itself; namely, that verse measure which I have already spoken of (p. 129) and which one will recognize especially as belonging to "The Betrothed in the Grave" (No. 90). I shall here cite several stanzas from "Proud Elin's Revenge" (No. 209):

3. Og saa förte de den unge Brud
i Hr. Renoldts Gaard:
der var ikke det röde Guld
for Legeren spart.

4. Saa fulgte de den unge Brud
i Salen ind:
for gik Ridder og Svende,
de bar hendes Skind.

5. Og saa satte de den unge Brud
paa Brude-Bænk:
frem gaar Ridder og Svende
de bar hender Skjænk.

6. Op stod stolten Ellind,
hun tog sig Kanden i Haand:
saa gaar hun at skjænke Vin,
men Dagen vaand [mens Dagen randt].

7. Saa gaar hun at skjænke Vin,
men Dagen vaand;
saa vredlig tog hun Sölvkar
af Brudens Haand.

3. And so they led the youthful bride
To Sir Renoldt's yard;
There was plenty of the red, red gold
To the players spared.

4. So followed they the youthful bride
   Within the door;
   Before her marched the knights and squires,
   Her furs they bore.

5. And so they set the youthful bride
   On the bridal chair;
   Forth then stepped the knights and squires,
   With gifts so rare.

6. Up then stood proud Ellind,
   She raised the cup on high;
   So she poured around the wine
   The livelong day.

7. So she poured around the wine
   The livelong day;
   Angrily she snatched the cup
   From the bride away.

Here is a marked contrast between the rhythmical swing of the first and third lines, and that of the other two lines. While the latter move like a marching step, the long lines of the former hasten on with a certain flying momentum. If one is not inclined to grant, however, that this difference is necessarily a result of a change in tempo, — in no case do the melodies preserved contradict my theory, — yet one must surely concede that it points, at the entrance of each line, to a change in the manner of dancing.

Ewald's romance of "Liden Gunver" has imitated in part this verse measure, in that two of his lines fit in perfectly with the rhythm of the ballad:

Liden Gunver vandrer som helst i Kvæld,
    saa tankefuld.
Hendes Hjerte var Vox, hendes unge Sjæl
    var prövet Guld.

Liden Gunver meder med Silken-Snor
ved Havets Bred;
da hævedes Bölgen, og Vandet foer
saa brat afsted.

Little Gunver walks about at even-time
Lost deep in thought.
Her heart was wax, her fair young mind
Like gold well wrought.

Little Gunver fishes with the silken thread
At the sea's brim;
The billows heaved, and the waters spread
Away so dim.

A comparison of the modern poem with the ballad, however, will make evident how great is the gulf between the rhythm of the two. The contrast between the two pairs of lines is not felt in Ewald's poem to the same degree as in the ballad; the first line has a far steadier movement in place of the hasty run of the ballad, a consequence of the strong use of anapæsts, and of a regular structure of the strophe consistently carried out.

CHAPTER VI

THE SUBJECT MATTER AND PURPOSE OF THE BALLADS

It lies outside the province of this work to consider all the themes which furnish material for the ballads, to trace out all the relics of old, mythological beliefs in the poetry of the Christian period, to inquire into the kind and nature of the superstitions, to see relations with the poetry and the world of tradition in other lands,[1] to paint pictures of the life of chivalry, of the doings of the common people, of moral aspects and customs — all of which our ballads unroll before us. All that can be thought of here is to bring to light general features of ballad poetry regarded as a specific form of poetry, to see in what degree it adapts itself to that epic scope of action with lyrical backgrounds which it has chosen, for better or for worse, as a scene of action; to indicate the general point of view of ballad poetry respecting religion and the instinct of patriotism. But these various researches may also be undertaken in order that the boundaries of the ballads may be drawn more distinctly, and thus what is new and what is old be determined more sharply. Finally I shall endeavor to throw some light upon the means used by the ballads to further their poetical ends.

[1] Both Child and Grundtvig have laid the student under great obligations in this respect in their introductions to the ballads. — Translator.

I. Nature

In a consideration of the ballad's point of view as that of the epic with a lyrical background, the first question that forces itself upon the attention is, What is the attitude of the ballads toward nature?

Nature is always depicted in the ballads only as a background for events; almost without exception what we meet with is intimations like "Late in the evening when the dusk drew on" or a remark like "Now crows the cock." The place is always indicated in general terms — on the strand, on the mountain side, under the linden, in the orchard, in the rose grove, by the castle gate, upon the grassy field. Of flowers there are named only the rose — but its realistic thorns are never mentioned — and the lilies; we have found once "She made a garland and 't was violet blue" (No. 189, B 8). Only in the refrain does the joy in nature come out at all decisively, but it is never a pleasure in nature's many details. Here rings out clearly the delight in the linden tree, the favorite tree of the ballads,[1] in spring and in summer. The birds sing, but their names are not given; and it is only in the later ballads that the nightingale is allowed to be heard. In the colors also there is shown but little naturalism; the standing expressions constantly appear. The maiden's arms are lily-white, the steed at times can be white as a wall (No. 182, E 5); but the silver especially gleams white and the gold red. The eyes of the dying queen Dagmar are red as blood (No. 135, A 19); otherwise they are preferably likened to the red of roses. The ground is black and so is the moor; "what is blacker than the sloe?"

[1] Johannes Steenstrup, Normannerne, I, 182 ff.

Svend Vonved asks, and gets for an answer, "Sin" (No. 18, A 29). "Blacker than the sloe" is furthermore an expression belonging to the Romanic languages (IV, 751). "Like doves so blue" appears once (No. 181, E 15). In short, a very limited choice of figures is permitted to colors, and these are far from being realistic. Such verses as these have ventured pretty far out from shore:

No. 73, A 26. By the river's side I wandered down
I looked at the flowers both blue and brown.

27. I looked at the flowers both blue and brown,
The fairest I thought to pick for my own.

28. I looked at the roses, both red and white,
They stand in their fairest growth bedight.

These verses are noted down as early as 1550; but from the text recorded by Kristensen (II, No. 34), a text which goes back independently to the original version, they have disappeared.

In the refrain, on the other hand, delight in the world of nature is allowed expression. And, since we have already seen how closely related the first stanza often is to the refrain, we need not be surprised to find that some praise of nature creeps out in the first stanza. Accordingly the oldest text of the "Faithless Bride" (Kristensen, I, No. 90; II, No. 73; III, No. 57), from Karen Brahe's Folio Manuscript (No. 355) runs thus:

1. There 's come so merry a summer this year,
Cold winter is fled away;
Roses and lilies are springing up,
The forest is decked so gay.
Now comes the pretty time.

2. It was the bold Sir Nilaus, etc.

The stanza has all but assumed the burden of a refrain. The same stanza appears in No. 356, and a stanza of similar nature turns up here and there and in an odd ballad; in any case, it belongs to the framework and not to the text itself. We might well wonder why a stanza concerning nature does not appear far more often in our ballads, for such an introductory reference to nature is very general, for instance, in the German ballads; in fact, it is found in all folk poetry the world over, from the songs of the Romanic peoples in the west to the poetry of the Chinese and the Malays in the east. Of a very different order, on the other hand, is that endeavor to harmonize the natural environment with the poet's own feelings, such as we find in the German poetry of art; namely, the minnesongs.[1] No such element is to be found in our popular ballads.

The statement just made will be illuminated by a discussion of individual ballads which form exceptions. The famous ballad "The Game at Dice" (No. 238) — "And do thou hear, thou bonny boy, come play at dice with me" — has been noted down also in Iceland, and concerning it Grundtvig remarks that "scarcely any other of the Icelandic popular ballads bears a more decided stamp of its Danish origin." At the same time the Icelandic version departs very widely from the Danish, the cause of which presumably is that it represents a much older Danish tradition than does that which meets us in the records of the seventeenth-nineteenth centuries. "The Icelandic tradition gives us, if anything, the ballad as it ran in the twelfth

[1] See *Zeit. f. d. Altertum*, XIX, 199 ff.; XXIX, 192 ff.; *Zeit. f. d. Philologie*, XIX, 444 ff.

and thirteenth centuries." It seems to me, however, that one must be somewhat cautious in venturing to say what the poem was like in the twelfth century; it would certainly prove a difficult matter to furnish any evidence of what the ballad was like at that precise period. On this point, however, I shall dwell no longer. Here follow the opening stanzas of the Icelandic version (translated by Grundtvig into Danish, "Íslenzk Fornkvæði," No. 38):

1. It is so merry on a summer's day
   Every maid grows gentle and gay.

2. The maidens deck them one and all:
   Some in silk and some in pall.

3. In softest silk their limbs are arrayed,
   They rest beneath the linden's shade.

4. They rest them at the linden's foot,
   The stag his horn thrusts in its root.

5. The stag his horn thrusts in the tree,
   The fishes sport so light in the sea.

6. The maiden sits aloft in her bower,
   She plays at chess by the hour.

The earliest manuscript in which these verses are found dates from 1665. I need not affirm that this sort of verse never appears in our Danish ballads, and that if such a form of composition had prevailed in the twelfth and thirteenth centuries or throughout the entire Middle Ages, and if such detailed sketches of nature had been drawn, they certainly would have left their mark on the ballads. But, as a matter of fact, they are absolutely wanting.

One version of "The Maiden transformed into a Bird" (No. 56), which is found in a manuscript of the time of Frederick II, begins thus:

C 1. I know well where a forest stands,
It stands far out by the fjord;
Within it grow the fairest trees
That are known to knight or lord.

2. Within it grow the fairest trees,
Willows and lindens, their name;
Within it sport both hart and hind,
The honest beasts so tame.

3. Within it sport both hart and hind
And other beasts are seen;
There sings a little nightingale (*Nachtegal*)
In a linden tree so green.

4. This asked then Niclaus Erlandssön. . . .

These stanzas are not included in the other forms; on the other hand, they haunt a number of Norse and Swedish ballads and also turn up elsewhere in Denmark. They are not native to the "birdskin ballads" and their origin is betrayed by the German word *Nachtigal;* in German songs similar stanzas appear very frequently (cf. Grundtvig, III, 834).

Just as the lyrical element in the ballads is seldom satisfied with pictorial images of nature's details, so is the ballad temperate in its use of nature for allegorical ends as well as in the practice of framing thoughts in pictures. It is certainly startling to come across such stanzas as the following from "The Maiden in the Woods" (No. 416). A knight finds a maiden in the woods and rests the live-long night by her side. When he meets her brothers the next morning, he is asked where he has been. They accuse him of having slept with their sister, upon which he replies:

> I rode me out to chase the deer,
> Your sister I never knew;
> I baited me the fairest deer
> That came first to my view.
>
> It hid itself under my scarlet cloak,
> With me was well contented;
> That suited me well and made me glad,
> Of that I 've not repented.
>
> I made the wild deer run to the forest
> Before my hounds so fleet;
> The tame deer to my bosom I pressed,
> Our hearts with joy did beat.
>
> A maid she was both fine and bold
> As man could wish to see.
> If she 's your sister, I pray you then
> You let our wedding be.

Thus a modern poet might well sing; but the lengthy comparison and the great amount of pictorial language have no connection with good ballad style. None of the manuscripts have these stanzas, neither are they to be found in the modern copies. They were composed by Vedel, who probably discovered his models in various German ballads.

There exist a number of vagabond verses which have taken root in every possible place, and which are really acknowledged by no one:

> To hold a young man to his word
> Is like taking an eel by the tail.
>
> To hold a young man to his faith
> Is like riding over a rotten bridge.

In Queen Sophie's Ballad Manuscript these verses stand unattached to any ballad; in Vedel's "Tragica" they form the conclusion of a ballad, and likewise of ballads from copies of the seventeenth century. Even in our own time they flit about and attach themselves to other vagrant stanzas (see Nos. 230, 462). In this way these lines, along with others, have connected themselves with two other lines, which also belong to the vagabonds of the world of later folk songs:

> Ah! had I the door-key to this day,
> To the bottom of the sea I 'd cast it away;

or with clearer application in the ballad of "The Bridal" (No. 88):

> And if they 'd had the key to lock the morning's door,
> They would have wished the night would ne'er be o'er.

However excellent these figures may be otherwise, they are wholly foreign to the style of our ballads; on the other hand, these lines belong to the conscious, intensely lyrical songs of Germany. And it is an easy matter to point them out, since they are very general in old German and Dutch ballads. In these the lovers express a wish that the night would never end, that they could lock up the dawn and the day and throw the key into the water. As early as the fifteenth century these verses are found quoted in a Netherlandish manuscript and run as follows[1]:

> Had ic den slotel vanden daghe,
> ic weerpen in ghender wilder Masen
> oft vander Masen tot inden Rijn,
> al en soude hi nemmer vonden sijn.

[1] Since the above was written these shifting verses have been thoroughly discussed by Richard Steffer, Enstrofig nordisk folklyrik. Nyare bidrag till kännedom af svenska landsmålen, hefte 63.

II. Religion

Let us turn from the feeling for nature in the ballads to their attitude toward religion. Here we meet first of all the legendary ballads, for which Grundtvig seems to have had an especial affection — he has included no less than fourteen in his "Selected Danish Ballads." I confess that in regard to these ballads I entertain some critical doubts. That legendary ballads were composed in Denmark during the Middle Ages is probable enough. I shall not deny that several of the ballads preserved were written in that period; very possibly Peter Palladius had these in mind in his "Visitation Book," when he forbade pipers at weddings and banquets to sing "their ungodly ballads on the invoking of saints and other such" (p. 79). At the same time many of them are not substantiated by evidence of any kind. They appear in broadsides of the eighteenth century, and their form is not such as to warrant the supposition that they are old.

In all probability the rupture with Catholicism here in Denmark was so sharp that everything which bore marks of the old faith was grudgingly allowed to live. Nevertheless it is strange that not a single one of these ballads is to be found in manuscript; several of them, however, contain in reality very little Catholicism. On the other hand, one can very readily admit the possibility of a new immigration of legendary ballads from abroad in the sixteenth and seventeenth centuries. We know assuredly, as has been pointed out a number of times, that new varieties of ballads made their way into the country during these periods. Apparently there was nothing to hinder our soldiers of the Thirty Years' War, or our troopers in foreign service, or our seamen in harbors abroad, not to speak of various wandering warriors and artisans, from bringing back such ballads. I need not go farther into this phase of the subject, since a notice of these ballads is not necessary to establish the statements which I wish to lay down. Precisely because the old records are not forthcoming, the history of these ballads escapes our eyes. I own to a certain fear that much of what is given for ancient in reality is not.[1]

We shall leave out of consideration therefore the genuinely religious or legendary ballads. Concerning all others the rule holds good that however many remarkable and marvelous things happen, miracles never find a place. It is not by prayers and petitions to God and to the saints that metamorphosed knights and maidens get their own shape back again, nor is it by making the sign of the cross nor by reading the Scriptures that evil is bested. The intervention of the Virgin Mary or of holy men is unnecessary; that which heals or reshapes, that which draws the frigid lover to longing is mysterious remedies, the various instruments of superstition, the token and the mystic word. Runes have a wonderful alluring power, a man's life is bound up in his name as if in a mathematical

[1] In any case the real legendary ballads may assuredly be regarded as being farther removed from folk poetry. In the field of German folk poetry — but consequently in the realm of the lyric — some German writers, as, for example, Vilmar, show no inclination to recognize a clerical or religious popular ballad. Even Böhme remarks: "Upon the whole, one cannot call spiritual songs true ballads even though they exhibit no ecclesiastical marks and would be nothing more than religious poems; there is wanting the genuine folk tone, above all naïveté" (Altdeutsches Liederbuch, pp. xlvi, 676).

power, and with or against this one can work precisely as though it were the man himself. In a kiss lies witchcraft, which releases that which is bewitched, and drinking a man's warm blood and tasting of his flesh leads to metamorphosis.

Grundtvig has incidentally said the same things that have here been asserted, and in an excellent manner. That which gave him the occasion was "The Dalby Bear" (No. 64). A bear goes into Dalby's fields and knocks everything down, causing the farmers great annoyance. In reality the bear is the king's son, who has been transformed by his stepmother. The old copy of the ballad omits the explanation of how the bear regained his former shape; one learns that he engages in conflict with a man, but nothing further. The diffuse text of Anders Sörensen Vedel, on the contrary, reads that the man, after fighting with the bear and hearing how the latter has been transformed by his stepmother, who has laid an iron band on his neck, says:

> 22. "I shall release you from your plight:
> Mary's Son, who sets all things right,
>
> 23. He will loose for you that hard band,
> So great is the power of His right hand."
>
> 24. The knight made over him the sign of the cross,
> The band it broke, and he was loose.
>
> 25. He then became a knight so bold,
> His father's kingdom he came to hold.

These verses, and, in fact, almost all of Vedel's contribution, Grundtvig would not admit to be genuine; there is nothing in the language, style, or rime that suggests any great age, "and as far as the substance is concerned, it is very suspicious that the bear's release is brought about by a miracle, a procedure that is never met with in any of the many tales of transformation and deliverance which we find as the subject of our old ballads. For the remarkable circumstance connected with these, and one which indicates great age, is that the trace of Christianity which appears in them never touches their essential nature; the action itself goes on everywhere (if one may so speak) according to Nature's own laws of the supernatural. In contrast with this hard and fast situation, stands here one in which only through divine assistance the knight is enabled to break the band that held the bear imprisoned." These words are true and pertinent, and can be substantiated by many ballads.

But Grundtvig has not always applied his true perceptions nor has he always followed them out to their consequences. Precisely because the religious impulse and the encroachments of the God of Christianity in events are so rare, Grundtvig's remarks on "The Game at Dice" (No. 238) are, it seems to me, incorrect. This is the excellent, well-known song, "And do thou hear, thou bonny boy, come play at dice with me," in which the maiden plays away everything she owns and finally her honor and her faith. She desires to purchase her freedom, but the bonny boy will not accede, and already she sighs despairingly over the match she has made. The youth then discloses his identity as the king's son. In one of the later versions which Kristensen has collected (II, No. 40), the story runs that the maiden was lucky at the beginning of the play:

A 13. The knight goes into the garden, lets fall the bitter tear:
"I've rolled the dice with the maiden, my luck went against me here!"

14. There came to him from heaven a voice both loud and clear:
"Go roll the golden dice with the maiden one time more."

He ventures one more trial and wins thereby her honor and troth.

According to Grundtvig, the recent forms deserve especial attention because they give us the ballad in an older shape and closer to the original form of the legend. In them the old legend is serious in tone, whereas the later versions are facetious. Now it is unfortunate that these recent forms are wholly meaningless. We can repeat Grundtvig's own words: "In version A the knight has played away horse and saddle and eighteen farms in Skaane; in B even two kingdoms and seven ships at sea. After all this the maiden surely cannot look upon him as a simple boatman." This statement admits of no question, and here we have one of those not infrequent cases in which it is the late recorded forms that have so very slight a value and are rather misleading than instructive. And to this should be added that the proud king's son steps entirely out of his character when he goes down to the garden and weeps over having lost eighteen farms in Skaane. When moreover he is said to be assisted by a voice from Heaven, a voice which can call out that things will once more turn out well for him if he but venture another cast of the dice, then we have entered the realm of the ludicrous, the tasteless, and the profane.

Grundtvig points to the Icelandic version ("Íslenzk Fornkvæði," No. 38) as the one which is to give us the ballad in its oldest shape — in fact, "in the shape which was current in Denmark during the twelfth and thirteenth centuries." Here the ballad strikes a serious tone; it is no disguised prince, but a knight who has fallen a victim to passion and plays away everything; then he goes out and calls upon God for better luck and wins. But to what extent the ballad has become Catholic will appear from verses such as these:

> He then went out by the garden wall,
> On God and Saint Canute he calls.
>
> He calls on God and the holy Cross:
> "Let not the maiden play our life from us!"
>
> He calls on God and Saint Paul,
> The tricks of the game, that he win them all.
>
> He calls on God and the holy Shrine,
> That the maiden should belong to him.

I believe that our ballads, taken as a whole, will testify to the fact that such a sudden, solemn invocation of higher powers is as wholly unknown to the earliest versions of the ballad as is the intervention of these same powers. Furthermore it is truly remarkable that all the various Danish, Norwegian, and Swedish texts, however diversified they may appear to be, exhibit absolutely no trace of the interference of Heaven, if we set aside the two meaningless texts which have turned up last. That the ballad dates from the Middle Ages can well be doubted, since it cannot be traced farther back than Peder Syv's time (c. 1695 or 1700). The Icelandic ballad has taken on such a priestly and learned character that it might well arouse suspicion;

with the exception of the last stanza, the lines quoted above are found in manuscripts as early as 1665. Nevertheless the ballad, even in this form, is forbearing enough not to allow Heaven itself to speak, nor does it give instructions to the knight how to play the game. But can these lines attest anything else than the taste which prevailed in the seventeenth century? To shift the ballad back to Catholic times, on the ground of its invocation of the saints, would be to leave out of account the learned hands by which the ballad has been preserved.

On the other hand, a similar use of a voice from Heaven is found in a ballad (Unpublished No. 101) which tells how a mother, during the bridegroom's absence, had his truelove, Amor, buried alive:

> One must have heard far over the sound
> How Amor shrieked beneath the ground.
>
> One must have heard in foreign town,
> How Amor cried beneath the ground.
>
> There came a voice to the knight's own door:
> "Your mother has buried alive Amor."

Now one would think it sufficient if Amor's complaining cry reached her lover's ears in the foreign land; but the poet, who, on the whole, is lacking in taste, has introduced Heaven. The ballad is found in only one manuscript, which dates from 1650.

I shall cite further several examples to make good the assertion that miracles do not happen in the ballads. As far as "The Maiden in the Linden" (No. 66) is concerned, one will be able to note a difference according as a copy from the sixteenth or from the seventeenth century is used. In A and B it runs naturally and prettily:

> A 24. He gave a kiss to the linden root,
> So she became a maiden good.
>
> B 22. He laid him down and kissed its root,
> So she became a maiden good.

On the contrary, C (written down in 1650) relates:

> 28. King Magnus he laid him upon the green earth,
> And then he kissed the linden root.
>
> 29. He kissed it once, he kissed it twice,
> The root stood ever as it was.
>
> 30. The third time he called on the Son of Mary,
> Then the linden became a maiden fair.

That these three stanzas neither fly the old ensign nor outweigh poetically the simple lines of the other two forms may be taken for granted.

The three versions of "The Trold and the Housewife" (No. 52) which are known from old manuscripts assert that the *trold* is released and transformed by the kissing of the farmer's wife; Vedel alone relates that when he would kiss for the third time she called on the Son of Mary, and then the *trold's* skin fell off. In the "Lind-Worm" (No. 65) Peder Syv has, as Grundtvig points out, added a stanza in which the Son of Mary is invoked.

There is one ballad, "The Water of Life" (No. 94), which we might believe has lighted upon a miracle. The king has found a suspicious relation existing between the queen and the count, for which he has had the count put to death, chopped to pieces, and placed before his wife as a dish. She discovers what is offered to her, collects all the pieces, and carries them to Maribo's well:

> A 20. In clearest water she then dipped them:
> "Stand up, stand up, thou Christian man!"
>
> 21. The man stood up and thanked God,
> So from his country he fared abroad.

Thus runs the ballad with Peder Syv. But a copy from popular tradition reads:

> B 15. She picked up the fingers, she picked up the legs,
> To the living water so fared she then.
>
> 16. She washed the fingers, she washed the legs,
> "Stand up, little Löfgren, and be a man!"

What is referred to in the expression "det levende Vand" (the living water) is the old German *heilawâc*, that is, healing water or healing; in an old English magic formula it is *hálewǽg*, and *heilivágr* in several Icelandic sagas; it also appears in Norse and Faroese ballads and in the Danish ballad of "The Valraven" (No. 60; A 16, 17):

> So flew he then to Hileva's well,
> So dipped the maiden in Hileva's flood

(see Grundtvig's remarks, III, 835). Here then we are constantly within the bounds of the supernatural; the word has nothing to do with *hellig* (holy), but with *hel* (healthy); in the Laws of Skaane it runs: "hel ællær siukær,"— that is, healthy or sick (*Helbred*, *Helse*, "health"),—and the collecting and resuscitation of dead men's bones are found in many sagas and tales as well as in the myths of Thor's goat. Peder Syv has had this healing take place at Maribo's well.

We saw that healing waters are found in the ballad of "The Valraven" (No. 60). In this ballad various transformations take place. The maiden's betrothed, who was metamorphosed into a bird, drinks her blood and is released. Upon this the dead maiden is recalled to life by being washed in Hileva's well. Finally their child, who was to fall to the raven as the price of his assistance, speaks three words as soon as it is born, and by this means effects the release of the Valraven, which is transformed into a knight. So goes version A; versions B–E, however, run somewhat differently: the Valraven drinks the child's blood and thereupon is transformed; the child is revived by all falling upon their knees and praying to God to restore it to life, or by its being carried to the holy place. One feels upon reading these texts that the picture as a whole is wanting in something, that a certain logical order in the management of the universe is lacking. When it is possible to effect transformations and other wonderful deeds by means of legends and superstitions, it seems a little strange that final recourse must be had to a Christian miracle, to an invocation of God. If one could prevail upon God through prayer to interfere, why did he not let Him assist him from the very beginning? Accordingly the text quoted first appears to be the more reasonable; right from the start it allows the knight to be metamorphosed into a Valraven upon the condition that upon the first words of the child which is to be born to the maiden he shall be released. Grundtvig must have come to a like conclusion, for in his popular edition of "Selected Popular Ballads" he says nothing of this calling upon God for help. With reference to the assistance rendered by the dead in

"St. Gertrude" (No. 93: St. Gertrude, whose land has been attacked and laid desolate by a count, conjures her godfather up from the grave and gets his help), I shall content myself with pointing out what Grundtvig has said upon the subject. It is a cross between a legendary ballad and a ballad of magic. In the narrative concerning St. Gertrude heathen elements seem to be present, and in some countries a use similar to that of "Cyprianus" has actually been made of "Gertrude's Book" (III, 875).

Of all our ballads, however high and surely they have aimed and struck, there are none which can be compared with the ballads of magic. These seem also to have looked deepest into the human heart; they have depicted not only love, but other joys and sorrows that befall humankind, and in matchless words and pictures have brought comforting thoughts and refreshing promises. As a notable example I shall name here "The Buried Mother" (No. 89) and "The Betrothed in the Grave" (No. 90). If guessing were allowable, I should say that these two were written by the same ingenious author. But even in the case of these ballads, which conduct us to places the other side of the earth and earthly life, we can perceive to what small degree the ecclesiastical, or the strictly Catholic, element, or whatever we should like to call it, gets leave to appear; although these ballads are, as a matter of course, like all our ballads, certainly built upon a Christian basis. When the buried mother, observing how her children are neglected by the stepmother Blide, is irresistibly impelled to see her children again, naturally she must first gain permission of God to return to middle earth (*Middelhjem*, corresponding to the Old Norse *miðgarðr*, that is, the world of men; Grundtvig, III, 870):

On Saturday night at eventide,
Then should all souls in peace abide.

To the home of angels she took her way,
Of Jesus Christ a boon did pray.

She prayed that to earth she might return,
And talk again with her small children.

"Yes, indeed, go you may,
But do not remain too long away."

This is all we hear of God or of Christ. It is not to preach any Christian lore that the dead one appears; she indulges in no threats, but merely tells her former husband, Sir Björn:

An I must come to you any more,
Blidelil shall die a death right sore.

When you hear the hounds a moaning,
Then you may know the dead are roaming.

The punishment of the stepmother she promises here as a natural, inevitable revenge, and she says nothing of the punishment which God inflicts upon all wicked people. Thereupon she departs, having accomplished everything:

No sooner was she beneath the mould
Than her children on bolsters blue did roll.

Blide brushed them clean and combed their hair,
She raised them up and eased their care.

She gave them wine, she gave them bread,
And never again did they suffer need.

Whenever she heard the hound a baying,
The children with gold so red were playing.

Heiberg, in his criticism of Hertz's "Svend Dyring's Hus," pointed out that the latter, in the chorus of angels at the end of the play, carried the use of the supernatural far beyond the stage that gives success to illusion; and here Heiberg has the support of the ballads, which hold the other world off at a great distance.

The same is true of that other noble ballad, "The Betrothed in the Grave" (No. 90). The distinctly Christian features are repressed as much as possible, even in the scene where the knight knocks at the door of his truelove's bower:

9. Then spoke the little Elselille,
With tearful mien:
"And you can name the name of Jesus,
You may come in."

10. "Get up, get up, proud Elselille,
Open the door!
I can name the name of Jesus as well
As I could before."

When she follows him to the churchyard, he reiterates that she must sorrow for him no more:

29. "Get up, get up, proud Elselille,
And get you home!
And never weep again
For your bridegroom.

30. "Look up to heaven high and see
The stars so small;
So you will come to know
How the night doth fall."

31. And quickly slid the dead man
Into the ground;
So sorrowfully goes proud Elselille
Homeward bound.

It is indeed possible that stanza 30 has been changed and that originally it ran otherwise; but, as it lies before us, it contains at any rate no reference to the search after religious consolation. At the most, it directs attention to the pleasure of gazing at the stars in heaven, and first and foremost Sir Aage refers to heaven in order to turn away Else's gaze, which holds him fast, so that he may "slide" into the earth again. No, throughout the whole ballad there sounds rather a consolation of a more general human order, — even if, as has been said before, the Christian faith is always conceived of as lying behind, — and, above all, in the sublime stanzas which have an inherent healing power of wonderful strength:

"As often as you do weep for me,
And sad your mood:
Then stands my narrow coffin filled
With clotted blood.

"As often as you do sing,
And glad your mind;
Then is my narrow grave within
With rose-leaves lined."

I shall now leave the miracles and shall briefly discuss in conclusion the reserve with which even the naming of God's name is practiced. The way in which God is drawn into one form of "The Trold and the Housewife" (No. 52) deserves notice. I have already mentioned that version C shows a distinct attempt to bring about alliteration, whereas the older texts avoid it. But in another respect also this version points to a later date:

C 6. He 's hied him to the farmer's croft
Right late it was one evening;
The hound it growled in the farmer's croft,
For so our good Lord had willed the thing.

The meaningless intrusion of God in the fourth line certainly requires no comment; nothing corresponding to it is found in the other versions. But farther on in the ballad we read:

> 14. Up then stood the wretched farmer,
> O Lord, hear well his moan;
> Elline he gave, his own true wife,
> To the ugly trold for his own.

The exclamation contained in the second line, the poet's own utterance, is surely not original. The copyist misunderstood an exclamation that had been put into the mouth of the farmer thus:

> This then spake the wretched farmer:
> "Lord God, hear well my moan."

In like manner we find God invoked in the other forms, as, for instance, in the verses from C below. It is not the singer but the actors that call upon Him:

> A 11. The housewife became right heavy of heart:
> "Now help me, our dear Lord's Son!"

> B 10. "May God that now forbid
> That ever I whore with a trold!"

> C 15. "O Lord, be gracious to my poor woman,
> My fate is hard to bear."

How later times have changed the tone one can see for one's self by noting the way a ballad sings in the period of the Reformation. It is indeed in a ballad that we come across such a beginning as "Will ye listen and hear, A ballad I'll sing to you." In No. 172, "Christian II in Sweden" (1520), we read:

8. They marched forth both over hill and dale
Through the gloomy forest;
In God, in whom reposed all their faith:
Not in man they set their trust. . . .

11. The captains called their riflemen out,
They bade them level their weapons;
"We will advance if it be God's will,
Despite what the Swedish threaten." . . .

13. Sir Sten his leg was shot to pieces
In the second shot;
This I say to you in sooth:
It was foreseen of God. . . .

30. Praised be God, our Father in Heaven,
The Danish men the glory have won!
God give us rest in Heaven at last,
With him to dwell forever at one.

From all the above discussion, two things, I believe, will stand out clearly. First, the reader will notice the great difference between the ballads and the rimed romances, in which we usually meet with allusions to Christian dogmas and Catholic doctrines, and in which the language in so many ways reminds us of ecclesiastical speech. Second, the evidence all goes to show that clerical people are not the authors of the ballads. In other words, there is found in no genuine ballad any indication that men of learning or of wide knowledge, least of all, ecclesiastics, are the authors of the ballads. It is related in a chronicle from Limburg[1] that a leprous monk was the composer of the very best songs and melodies, and that he had no equal on the Rhine or elsewhere. It is very possible that in Denmark such monks were to be found who composed ballads; but in any case these have an aspect which does away with the necessity of considering such an origin.

[1] Böhme, Liederbuch, p. xxii.

III. Morals and Wishes

In close relation to the subject just discussed stands the question, How near do the ballads come to the goal at which they aim; namely, the ethical and æsthetic impression they wish to produce?

On this point the rule holds good that the essentially objective movement of the narrative is never interrupted by any application to the listeners. We have already seen that all references to the setting find their place in the refrain. Here it is interesting to note the parallel offered by the Norse poetry of antiquity in the course of its development. Not until we come to its final flowering do we meet with poems whose conclusions confess that pointing a moral or uttering a wish was their object. "Gudrun's Incitement" (*Gudrúnarhvöt*), for instance, ends as follows:

May every earl's
Fate grow better,
Every woman's
Pain grow lesser,
When this song of sorrow
All men sing,
Gudrun's incitement,
Before all peoples!

Counterparts to this are found in "Atli's Song" (*Atlikviða*), but not in the older poems.

Blessed will he be called
Who such a son begets,
Such heroic offspring
As Gjuke begot.
His praise shall live
Through all the lands
So long as folk listen
To conflicts of passion.

Such applications or concluding observations discover themselves in a few ballads. We can easily make clear, however, what the true conditions are. "The Linden on Lindenberg" (No. 205) ends so:

F 28. God pity the maiden wherever she be
Must live without a friend!
She bargains with God that she be not tempted
And guards her honor to the end.

Grundtvig has already recognized the fact that F is "a worked-over text, which for one thing changes the phrasing to suit the rime, and for another adds this moralizing closing stanza." The stanza is found only in Dorothea Thott's manuscript of the time of Frederick III or Christian V. Belonging to the same period is a broadside ballad with rime in all four lines and with an entirely different, but likewise moralizing, conclusion:

27. God grant him luck and happiness
Who regards his honor rightly,
And from that man withhold His peace
Who treats his truelove lightly.

The ballad is extant, however, in five other versions, which are both older and better than these two corrupted texts, and from them the above stanza is absent.

In "Proud Elin's Revenge" (No. 209) it runs:

This is a rede for every young man
Who wooes so far away,
That he makes no promise for the sake of spite (*Hadings Ret*)
To any honest may.

He should never go back on his plighted word
Whatever is in his power;
For falsehood strikes its lord on the neck
Mayhap at any hour.

These stanzas, which read as if they were copied from a book of precepts, were added arbitrarily to the ballad by Vedel. In its sole genuine form it is extant in Karen Brahe's Folio Manuscript. Indeed, on the whole, fabrications of this kind constantly emanate from Vedel's hand (see, for example, Nos. 145, 149, 156, 295).

But with respect to another ballad the last-named manuscript leaves the theory which I have here defended in the lurch. In "The Maiden's Morning Dream" (No. 239) we read these two closing stanzas:

B 37. Let no one say nay to another's desire,
They know not what fortune they may yet acquire.

38. Let no one hinder another more,
They know not what fortune God has in store.

Though it may well be that in the great collection of ballads preserved in this manuscript we shall not find another single ballad which ends with such a moralizing stanza, yet it appears from these lines that not only in Vedel's day but also in 1550 there existed a fondness for this sort of talk. When the question touches upon the genuine stamp of our ballads during the Middle Ages, then we can assert without regard to these two exceptional and homely stanzas that such ballad endings were wholly unknown. Luckily we have a test by which we can determine in some measure whether or not such a condition as this text reveals is out of the ordinary. There are found, in all, twelve different texts of the ballad, of which six belong to old manuscripts and six to modern records. Moreover the ballad is extant in Icelandic, Swedish, and in eight Norse forms; but halfway between all these variations stands this version B in apprehensive solitude, unattended by any parallel whatsoever to its over-moral concluding verse. Therefore we need have no hesitation in declaring it to be unoriginal in the ballad.

On the whole, there is much interest attached to the study of those ballads which exist in a great number of copies dating from olden times. Thus one has the opportunity of seeing how a certain taste, working its way down, sought to impress the ballads with a character which at first they did not possess. For instance, in five versions (B, C, E, I, M) of "The Youth of Vollerslöv" (No. 298) we meet an *I* in the opening stanza:

> I know a right rich maiden
> By a brook south in the land;
> And she prayed that the youth of Vollerslöv
> Might never win her hand.

The other texts which were written down in the sixteenth century, begin, on the other hand, in this fashion:

> There lives a woman in Vermerland,
> And she has daughters two,

or

> There lives a right modest woman
> By a brook south in the land;

that the latter is the correct form admits of not the slightest doubt. Corresponding to this intrusion of the *I* appears an *I* in the concluding stanza. L, N, O end so:

> Praised be God the Father in Heaven,
> From evil he is able to defend;
> Never did I hear of a worse journey
> Which came to a better end.

In K and P these lines are the concluding words of Lady Mettelil, and do not concern the singer at all. And where B, C end with "Thanks be to young William," etc., A (cf. K) gives as Lady Mettelil's last words: "Many thanks, young Sir William," etc.

Finally D closes with a stanza which is unique in the whole fifteen different versions:

> Now I warn both women and maids
> Who wish to live with honor,
> That they mock no man, neither rich nor poor,
> Even though he be yet unborn (sic!).

One will thus see how unauthentic are all these expressions on the part of the singer; and since such stanzas are wholly wanting in A, E, F, G, H, I, K, M, it can serenely be maintained that the taste of the sixteenth and later centuries bears the blame.

In version D of "The Test of Fidelity" (No. 252) we find this closing stanza:

> 44. This it is to be firm and loyal
> To try his truelove with honest toil.
>
> 50. It ever happens as God so wills,
> He helps neither falsehood nor scandal's ills.

This form is referred to by Grundtvig as "a late, — perhaps made over in the seventeenth century, — untraditional dilution of a genuine basis best represented in A, B." Since therefore the three older forms, A, B, C, omit this stanza and bring the ballad to a close in good, old, popular style with holding a wedding; and since the four copies of the present time, as well as those from the Faroes and Sweden, fail to recognize it, we may well feel ourselves justified in saying that such stanzas are not native to the ballads.

A ballad which to an unusual degree preaches a moral, but which has concerned itself especially with a certain phase of the moral, is "The Sacrilege" (No. 112). It emphasizes in its narrative how unlucky it is to go hunting on the Sabbath,—"All on the holy Eastermorn." The two hunters who are guilty of this sin fall into a quarrel over their horses and hounds and end by killing each other. The ballad gives no utterance, however, to any general moral sentiment until it reaches the end. Seven of the texts have nothing whatever to say in conclusion which is in any way indicative of the quintessence of the ballad. Only in the eighth form, written down in the beginning of the seventeenth century, do we meet with the stanza:

G 23. Now I counsel you, each one and all,
Who early ride to the wood;
That you ride down to the church
And fear Almighty God.

"This moral is manifestly a later addition," as Grundtvig very truly observes. But is it not significant that the taste of later times deemed it necessary for practical purposes to state expressly the moral of the ballad, instead of allowing the fundamental tone of morality to find its own echo in the minds of its hearers?

In conclusion, I shall merely add that in "Anna Urop's Ballad Book," the ballad of "The Faithless Bride" (see above, p. 172) ends as follows:

Then up spake little Kirsten,
As he ran the sword in her side:
"I thought to find a better fate,
Now sorrow I must abide.

"I warn every proud young maiden
Who thinks to keep her estate:
That she plight her troth to only one man
And hold to him in good faith."

Here it might appear as though the ballad poet himself had spoken this concluding moral, but in reality it is a part of Little Kirsten's speech, as is evident from Karen Brahe's Folio Manuscript. It is purely by accident that the ballad in Anna Urop's manuscript concludes with this stanza.

Ballad style demands a narrative of events that is wholly objective. The singer never mingles his judgments or remarks with the narrative stream. If by exception he steps into view, it is at the beginning of the ballad, or rather in the first stanza and possibly in the last. This is so marked a characteristic that any arrangement to the contrary is sure to shock the reader. Now let us read the following stanzas taken from the middle of a ballad on "Burd Ellensborg and Sir Oluf" (No. 303), beginning after the point where the maiden had plighted her troth with a knight who had slain her maternal uncle and who was in consequence in danger of his life from her brothers:

> 12. The young pair bade each other good night
> With many a grievous groan;
> May God the Father who dwells in Heaven
> Grant that they meet right soon.

Then follows a narrative of how the brothers kill Sir Oluf and of how the maiden mourns for him. The detail cited in the above stanza is wholly foreign to ballad style, and should one investigate more closely the sources, he will find that it is Peder Syv, and after him Abrahamson, who has altered the old text, which in all four versions runs:

> The young pair bade each other good night
> With many a grievous groan;
> "May God the Father who dwells in Heaven
> Grant that we meet right soon."

At the close of the ballad a wish is sometimes in place. Examples of this, however, are not many. In one of the concluding stanzas of "The Wager" (No. 224) we meet with a "thanks":

B 24, C 21. Thanks be to every gentlewoman
Who brings up her daughter in honor!
Sir Peder rides out to the Landsthing,
He woos her with glory and honor.

This stanza, however, is found in only two texts out of the nine, and both of these were written down in the first quarter of the seventeenth century; whereas several of the other texts were written down half a century earlier. The corresponding stanza found in the other manuscripts is in keeping with normal ballad style, and runs with several variations as follows:

This got Ingerlil, Thorlof's daughter,
For giving Sir Peder such answer:
Sir Iver rides off to her father's court,
And demands her hand in marriage.

On the other hand, this same verse with "thanks be" occurs in all the forms of "In Chastity and Honor" (No. 225), and here too in manuscripts of the sixteenth century; likewise in "Proud Ellensborg" (No. 218), a ballad preserved also in old copies, where the expression is even bound up with another tramp line, "Where will such another be!"

Thanks be to proud Ellensborg,
Where will such another be!
She dared to fetch her own truelove
From the Easter king's country.

Somewhat improbable is the exclamation contained in stanza 12 of No. 202. Finally, one of the best known examples of the "thanks be" is found in the last stanza of the ballad "Niels Ebbesön" (No. 156), with which one should compare "Magnus Algotsön" (No. 181). As another example of how a wish can form a part of the ballad's conclusion can be named "Sir Bugge's Death" (No. 158), where we find in all four texts:

> The Medelfar men, Christ give them bad luck,
> They shot Sir Bugge under a safe-conduct!
>
> The Medelfar men, Christ give them shame,
> They shot Sir Bugge, the well-born man!

IV. Fatherland

A conception of which no mention is made in our ballads is that of fatherland. Neither does it appear in the ballads of Germany. But here I must lay special emphasis upon the fact that we are concerned only with the abstract notion of fatherland. Certainly we should clearly distinguish between whether the name is missing, whether the idea is wanting, or whether, on the whole, the feeling which we call love of one's native land is nonexistent. That such a feeling did exist in the fullest measure does not admit of question. Our Danish nationality was defended against the Wends, Germans, and Swedes by the men of the Middle Ages as bravely as by those of any other period; but with us, as with other peoples, the prince stood as the incarnate representative of the folk, its will and wishes. The struggle for the land became fused in a peculiar manner with the struggle for the king.

The question has been raised whether the word "fatherland" appears in the ballads. In the ballad "Marsk Stig's Daughters" (No. 146) the two daughters ask:

> Nothing else of you we desire
> Than you let us go home to our *Færne* (our father's land?),

and the queen orders the five knights:

> "Ye shall lead the maids home to Kollen!"

In version A the maidens are not daughters of Marsk Stig but of "the king out of Kollen," which is a land of adventure. The place is mentioned also in other Scandinavian ballads, and perhaps was originally Colonia, now Cologne. Meanwhile the word *Fædrene* comes closest in meaning to "vor Faders Land" (that is, our paternal possessions).

> 33. They came not ere Yuletide to their fathers' land (*for deres Faders Land*)
>
> 44. Promise us to remain in your fathers' land (*i Eders Faders Land*)

Again *Færne* possibly means "paternal ancestry" (*fædrene Slagt*); in both these senses it is used very generally in the "Provincial Laws" and in later works (cf. also "The Maiden at the Thing" (No. 222, A 17): "I will give your Grace my patrimony (*mit Farne*)"; "The Maiden transformed into a Bird" (No. 56, B 14, 15). As is well known Marsk Stig's exiled adherents fought to win their inheritance, and Huitfeld says that at length it is granted them "to enjoy their fathers and their mothers" (I, 344). Kalkar in his dictionary translates *Færne* of the above ballad as "fatherland" (*Fædreneland*), but he cites no similar instance; on the other hand, there are numerous examples of its use in the sense of paternal estate or family.

In B 2 and D 2 of "Ribold and Guldborg" (No. 82) it runs: "To my fathers' land (*Fædrene Land*) I shall thee lead"; but the discrepancy between these texts from Sophie Sandberg's manuscript and those from the great Stockholm manuscript of the beginning and middle of the seventeenth century, as well as the numerous other texts, speaks very decidedly against the supposition that *Fædreneland* was original here. Indeed, by comparing "min ferne land" (my paternal land) of B 2 with *til en halfieer land*, that is, *dobbelt saa fagert Land* (doubly so fair a land) or *det feierste Land* (the fairest land) of D, one will see how the words originally ran.

Although I can find neither that word nor *Fosterland* (native land) in Danish sources of the Middle Ages, yet it may well have been used, for we read in Magnus Smek's "Town Laws" the words *fadhurlandh* and *fædhernis land*, and in old Swedish laws likewise *Fosterland*, with reference to both the native province and the country.

But as has already been stated, love of one's fatherland does not, on the whole, show itself in our ballads. The same thing holds true of Sweden in the Middle Ages. The individual provinces as yet stood opposed to each other with so strong a national independence that it is difficult to see how any very marked degree of feeling for the fatherland could be expected of the Swedes. The monarchical unity, says Henrik Schück, in his excellent "Literary History of Sweden," and the notion of Sweden's being one land for everybody, Uplanders as well as West Goths, had not yet come into being: "It follows as a natural consequence that in Swedish literature, even down to the days of Albrecht of Mecklenburg and Engelbrekt, Swedish patriotism is conspicuous by its absence." In what is supposedly the oldest work preserved to us, St. Sigfred's legend, dating from 1206, one can notice how the author warms up to his subject when he speaks of his native parish, — the beautiful Värend, — but farther than local patriotism one never reached. The author of the oldest of the rimed chronicles, that of Erik's, is an enthusiast of the first water, but a proper patriot he is not. "In the introduction he has only a few words to say of Sweden's renown, and these are quite trivial; but in 1452, when this introduction was rewritten, the tone changed. The new writer, in poetic respects, can by no means sustain a comparison with his predecessor; . . . but in one thing he is a skald, one can almost say a great skald, and that is when he speaks of his fatherland. The nearer one comes to the end of the Middle Ages the higher this note of patriotism mounts up. Its form manifests itself in an increasingly wilder hatred of the Danes" (p. 85).

The same conditions obtained no doubt in Denmark, and if our ballads bore a date, we should perhaps discover a similar change in the national feeling. For instance, a new national tone emerges characteristically in the ballads on Svend Felding. This famous hero rides to Rome, visiting en route a certain maiden. When she sees his gold-stitched shirt she exclaims that he must be either king of Denmark or else of the highest rank. She has heard all her days that the Danish men are very brave; therefore she is very glad to see one of them, for a *trold* has been plaguing her land and carrying off women and girls for food. Svend Felding is sufficiently desirous of breaking a lance with the *trold* for her sake, but he must have such a horse and armor as will suit him. The Spanish horses which were led out for him fell to the ground when he barely laid hands on them, upon which he exclaims:

A 14. "Oh, I would give the red, red gold,
But and a thousand marks,
If now I had a Danish horse
Was born in Dennemark."

15. And by there came a miller good,
And speak right well could he:
"Oh, I have a right good Danish horse,
But ridden he dare not be.

16. "Oh, I have a Danish horse,
Was born in Sæbylund,
And every time he goes to mill
Bears fifteen hundred pounds."

17. "Hear me, thou good miller,
That horse now let me see;
Then we ourselves, we two Danes,
Will fight with Southrons three."

Svend Felding then draws the saddle-girths so tight that the horse falls down on its knees, and at once he rides into combat against the *trold.* His spear breaks, however, and his shield rolls on the ground.

27. Then sped he off to the church,
His sins he there confessed;
He bore away the sacrament,
To the spear he made it fast.

28. "Now put away the crowned spear,
It failed me in time of need;
And fetch me hither a good sloop mast,
Then well I can me speed."

In the second tilt Svend Felding breaks the evil one's neck. Then the bold warrior was offered the maiden and land and kingdom; but he is already plighted to another and he will not betray her. "But if a Danish pilgrim visits you, Spare neither bread nor wine."

Evidently this is a ballad that would commend itself in the highest degree to the Danish national feeling. The renown of the Danes had already reached foreign lands before Svend Felding made his journey south, but he gave a brilliant exhibition of the might that lay in a Danish man's arm and of the strength that resided in a Danish horse. There is only one vulnerable point in all this glory, which, when viewed closely, proves to be an Achilles' heel; that is, the circumstance that all this strength is absolutely of no avail. Only after Svend has laid the Host on the spear does he gain the victory. As a matter of fact, that is a very stupid piece of business, for it is, if anything, by a trick or stratagem that Svend Felding bears off the victory. I can think of nothing else than that two ideas here run counter to each other. Moreover it is unintelligible why Svend Felding takes the mast of a sloop for a weapon, since it is not the weapon but what is concealed on it that counts. Here again one feels, as I have pointed out in many other ballads, that the religious, the ecclesiastical, the Catholic element has been clapped on later, and that it is a disturbing and jarring force. Svend Grundtvig must have had the same feeling, for in the text which he published in his "Selected Popular Ballads," he leaves out altogether the stanza dealing with the Host on the spear for the reason that it is wholly superfluous.

The second ballad on "Svend Felding" (No. 32) also makes use of the Host, but in a more rational manner:

> A 64. He bids consecrate God's body,
> Bids set it on his spear-shaft;
> Right soon then fled the loathed *trold*
> That sat on the warrior's back.
>
> 65. The second tilt they together rode
> The heroes were strong enow;
> It was Sir Peder Kæmpe,
> His neck was broke in two.

The German warrior has a *trold* sitting behind him on his horse; it is he whom Svend Felding overthrows by means of God's body. Upon this the strife between the German and the Dane becomes equalized, and now the Dane wins the victory. In texts B, C the motif respecting the Host and the *trold* is wholly wanting, thereby showing very clearly that it has been stitched on.

In this ballad Svend Felding is sent out by the Danish king to propose by proxy to the Lady Juttelil. She is much prejudiced in advance against the Danes and makes sport of them in various ways; but she gets a rough answer from Svend Felding. Moreover, when Jutta comes to Denmark, she is far from being pleased; she does not think the bridal house good enough, and she rejoices when Svend Felding is overthrown in a joust by Peder Kæmpe. But at the next onset when Svend Felding breaks the German's neck, the queen weeps. The way in which B (in the burden) forms its refrain indicates the drift of the ballad:

> 1. There are setting out for Denmark
> Many a renowned knight,
> And so many Germans,
> I cannot count them quite.
> *There are setting out for Denmark.*

Whoever Svend Felding may be, whether, as Bugge supposes, the mythical hero Sinfjötli in a new guise, or, as Grundtvig assumes, "a popular mythical personage who was certainly called into being in comparatively late times, but wholly in the old style (III, 804)," I shall leave unsaid. But Grundtvig's conjecture that the ballad on Queen Jutta was composed on the occasion of Erik Plovpenning's marriage with the Saxon Princess Jutta (1239) seems to me highly improbable. In Ryd Kloster's Annals, to be sure, one comes upon decidedly strong expressions of feeling against the Germans in consequence of King Valdemar's imprisonment: "And you should know that the Germans have seldom or never won any advantage or victory over the Danes without using treachery or deceit, as may be evidenced in the case of these two kings, and in many other ways." But this is merely a temporary blaze which was quickly put out and which was followed by a still closer alliance with the Germans, bringing in its train even greater misfortunes for Danish nationality. Neither the positive side of national feeling, satisfaction over what is Danish, nor the negative, hatred for what is foreign, crops out very noticeably in the earlier periods of the Middle Ages. It is not until the fifteenth century, when our kings took up the fight against the Germans whether the latter came in the likeness of merchants or of warriors, that the national feeling flames aloft. Who knows but that it was the journey of the gigantic King Christian I to Rome, and the sensation and renown that his trip aroused, which may have given rise to a new conception of the story of Svend Felding and to the treatment of the subject found in these two ballads?

In conclusion I shall mention that the tradition of Holger Dansk, as all know, is not of national origin, but that it found its way in during the latest period of the Middle Ages, and that in any case the ballad of "Holger Dansk and Burmand" (No. 30) cannot be said to manifest any marked patriotic stamp. Such a character, on the contrary, appears rather in "King Didrik and Holger Dansk" (No. 17); but this ballad also bears every mark of youth. Grundtvig regards it as "certainly the youngest of the Didrik ballads, and in one respect distinct from the others, in that it is not a spontaneous, naïve rendering of the old legend, but rather a conscious use of this for patriotic ends." Gustav Storm assigns the ballad to the sixteenth century.[1]

V. Romantic Ballads

As a distinct group must be segregrated those ballads which Grundtvig has incidentally called romantic ballads. Since he has not described these ballads in detail, I shall attempt to throw into relief various features of their physiognomy. The best known of these ballads is "Axel and Valborg" (No. 475, in 180–200 stanzas); others are "Malfred and Magnus" (No. 49, 89 stanzas), "Flores and Margrete" (No. 86, 30–40 stanzas), "Karl and Margrete" (No. 87, 50–70 stanzas), "King Apollonius of Tyre" (No. 88, 25 stanzas), "The Cloister Robbery" (No. 476, 94 stanzas), "Terkel Trundesön" (No. 480, 207 stanzas!), "Oluf Gudmundsön" (Unpub. No. 306, 152 stanzas)

I shall give the substance of one of these ballads in order to make their character plain. Earl Iver Ulfsön,

[1] Gustav Storm, Sagnkredsene om Karl den Store, p. 187.

the standard bearer of the king, falls in battle. He has intrusted his three daughters to the queen's care, but when she learns from a sibyl that the youngest one, Malfred, is to marry Magnus her son, she sends this daughter away on a ship. The boat is stranded on the shores of Spain, and the girl is led away to become the bride of a chieftain. Before her wedding she catches sight of Magnus, who has been captured by pirates and carried off to a foreign country and forced to sit at the oars and row. She manages to have him ransomed. Magnus kills the bridegroom and flees with her. One day during their sojourn in the forest Malfred was lured into the mountain by a *trold*, and Magnus journeys home alone. After the lapse of nine years he engages to marry Thorelille, but just then Malfred, who has slipped away from the mountain, comes sailing home to Norway. The two women agree to share Magnus as a husband.

As is very evident, strict unity of treatment is abandoned. Of dramatic force there is not a tittle; its place is taken by a whole string of adventures. A similar peculiarity marks the narration of "Flores and Margrete." Flores loves Margrete, but her friends wed her against her will to Sir Herman, the rich count. When Flores meets Margrete in the church, she confesses to him that she still loves him. Her husband, on his return home, notes that she has been weeping, upon which he declares that after all he intends to relinquish her to Flores. But Flores' mother has in the meantime come to his rescue by sending out a *trold* in the shape of a hart at whom the count shoots; the bullet, however, turns against the count himself. Now Margrete is a widow, and Flores woos her;

but she will remain a widow a year. Thereupon joy and mirth prevail. In this ballad the want of unity in the thought as well as in the treatment is likewise conspicuous.

The length of the ballads is remarkable and seems designed to supply a want in the substance. But this feature indicates their purpose; namely, to provide entertainment for long evenings. In addition the ballads seek to fix the interest by new means; they concern themselves with foreign lands; as, for instance, Spain (No. 49), Tyre and Naples (No. 88); they use foreign personal names (Flores), and they are erudite; as, for example, the ballad of "Malfred and Magnus," which allows Earl Iver to say, as though it were modeled on the classical style of the sagas, "So help me, Lady Freya and Thor, and keep my life free from pain" (No. 119, A 10). Furthermore, instead of employing good dramatic diction, which goes straight to the point, they take up much time and use many words on matters of inquiry, reflection, and persuasion. Altogether they have a character of long, spun-out precision.

In the next place the moral force is lost, or rather the ballads are morally bungled. No. 49 unblushingly allows the narrative to end with Magnus becoming the husband of both Malfred and Thorelille.

> It has come to pass in Norway's land
> And it comes to mind full ready,
> Sir Magnus lived for eighteen years
> With two fair noble ladies.
>
> They lived together for eighteen years,
> With love and right good feeling,
> And never mortal man has heard
> A quarrelsome word between them.

To such bad taste had the times fallen. The heroes of the ballads dare not do evil nor dare they do good. Margrete will not permit Flores to kill Count Herman; Count Herman would gladly resign his wife to her lover; Flores is to be rewarded for his languishing fidelity. But why does the ballad lug in here the ugly story of his mother's magic arts? And yet Count Herman up to the last is so virtuous that when dying he bewails the fact that he and his wife have no child, — not because he wishes to leave an avenger behind him, — but because the inheritance will go to relatives instead of to Margrete. It would be wrong to say that these ballads are immoral; rather are they fairly tricked out with virtue.

A sentimental tone, on the whole, has crept into these ballads. In his great sorrow Flores resolves: "I'll lay me in an upper room and grieve myself to death." And the same holds good of "Axel and Valborg" (No. 475), however beautiful it may be otherwise. A master like Oehlenschläger can annihilate doubt and make us believe that Valborg dies of a ballad. But a too bounteous measure of virtue finds expression in such stanzas as

118. "Deep is my love for Valborg fair,
She was my highest bliss.
But never once did I come so near
As to give her a single kiss."

119. She laid her hand on the mass-book nigh
And swore with right good grace:
"I was ne'er so bold as to lift my eyes
And look him full in the face."

Though both in ancient times and the Middle Ages men and women were found who conceived love for one whom they never saw, for the might of runes and love is strong, yet surely they dared to look upon one another when they met. And it is precisely because the lovers themselves speak of their great bashfulness that something of the naïve beauty is lost. On the one hand, we can readily agree with a Swedish author, who said of these lines: "Over all these stanzas there is diffused a fine blush"; but, on the other hand, we realize that we have approached tolerably near to the edge of the truly natural, and we can understand why the bailiff of Anholt, in Holberg's poem of "Peder Paars," reproached his wife with being almost drowned in a flood of tears at the last festival because some one had read to her a little of Axel Thorsen. Here we feel as if we were present at the wind-up of the days of knighthood. And in reality, after one has lingered a little over these ballads, he needs but to glance around the corner to see that familiar Spanish knight of the lanky figure approaching.

Furthermore these ballads are difficult to remember because of their great length and especially because of the lack of continuity in their plots. Adventure succeeds adventure and speech follows upon speech. If ballads ever required the services of professional singers, they may well have done so in these instances. Such ballads show clearly that they are at home among the romances. The subject of the ballad of "King Apollonius of Tyre" (No. 88) is derived from the romance of the same name. "Malfred and Magnus" (No. 49) treats of a familiar German legend of the Count of Gleichen and the two women. The sentimental ballad of "Sir Sallemand" (Abr. No. 153), who loves his sister's child, ends with the statement that such love was never seen "since Tristram and Isald died." Such a beginning as opens up "Flores and Margrete" (No. 86),

> 1. A ballad I will sing to you,
> Which many a time I have sung,
> All how the lovely Lady Margret
> Was loved by Sir Flores Bendiktsön;

or such a conclusion as that which appears in the last stanza of "Oluf Gudmundsön" (Unpublished No. 306, 152 stanzas !),

> Of nothing was this ballad made,
> The truth I tell to you,
> Now must another begin
> Who better can do,

is likewise found continually in the romances. In his manuscript collection Grundtvig has written concerning this last quoted stanza: "The last stanza is noteworthy for showing us the use the ballad was put to in social entertainment when delivered by a single, let us say a professional, singer. People of this class have, I dare say, composed ballads of this sort."

That such ballads belong to a very late date may well be regarded as certain. The ballad of "Axel and Valborg" (No. 475), judged by its costume and apparatus, cannot, as R. Bergström has pointed out ("Historiskt Bibliothek" III, 419 ff.), be set farther back than the fifteenth century. Finally let me call attention to the fact that these ballads commonly lay their scenes in Norway; this is true, for example, of "Malfred and Magnus" (No. 49), "Axel and Valborg" (No. 475), and "The Cloister Robbery" (No. 476), in which a son of a Swedish king robs the daughter of a Norwegian duke in the Lyse Cloister. How far "Karl and Margrete" (No. 87), which, as Grundtvig says, shows "a good deal of similarity" to the last named ballad, has anything to do with Danish personages, might well be questioned; it concerns itself chiefly with Sweden. "Terkel Trundesön" (No. 200) treats of Denmark and the king of Iceland.

These remarks by no means imply that these ballads are wholly lacking in poetical qualities. A number of them, in addition to a certain amount of dilution and dullness, contain good stanzas and good scenes. Regarded as a whole, however, they can be taken only as a medley.

VI. Ballad Style

I now turn to the various peculiarities of ballad style.

We commonly understand by inversion that a word does not occupy the same place in a sentence it would in ordinary speech. In daily speech we often shift a word about for the sake of emphasis and accentuation; in poetry the same causes operate, but most frequently with a view to rhythm and rime. There is a great difference in the extent to which various poets use inversion; mediocre poets will often resort to it to secure rime, or because they are misled by the belief that this is the only means available of drawing the attention. The poet who is imbued with a strong didactic sense will knit words together in weighty sentences. There is no question that those poets must be ranked highest who, with the simplest means, gain the same ends as those who must rely on the aid of embellishment.

In this respect, then, there is a very great deal to be learned from the ballads, which are extremely moderate in their use of inversion as an aid in the construction of the verse and in the securing of rime. One can find "son mine," "the knights good," "maiden fair" (or rather "maiden so fair"), and the object before the verb; but, on the whole, inversions are not frequent and in any case never violent. When in "Ribold and Guldborg" (No. 82) we read:

> G 62. Ribold was dead ere the cock crew,
> Guldborg died ere rose the sun,

we see that the last line, even when the license of our own time on this point is considered, contains an all too violent inversion. But it happens that this verse is found only in Peder Syv and that in the remaining eighteen forms it is wanting. A corresponding verse is found in several texts, dating from the middle of the seventeenth century, of "Söborg and Adelkind" (No. 266), but the oldest form of the ballad in Karen Brahe's Folio Manuscript has a far more unobtrusive inversion:

> E 2. She was born at eventide,
> Her mother was dead ere rose the sun.

In the "Kinsman's Revenge" (No. 4) we read:

> C 44. Hun redte deres Senge paa Dunen blöd,
> hun vilde dennem unde Sövnen söd.
>
> She made their beds of down smooth,
> She wished them well sleep sweet;

but only under Vedel's hand could the stanza get those two inversions. His only source, as Grundtvig points out, is A 32:

Stolt Ellind gjorde deres Senge paa Dune:
hun vilde [dennem] Sövnen vel unde.

Proud Ellind made their beds of down,
She wished that they might well sleep sound.

Here we have a familiar inversion in the second line, if it is an inversion. One must remember, on the whole, that many word orders which depart from the popular usage of to-day were at that time natural and common features of daily speech. Two inversions in succession, however, the balladists would regard, I believe, as inadmissible.

A familiar inversion is to be found in "Niels Ebbesön" (No. 156):

E 15. "Hear now this, Sir Niels Ebbesön,
I talk with you too long;
You shall either from Denmark flee
Or I shall have you hanged."

16. "Thieves you may on the gallows hang,
Both for owls and erns;
But I shall surely in Denmark live
All with my wife and bairns."

For all that the "Thieves," when placed at the beginning, rings out so boldly, yet it seems to take one by surprise and to sound so harsh that the line almost becomes top-heavy. The other three texts have preserved the following version of the stanza:

Must I out of Denmark flee
From my wife and bairns so small;
Unlucky shall you think it then
That ever you me saw!

Grundtvig may allow therefore that "this proud stanza (E 16 above), which, when looked at from a poetic standpoint, is certainly a gain to the ballad, in originality must give way before the stanza found in the other three copies." "There is the greatest probability that it was added at the same time with the renovation of the expression, which E in several places exhibits; and by one possessed of an undoubtedly poetical talent, which knew how to patch up in masterly fashion the weak spots in the memory, which overtake, however, the expression more frequently than the contents." Nevertheless, Grundtvig has included this stanza in his popular edition of 1867. In A 84, 85 of the same ballad appears "sige Dronning Tiding slig" (tell the queen tidings such), likewise a violent inversion; Vedel has more correctly: "Dronningen Tidende sige" (the queen tidings tell); cf. Ab 84: "sige Dronningen sligt Men" (tell the queen such hurt).

In many other places we could point out inversions that have originated in later times; as, for instance, in C 9 of "Sir Ebbe's Daughter" (No. 194): "Up then waked the maidens shrewd." This is a labored text with rime in all four lines; the older forms omit this line.

Inversion is found by far most frequently in the refrains; I cite the following examples:

No. 130. Selv lader hun sig vel.
No. 142. Og saar er min Haand af den Brynje.
No. 167. Saa glad rider Erik Stygge imod sin Jomfru.
No. 174. Til Meissen kom den Fröken med stor Ære.
No. 195. Deraf al vor Sorg matte sig vel fordrive.

No. 130. So behaves she well.
No. 142. And sore is my hand on the breastplate.
No. 167. So gladly rides Erik Stygge to his truelove.
No. 174. To Meissen comes the lady with great honor.
No. 195. Thereby all our sorrow must be driven away.

As one will notice, there is not a single inversion here which could not be found in an ordinary prose text of the same period.

The connection between sentences is marked by a great simplicity. Parallel structure is the general favorite; all involved constructions are avoided. The apodosis follows in the next verse-line; in the case of a four-line stanza the first two lines readily constitute an entity, and seldom or never do we find the third line knit grammatically with the second. At as late a period as after "Sir Tyge Krabbe's Fight in Skaane in 1510" (No. 171) one could still write:

C 21. Sir Tyge orders the spies to go out,
They should in truth discover
What the enemy had in mind to do,
And what way they meant to manœuvre;

the older forms, however, have no such ponderously constructed stanza, nor any like it. "It runs contrary to good, old ballad style to have an antecedent in one verse and an apodosis in another," says Grundtvig in his introduction to No. 220 (A, stanzas 287–288). Nevertheless in all manuscripts of "The Buried Mother" (No. 89) are to be found the verses:

16. She 's ta'en her way to the angel's home,
She begged of Jesus Christ a boon,

17. That she might to earth return
And speak again with her little bairns;

but evidently the first line in stanza 17 should be amended to:

She begged she might to earth return.

In his popular edition of the ballads (1882) Grundtvig also has made this change in the line.

On the whole, repetition aids in avoiding any heavy or involved construction. Simplicity in sentence construction is a striking feature in the ballads and sets them apart from the style of to-day. They may indeed vary widely in this respect from the style of the romances. And such constructions as are found in the "Nibelungenlied" would be wholly impossible to a ballad poet. One need but glance at the first stanza of that famous poem to see the difference:

Uns ist in alten maeren
wunders vil geseit
von helden lobebaeren,
von grôszer kuonheit,
von fröuden hôchgezîten,
von weinen und von klagen,
von küener recken strîten
muget ir nu wunder hoeren sagen.

As on many other occasions, counterfeit stanzas are instructive also in the matter of sentence formation.

No. 4, C 22. She placed beneath their side
Their knife upon which they relied.

This is a stanza of Vedel's; the old text runs:

B 17. She placed beneath their side
Their sword and a bared knife.

"Hagbard and Signe" (No. 20) has the following stanza in form A:

10. Hear me now, proud Signild,
To me you will allow it:
That I may handiwork learn from you,
So few are they that know it.

Not one of the other seven versions, which are found in copies equally old, has in the corresponding stanza so heavy a construction. In its place appears, for example:

> C 13. Here you sit, proud Signild,
> You spin the silken twill;
> Hafbard, the king's son, has sent me to you,
> If me you would teach like skill.

Karen Brahe's Folio Manuscript contains the following stanza:

> No. 30, A 18. He swore by God on high,
> That he his word would hold,
> If she could hand to him the man
> Would dare to strive with Burmand so bold.

The other two texts have no stanza answering to this; and Grundtvig in his introduction to this ballad calls attention to the fact that that manuscript "expands and revises the traditional texts" (IV, 782).

A striking parallelism occurs in a stanza of "Magnus Algotsön" (No. 181, B 8, E 17):

> Sharp are their swords
> And bent are their bows;
> Wrathful are they in mind,
> And hard are they in mood.

This stanza, which from a modern point of view would be regarded as excellent, is found in a manuscript of 1590 and in one of 1610; but it is interesting to see what the stanza is like in other texts:

> A 7 (1550) Here stay three hundred armed men
> In front of our courtyard;
> Without they all in silk are clad,
> Within in steel so hard.

C 8 (1650) Above they wear the silk,
Beneath the cuirass blue;
Wrathful are they in mind,
And rough are they in mood.

D 9 (1625) Here stay three hundred brave lordlings,
All blue as any dove;
The horse he is in silk bedecked,
The lord he rides above.

This fourfold parallelism is found therefore in only one form, and it can hardly be said to be well certified.

And very seldom is antithesis used. Professor Peter Hansen has quoted the following stanza from the ballad of the "Cloister-Maiden" ("Danish Heroic Ballads," 1867, No. 20) as an example of this artifice:

Now sits the swain in the bower aloft,
He plays with the silver so white;
So little heed the swain pays to me,
So grievous is my plight.

Now sits the swain in the bower aloft,
He plays with the gold so red;
So little the swain now thinks of me,
So grievous is my dread.

But nothing definite may be gathered from this ballad; it is, as has been pointed out, scarcely older than the sixteenth century. Professor Peter Hansen cites further the words between Agnete and the Merman (in the ballad of that name, No. 38):

"But when you to the church are bound,
You must not wear the red gold on your gown.

"And when you to the churchyard repair,
You must not unbind your fair yellow hair.

"And when you within the church door step,
You must not smile under your scarlet cape.

"And when you walk up through the aisle,
You must not sit by your mother the while.

"And when the priest names Him most dread,
You must not then bow down your head."

And when she to the church was bound,
She wore the red gold on her gown.

And when she to the churchyard repaired,
Agnete unbound her fair yellow hair.

And when she within the church door stepped,
Agnete she smiled under her scarlet cape.

And when she walked up through the aisle,
Agnete sat by her mother the while.

And when the priest named Him most dread,
She then bowed down her head.

Here we have parallelism carried out in full, together with what in the truest sense can be called antithesis; and herein we are again brought face to face with the purely artistic. We now stand on the exact border line of the rigid and the uniform, at the very threshold of the Learned Period; whereas our ballads of the Middle Ages speak in the fashion of children, or rather as a mother speaks to her child. The proof that "Agnete and the Merman" should be dated back to the Middle Ages, when its eccentric form and its late appearance certainly relegate it to the eighteenth century, has meanwhile not yet been brought forward, and he who is to adduce this will have his work cut out for him. Until that has been done, we ought to leave this ballad out of consideration when the question deals with the qualities peculiar to the ballads of the Middle Ages.

It will be evident from the foregoing discussion that the style of our ballads forms a complete contrast to that of our proverbs. In the latter we frequently meet with antithesis ("Speech is silver, silence is golden"; "Penny-wise and pound-foolish"; "It is sweet to get and bitter to pay") and with inversion ("To every cow belongs her calf"; "Little is the harm silence does"). Proverbs also attract alliteration ("Look before you leap"; "Plunder Peter and pay Paul"; "Cat will after kind"), and they affect disjointed speech ("A bad egg, a bad bird"; "Out of sight, out of mind"; "bad beginning, bad ending"). When therefore one asserts that many old proverbs lie hidden in the popular ballads, it seems to me that he misunderstands the language in which they are usually couched, for in the ballad there is found absolutely nothing of the sententiousness, the weighty thought, and the condensed expression that everywhere prevail in the proverb.

Perhaps one will be inclined to say that in "Marsk Stig" (No. 145) are to be heard not a few proverbs and sententious utterances. Especially does this apply to the bold conversation between the Marshal and King Erik:

A 42. Then answered young Sir Marsti,
He was sorrowful enow:
"It is a well-known adage,
Scorn and skaith together go."

47. "Marsti, thou dost not ride so hard
But well I can ward myself against thee;
If thou wilt naught of my friendship have,
Then thou must let it be."

48. "No, I do not ride so hard,
Thy might is more than mine;
Hast thou never heard it said before:
That strength takes the road before might?

49. "No, I do not ride so hard,
I am not so stubborn of mind;
One finds very often a greyhound
Puts to flight both hart and hind.

50. "Call this well to mind,
I have thee here defied!
It happens right often a little hump
Will upset a full great load."

All of this sounds splendid enough; yet I must confess that the other texts display more effectively the haughty spirit of Marsk Stig. That wealth of proverbs, which Marsk Stig even quotes as proverbs, makes him in my eyes look book-learned. It must be remembered that text A, in which these stanzas are found, has been freely worked over in a late period, and that additions or expansions, which propose a little too much of what is good, have certainly found a place here. In any case the older forms have nothing like these proverbs.

Vedel has allowed "The Death of Alf the Lesser" (No. 151) to conclude with a long soliloquy in which Alf confesses that he has been a horrible sinner, to the terror and warning of everybody. There occurs also this stanza:

19. I have robbed and stolen without any stint
Many long days and years;
What one with sin and wrong has gotten
With shame and sorrow disappears.

But Vedel must assume the responsibility of this.

At any rate a distinction must be made between two things. One is that current proverbs are used in direct discourse, and the other that the speaker utters the words which the event calls forth as if they were proverbial sayings. This is true, as we have seen, of Marsk Stig. And when Niels Ebbesön says:

> Never did you see me so afraid
> That I did not dare to shiver,

it is indeed possible that he is speaking a line that is original with the ballad poet; but it has been cited already in the collection of proverbs by Peder Laale. In the same ballad Niels says:

> Thc count offered me two terms,
> And neither of them was good;

which is an old expression occurring also in the sagas (cf. No. 300, 14: "There are two choices and neither is good"). But wholly different from this is the case where the poet strives on his own account to muster his impressions, his reflections, or his doctrines in sentences weighted with thought. Such a manner does not belong to the ballad.

In conclusion it may be illuminating perhaps to consider a stanza which is even yet to-day cited as though it were really a glorious relic of the Middle Ages. It is the concluding stanza of "Niels Ebbesön" (No. 156, F 83), in the form which Anders Vedel has communicated:

> Christ prosper every good Danish man,
> Who with both mouth and hand,
> Without jesting and scoffing, with heart and soul,
> Will serve his fatherland.

This stanza really deserves to be made the object of study, since it is a richly significant example of how stanzas were not constructed and spoken in the Middle Ages. In the very first line our attention is called to a wish or prayer, which, as has been pointed out above, never or seldom occurs in the ballads. In the second and third lines we meet with three parallelisms as well as with a relative sentence whose beginning and subject appear in the second line and whose conclusion and verb in the fourth. Finally, as has been shown, "fatherland" is a conception the ballads do not mention or treat of.

VII. Dramatic Structure

That which is so often wonderfully contrived in the ballads is the introduction. The first stanza frequently leads us straight into the situation, and every line of the stanza carries us a step farther into the story. Let me call attention, for instance, to the beginning of "Young Sveidal" (No. 70):

It was the young Sveidal
Was playing at the ball;
The ball bounced into the maiden's bower,
It made his color fall.

The ball bounced into the maiden's lap,
And the youth went in to get it;
Ere he out of that bower came,
His heart with sorrow was fretted.

"Hear thou, young Sveidal,
Why drivest thou the ball to me?
There sits a maiden in a foreign land,
She longs sorely after thee."

With this Sveidal's work is mapped out for him, and he must seek out this maid who has been bound to him by runes. In the same manner the task and the subject are set forth in "Karl and Margrete" (No. 87).

Can one call to mind a more compact narrative than that with which "The Betrothed in the Grave" (No. 90) opens:

It was the knight Sir Aage,
He rides so far away,
He wooed the maiden Elselille,
She was so fair a may.

He wooed the maiden Elselille,
All with stores of gold.
On the Monday after
He lay in the black, black mould.

It was the maiden Elselille,
She had grief untold;
That heard Sir Aage
Under the black, black mould.

Modern poets by the hundreds might well envy the singer of those vanished days the ability to lead us with such magical power and in so few seconds into the midst of his world of ideas, foreign though it may be; and in such a manner that we believe ourselves to have been conducted thither step by step, and are made to feel at home.

An introduction of another kind is mentioned above in which the singer evokes a universal mood, and in a few chords brings the listeners within his realm of feeling and action upon which the text of the ballad proper is built. In glaring contrast with these openings are the later "I shall sing to you a ballad" of the street ballads.

The truly dramatic narrative does not relate all that happens. The account does not seek to be absolutely complete; on the contrary, it strives to make everything stand out realistically and well defined. All intermediate stages are therefore leaped over, and only the most prominent are related. By this means the ballad attains to real energy and impressive strength. What a character thinks or decides upon is told as briefly as possible; it is by their actions that we learn to know the hero and the knight, their dispositions and peculiarities. The ballads are only now and then descriptive. The beauty of the maiden or of the sweetheart is never detailed to us; it is mentioned in general terms, and we believe in it because we hear how widely through the land its fame is spread, how many wooers it has lured, and how heavy of heart are the rejected lovers. A man's strength is vividly presented to us by his deeds; but his appearance is not described except again in the most general way. And only in the later ballads do we get so detailed a picture of his costume as those which are found in the rimed romances. In the words of a German writer, "With the *Aventiure* [Romances] appear the inane sketches of horse, saddles, bridles, tents, rugs, beds, cloaks, equipments, — which are so costly because they cost nothing." [1]

All pauses in the action are avoided. Scene is knitted to scene, and transitions are prepared for us, as when, for instance, it is related how "the watcher stands upon the wall" and sees what is coming. In the same manner the eye is led from scene to scene in the sketch of the Bayeux

[1] Gödecke, Grundrisz zur Geschichte der deutschen Dichtung, 2d ed., I, 75.

Tapestry.[1] The common use of the present tense of the verb, of the narrative in the present, conjures up the picture more clearly. Then the rise in the narrative awakens attention: "They were there in a month, they were there in three." When an offer is made, when an oath is sworn, there comes after several lesser statements, as a conclusion, the highest and most solemn one. When wealth is depicted, the possessions are not enumerated coördinately, but in a series from the less to the greater, from the commonplace to the remarkable. Yet withal, the repose essential to the picture is not wanting. The repetition often impresses the picture more deeply in the consciousness of the audience.[2] Several verse-lines recur intentionally, as in such cases when a messenger is charged with his duties and is made to repeat his tidings in the same words.

Speeches, questions and answers constitute a main ingredient of the ballad. Moreover it is noteworthy that time after time — in fact, in the majority of instances — dialogue is not assigned. As a rule we find no such introductory line as "he then replied," etc. "The Dangerous Maiden" (No. 184) relates the doings of the chief personages and intermingles with these a long series of speeches without saying once who is speaking, and yet without leaving us in any doubt concerning the speaker. This is true to a great extent of the dialogue of "Hagbard and Signe" (No. 20). In the old Norse poetry we run across the same thing; for example, the "Alvíssmál" consists wholly of dialogue between the dwarf Alvis and Thor.

[1] Johannes Steenstrup, Bayeux-Tapetet, p. 44.

[2] N. M. Petersen, Literaturhistorie, 2d ed., I, 146.

One might ask whether a number of the actors do not reappear with the same general traits in various ballads. This holds good, as a matter of course, with the well-known mythical heroes and heroines as well as of individual historical personages. Queen Sophie of the ballad world is sketched in the same outline in a number of ballads. This is not the case, on the other hand, with the knights and their ladies. No specific traits of character are bound up with Sir Iver or Sir Oluf [1] and scarcely with Kirstine or Margrete. Only thus much is certain: the first is always called "little" Kirsten (and not "proud"), while Margrete, Ingeborg, and Else are usually named "proud" Mettelil, Ingerlil, Elselil, etc.

VIII. Simplicity

Schoolmaster T. Kristensen mentions in one place [2] "the wonderful execution and expression with which an old woman can sing a ballad. For this is demanded a certain simplicity and a perfect ignorance of the great world

[1] Lave comes most readily to mind. Lave is, for example, violent. Lave Stisön flogs his betrayed (or innocent) wife to death with a bridle (No. 259). But he is also unfortunate. When Lave Stisön would use violence toward Proud Margrete, she slays him with her knife (No. 196). When Lave Pedersön breaks into the bower of the maiden Ludselille at nighttime, her brother cuts off one of his hands and he rides shamed away (No. 199). Little Kirsten loves Sir Peter, whom she may not have, and when she is to be forced into marriage with Sir Lave she dies of sorrow (Abr. No. 135). Sir Lave holds a wedding, but Sir Jon locks the door and sleeps with the bride; Lave complains to the king and a duel is fought, in which Jon comes out victorious (No. 390). Sir Lave seduces Eline at the night-watch party, but he is faithful and marries her (No. 282). In No. 122 Sir Lave must marry Tovelille, the king's concubine.

[2] "Jydske Folkeminder," I, viii.

and its motley press of business, a life with few thoughts and yet with a certain degree of poetry." But what is thus exacted of the singer must also be found in the poems themselves, and only through these means can they continue to live and be preserved in the lower stratum. Thus it levels for itself a new road and appears again in the literary cultured circle, where it will perhaps become invested with deeper significance.

It is therefore this incomparable singleness and simplicity that is the most unique quality of the ballad. It appears to a like degree in the body and soul of the ballad, in the antecedents out of which the ballad grew, in the means used to give a stamp to its style and tone, and in the object and end which the ballad has in sight. The language is simple and commonplace, like that of our daily talk, and the vocabulary used is that which is found in the mouth of the ordinary man; and only few expressions current in a higher world, such as meet one in all other poetry, occur. And the ballads are marvelously temperate in the use of imagery. The lass that is besung can shine like a star, she is called the rose, the lily maid, or the mirror of all women; but beyond such expressions the ballad seldom goes.

Here again comes to light the vast distance separating the poetry of antiquity from the ballads of the Middle Ages. For nothing could be farther removed from the former than the practice of calling a thing by its right name; rather it uses a conventional name which is to be translated into its real worth. The ballads never speak of "sea-trees" when they mean ships, nor of "army-wasters" when they mean heroes. A kenning appears in only one ballad, that of "Ironwolf" (No. 10):

15. Then answered the king of Blideuinder,
    He spoke as a man may dare:
    "I 'll meet in the morn in the chieftains' storm (*Hövdingens Storm*)
    If me a horse can bear."

Here the Norse and Faroese versions have *Odderstorm, Oddabragd,* a kenning for battle, which must also be the meaning of *Hövdingens Storm.*[1] This is such a glaring exception in a Danish ballad that it arouses all sorts of conjectures over the authorship of the ballad and its wanderings before it was written down. In the Faroese and Icelandic ballads kennings can be pointed out readily enough.

Everything that is of the nature of learning and is extraneous to the ballad is wanting. Every one can listen to them and enjoy them without any prerequisite knowledge or culture. They contain no mythological, Biblical, or historical references. The action takes place in Denmark or everywhere. The king of England, the king of Iceland, and the king of the Wends, all possess an equally high degree of poetical reality; they only want genuine historical and geographical ground to stand upon. Any one who has had an interest in human conduct and feelings can find pleasure in these ballads.

Abstractions or persons who impersonate abstractions never, as has been stated before, appear in the ballads. The wicked stepmother who calumniates, the cunning handmaiden who effects dissension, the faithless groom who betrays his master, are all admitted to the ballads and there they receive their punishment; but we learn,

[1] Grundtvig, Danmarks Gamle Folkeviser, I, 145; III, 783; IV, 687, 691, 697, 701.

however, their names, where they live, and whom they serve. They are real people, not Lady Invidia in her ethereal rôle; not, as in school comedies, the ghosts of Fallacia or of Perfidia. Directly opposed to this is the poetic product of the sixteenth century. In the truly lyrical poetry of that age calumny or backbiting lurks everywhere. The despondent tone which crops out in much of the poetry of that time harmonizes well with the daily use of the "backbiter."

If one will turn to the ballad book of the Swede, Harald Oluffson, of 1572 (edited by A. Noreen and H. Schück), he will find in the ballads the "backbiter" (*Klafferen*) (cf. No. 1, "Ah, Backbiter, how wonderful you are," etc.; No. 3, "God keep me from the backbiter"; Nos. 5, 8, "The backbiters are so many"; Nos. 18, 22, 23, 25, 29, 37, 41). One might think that the taste of the individual collector was responsible for this choice, but the same contents are found in Nils Larson's book; and from Bröms Gyllenmär's "Ballad Book," of about 1620, can be cited the songs Nos. 5, 7, 9, 10, 13, 27, 34, 36, 43, 47, 48, 50, 51, 52, 55, etc. In short, it had become a mania; wherever one sits, stands, or walks, he meets the "backbiter," even "at night, when I should rest at peace, I find myself thinking on faith and law." But that agrees well with the entire suspicious, pessimistic tone inherent in indolence which is struck in these songs, whose favorite subjects are the world, wickedness, friendship's unreliability, woman's faithlessness, and the backbiter's duplicity:

> Yea, a false tongue,
> It is most like a basilisk;
> Who catches it in a net,
> Catches a baneful fish.

We shall find the "backbiter" admitted into various stanzas of Danish ballads which have been stitched on in this period; examples have been given above (see pp. 60, 117, 199).

But now along with all this simplicity is not this poetry also monotonous and wearisome? Certainly the number of our popular ballads is remarkably large, but in appearance they resemble each other like relatives, and in their character and make-up there exists much uniformity; furthermore this poetry is able to represent only one side of a folk's poetic field of activity. As for the rest, what a German author has said of the minnesongs can be fittingly applied to our popular ballads: "There have been many complaints of their monotony, and, on the whole, the charge cannot be well denied. Nevertheless, the ear that listens more closely will find an endlessly stirring life within this uniformity. It affects us in the same way as when we enter a forest, and our ears ring with the voices from innumerable feathered throats. At first we think we hear only a hubbub of sounds, in which nothing can be distinguished; but a keener regard makes us aware of the individual emerging from the general. Yonder, skillfully interlaced runs and trills, here a capricious chirping; yonder again complaining tones drawn from the depths of the heart, here a tender seductive coaxing; suddenly in the midst of all this calling tone, like an audible conjuration, an unending series of tone colors and intervals."[1]

[1] Roquette, Geschichte der deutschen Literatur, I, 130.

CHAPTER VII

SOME REMARKS ON HISTORICAL TRUTH IN BALLAD POETRY[1]

The question has recently been overhauled, How far may a poet, in treating of historical facts and personages, depart from hard and fast reality, such as is familiar to every one? At the same time attention has been directed not only to the question, How free did the poets in olden times feel themselves to be when face to face with contemporary facts? but also to the matter of the narratives in our historical ballads.

A. D. Jörgensen would maintain that they who composed the ballads were very probably licensed to make very free use of contemporary facts, even to the extent of departing widely from what had actually taken place, notwithstanding that they had heard of or had witnessed the deeds themselves, and that the real facts were known to all. Professor Karl Erslev has indorsed Jörgensen's view by embodying it as the leading proposition in his book,—a work replete with interest,—on the criticism of historical sources. It will perhaps be worth our while to examine more narrowly the correctness of Jörgensen's theory.

Professor Erslev is right in his thesis that the use of many details awakens credence in an historical narrative, even though we are not in a position to verify them; but

[1] Reprint from *Historisk Tidsskrift*, 8th Series, 1907, I.

he adds that this does not hold true of the use of such details as, for example, the introduction of dialogue, in such artistic forms of historical writings as the classics and the sagas. "Still less does it hold true of details in a poetical composition; on the whole, the poet stands from the start far more emancipated from the shackles of his material than does, as a rule, the narrator in prose."[1] This is absolutely true of the poet who sings of the more distant past; but Professor Erslev may also have had in mind poems on contemporary events. This is evident from his next remark: "While formerly, with respect to our historical ballads, one laid down only two possibilities, namely, the historically correct, hence contemporary; the historically incorrect, hence later, A. D. Jörgensen has been the first to bring home to us the truth that a ballad poet, even though contemporaneous with his events, could subject his material to so free a treatment that the result would be far from historical reality. Examples of this are found in the ballads on Marsk Stig and Niels Ebbesön."

Now it is clear to me that those who differ from Jörgensen cannot claim to have had their views rightly interpreted. "Historically correct, hence contemporary," — the conclusion has not been drawn. A ballad can relate an historical occurrence so "truthfully," that is to say, so conformably to all the accounts at issue, that it appears for the most part to express the general, well-known run of traditions concerning it; hence there arises no temptation to overlay it with any synchronism, especially if it contains no details which bear witness of fresh and independent experience and interpretation. And furthermore,

[1] Karl Erslev, Grundsætninger for historisk Kildekritik, 1892, p. 21.

in those details which it communicates, a ballad can tally with a single source to such a degree that it seems to be founded upon that source. This I have pointed out with respect to the ballad "The Meeting of Kings in Roskilde" (No. 118), which Jörgensen identifies as the ballad that was sung before the battle at Grathehede; I accounted for its particularly close relation to Svend Aagesön's "Chronicle," and asserted therefore that it belongs to a much later day because of this very "correctness."

But neither can it be admitted that the second phrase, "historically incorrect, hence later," is an accurate rendering of the proposition laid down. It is here a matter of prime importance to know in what phases the incorrectness manifests itself. Those inaccurate features which a singer embodies in his song may have grown out of a false rumor which was current at the time; therefore just as we have no ground for surprise at its appearance in the ballad, so the audience had none at hearing it mentioned. Meanwhile the falsity of the report would in a short time become apparent, and it is doubtful whether the ballad, or the verses containing the false item, would be able to maintain themselves. The inaccuracy could furthermore have originated in the poet's assuming a certain attitude or in his belonging to a certain political party, so that he would most naturally view the occurrence in a certain light, or conceive of this or that causal relation between events. In this case incorrectness will far rather indicate that the ballad was written in the thick of events. In striking contrast to this situation is that in which the balladist, even though knowing better, distorts the true conditions to suit his own invention.

Let us now turn to the principle[1] which Jörgensen has laid down and which Professor Erslev has sanctioned; namely, that a poet is at liberty to treat contemporary events so freely as to drift far away from actual conditions. Here the question concerns only a ballad or poem that is narrative in content, one that is distinguished from a prose recital only by the nature of the portrayal and by the metrical form; the audience has had no hint that the subject matter of the song is not an incident drawn from Denmark's history.

Jörgensen has advanced this statement as his view or opinion without giving any proofs to substantiate its truth; consequently it is not easy for one who holds another view to attack it. If it were attended with some supporting explanations, one could perhaps expose its inaccuracy. As it is, one is reduced merely to pointing out the internal evidence of its improbability. Here then I shall make an attempt, by bringing to light various conditions, to show how slightly tenable it really is.

Would we in our own day approve of a poet who arbitrarily distorted familiar events to the extent of shocking our sense of what is true? Suppose that a poet represented King Christian IX of the twentieth century as having committed his duchy of Schleswig to the administration of his minister Estrup, or Queen Louise as having visited her grandson King Haakon of Norway,[2] — how

[1] Jörgensen published his view in the *Bidrag til Nordens Historie*, pp. 164 ff.; he returns to it in the introduction of my work, "Vore Folkeviser fra Middelalderen," in *Historisk Tidsskrift*, 6th Series, III, 58 ff., 60 ff.

[2] Schleswig was lost to Denmark in 1864; Minister Estrup resigned in 1894; Queen Louise died in 1898; and Haakon became king of Norway in 1905. — Translator's note.

should we submit to this, I wonder? Here I have invented such conditions of the present day as Jörgensen imagines a balladist of the Middle Ages was privileged to do for his own age.[1] Certain it is that we of to-day should find it intolerable nonsense, always assuming, of course, that the poet had no thought of travesty in his mind when he wrote the ballad.

Other times have other customs, one will perhaps say; but parallels to the above in one age or another can certainly be found, especially in the Middle Ages. It is accordingly worth while to investigate the situation in foreign lands.

The North offers to us in the Icelandic lays one of the most remarkable examples of poetical treatment of contemporary events. The scalds sing of the latest happenings, they relate the exploits of the king in whose honor they are singing, they use vigorous terms and a pictorial language; but they never fabricate, distort, or subvert. Thus to a great extent Snorri builds up his picture of Norway's past upon the lays. And he says in the preface to his work: "We regard everything we find in the lays as true concerning the chiefs or their battles. It is the practice of the scalds to extol most the prince before whom they are singing; but no one would have dared to relate to the very face of the prince such exploits as everyone, including the prince, knew to be lying boasts. This would have been an insult, not a eulogy." The other saga

[1] Jörgensen accordingly maintains that a contemporary of Valdemar the Victorious could well sing that the king owned seven realms; namely, besides Denmark, Sweden, the land of the Wends, England, Norway, Scotland, and Holstein with Mecklenburg.

writers own to the same views. In many of the family sagas and in all of the kings' sagas, the scald's verses are referred to as contemporary witnesses, and everywhere the notion prevails that the scald's utterances are historically true. Even scholars of to-day hold the same opinion regarding the trustworthiness of scaldic poetry.[1] Those who have objected have scarcely made good their point, that the scalds were independent of events, or that they fabricated outright,[2] even if they did regard the lays as strongly colored or incorrectly transmitted.

A notable study of the character of the lays was made not long ago by Gustav Storm in his researches on the exploits of Harald Hardrada in Greece and Italy. Munch had already maintained that the Byzantine material dealing with the subject should be compared directly with the statements in the lays, instead of with the sketches found in the sagas, which, as a matter of fact, depended on the lays and often no doubt misrepresented the foreign conditions. Moreover Storm had at his disposal a newly discovered Greek source, and thereby could carry on the investigation much further; he showed that the scald's assertions were borne out at every point by the actual events, so that the verses in part agreed with the Greek account and in part supplemented it.[3]

[1] See Finnur Jónsson's account in Den oldnorske og oldislandske Litteraturs Historie, I, 358 ff.

[2] A. D. Jörgensen has asserted in Den nordiske Kirkes Grundlæggelse, Tillæg, pp. 69 ff., that the narratives dealing with the events of Harald Hardrada's home-coming, and with his relations to Magnus the Good, ought to show how the scalds kept dark things which had taken place and to a certain extent distorted them. He is explicitly opposed to Finnur Jónsson, ibid., pp. 362–366.

[3] *Norsk historisk Tidsskrift*, 2d Series, IV, 354 ff., 379.

Let us turn now to another people.

In Germany there exists a wealth of ballads on historical subjects. A collection of these, 625 in number, has been published in four volumes by Von Liliencron. In the preface to the second volume, the editor acknowledges that he ought to have called the collection "political ballads." They bear so close a relation to the conditions of the day that they in reality enter into them and seek to influence the course of events. Consequently these "Neue Lieder" have quite a well-marked partisan standpoint, and therefore it is possible that their portrayal of occurrences is strongly colored. At the same time there is to be noted throughout the utter absence of fabrication on the part of the authors, who were contemporary with the incidents. The audience was not possessed with the idea that, because it is the world of song or because a narrative is rimed and metrical, other rules govern the presentation of reality. A search through the whole collection[1] will reveal that this is an altogether fixed, general principle, and that it is only after some time has elapsed and after events have become wrapped up in the haze of the past that the poet may run counter, either through personal bias or through defective knowledge, to the facts of reality. The worst fault of these ballads, in poetical respects, lies in this, that they are altogether accurate, that they follow too closely the succession and course of details without giving us a general survey of principle, and without striving for dramatic unity. Consequently the poetical worth of the ballads is rigidly circumscribed. If one still remains unconvinced

[1] Von Liliencron, Die historischen Volkslieder der Deutschen, I–IV. Cf. id., Deutsches Leben im Volkslied um 1530, pp. xxx ff.

after a perusal of Von Liliencron's collection or of his commentaries on the ballads, he needs but to examine other collections to find the same view holding good.[1]

Let us look still farther afield and come to France. Here it is of moment to ask how the Norman dukes and English kings were besung in the long, metrical romances of Wace and Benoît. These poems were designed to be recited in the presence of public assemblies; they related not only happenings of the more distant past but also events nearer to their own day. But the poets recorded as faithfully as they could, and they embellished their portrayals only with speeches and with anecdotes which they had heard. It did not occur to them to distort truth.[2] Now it is an utter certainty that these poets did not bring their recitals down to the period in which they were living themselves; it is wholly inconceivable, however, that if they had advanced farther — as was their intention — they would have allowed the narrative to shift the characters about, and have permitted fantasy to rule, particularly over the period which was best known to themselves and to their audience.

The poet Ambroise, who took part in the expedition of Richard the Lion-Hearted to the Holy Land, described immediately after, in poetical form, the deeds and achievements of this famous king, in which he showed himself to be an honest, straightforward, and accurate recorder. On this account he is a valuable source of historical material.

[1] Such as Erk u. Böhme, Deutscher Liederhort, II; Böhme, Altdeutsches Liederbuch. Cf. Rud. Hildebrand, Materialien zur Geschichte des deutschen Volkslieder, I, 183 ff.

[2] Gröber, Grundrisz der romanischen Philologie, Vol. II, Pt. 1, pp. 635–637; Gaston Paris, La littérature française au moyen âge, 2d ed., p. 133.

Among the Anglo-Norman poets the unknown author of the recently discovered great "Vie de Guillaume le Maréchal" occupies the place of honor. The explicit description of the Earl of Pembroke's private and public life was composed, according to the wish of his son, a few years after the earl's death (1219); the author was a highly cultured, clear-headed, and observant man, who was just as painstaking as he was solicitous of truth. The marvelous deeds of Crusading days may well have given rise to pictures wholly imaginative in character; but these very poems, as Gaston Paris points out, depended on older accounts, which in a higher degree retailed genuine history.[1] Such seems to be the evidence that French literature offers us. The poems cited are not, to be sure, historical popular ballads; since the latter are not to be found in France, I had to content myself with showing how the poets treated contemporary history.

It is only in English literature that we meet with ballads which, not only in respect to their form but also in respect to their portrayal of historical events, are comparable to our Danish ballads of historical content. Whoever goes through Child's great collection, or through that of any one else, will arrive at the same conclusion.[2] The balladist sings about that which has taken place as well as he knows how; but he does not consciously distort things. Nor, as far as I know, has any one accused him of composing

[1] Cf. chap. v. "Langlois" in Julleville's Histoire de la langue et de la littérature française, Vol. II, Pt. 2, pp. 280 ff., 292, 295; Gröber, Grundrisz, Vol. II, Pt. 1, p. 639; Gaston Paris, La littérature française, pp. 125 ff., 136.

[2] F. J. Child, The English and Scottish Popular Ballads, Vols. I–IV; F. B. Gummere, Old English Ballads.

contrary to his better knowledge. On this point I shall quote Talvj. After calling attention to the fresh, healthy blood of the English ballads, she goes on to say: "The simple, unadorned truth of history is here so poetic that not even the help of verse seems needed to impart to the ballads the highest degree of poetic interest. That is, of course, not objective but subjective truth; that is, not facts as they really were, for the historical ballads of the English have wandered far from conscientious fidelity, which is unfortunately the main excellence and often the sole merit of the historical ballads of the Germans." [1]

To this I can add that, as far as I am aware, none of the historians of literature in foreign lands have expressed themselves so radically on poetic composition of any sort as has Jörgensen. Apparently, then, people have had a natural antipathy to seeing those matters which every one knows of or can learn the truth of turned arbitrarily upside down by a poet.[2] Even to-day the people demand of a "new ballad" [3] that it give a true account of the last

[1] Talvj, Versuch einer geschichtlichen Charakteristik der Volkslieder, p. 480.

[2] No contemporary poet would have sung, "Mallebrok died in the war," seeing that Marlborough died on a sick bed many years after the war had ceased. True the ballad is not synchronous with the event, but sprang from a far older period, and seems to have been sung at an earlier day about the Duke of Guise. Cf. Scheffler, Französische Volksdichtung, II, 107 ff.; *Zeit. des Vereins f. Volkskunde*, VI, 459.

[3] The idea and the term "new ballad" is as old as it is popular, as will be seen from various references to it. Even in the twelfth century we read in one of the "Carmina Burana" that the maidens played in the meadow and sang new ballads:

> quarum nova carmina
> dulci sonant ore,

and in a manuscript of Lancelot there are mentioned "six puceles qui queroloient [carolaient, 'danced'] et chantoient une novele chançon."

murder or the latest accident; any ballad printed this year which departs openly from the truth would fail of popular acceptance and would forfeit the general confidence in such ballads.

And while the street ballads of the present day are probably read just as much as they are sung, in the Middle Ages the written basis was binding to a very limited degree; at that time the ballads virtually lived as song, they called an entire circle into coöperation by compelling it to take part in the proem or to sing in chorus the refrain. But that very community of possession with respect to the ballads must have madc it more nearly impossible for arbitrary distortion of contemporary history to get the upper hand. Such a course would have at once met with objections from all those who knew better, and would have given rise to a refusal on the part of the audience to share in the singer's unreliable account.[1]

These are the general views which may presumably be held by one who casts a glance over the literature of Europe as opposed to the hypothesis laid down above. I cannot therefore entertain any other opinion than that Jörgensen's statement, however brilliant it may otherwise be, tends to mislead with regard to the real state of things. The cast of

[1] For instance, a contemporary ballad poet might very well say that Count Gert was slain in the night, while another contemporary might say that he was slain in the daytime, "and not at night with all," — or rather he might add a rectifying stanza of such a nature to the ballad. The difference here is merely one of another interpretation, a varying piece of information. But a verse which relates that Niels Ebbesön marched to Norway and lived there care-free and happy cannot be charged to a contemporary; the latter could not in the presence of everybody turn upside down facts that were known to all. Cf. also Dr. Sofus Larsen's remarks in *Aarböger for nord. Oldk.*, 1903, pp. 121 ff.

mind belonging to the past, and the current attitude toward the true and the false, must have tended to sharpen the natural feeling against arbitrary distortion of recent experiences.

In conclusion I shall add a few remarks on the considerations which would of themselves hinder a poet from sacrificing truth to poetic effect.

In the first place, one spoke of and used the fictitious far more guardedly then than at present. A false report could produce far greater harm and was far more difficult to disprove than in our day, when the means of rapid communication and the widespread use of newspapers can easily reduce incorrect or false statements to their own proper level. Moreover those who carried messages which concerned the whole country and which might possibly bring about an uprising among the people must take precautions against bearing unauthenticated reports, if they wished to escape severe punishment.[1] There existed, too, in those days a public sentiment which resented being violated. In the next place, a false recital of contemporary events might happen to injure some one party or another, or certain circles of society, or a single individual or family, and they who felt themselves aggrieved would not suffer themselves to be represented in a false or perhaps malicious light. The feeling of honor was alive to such a degree that it would not allow an accusation to go unpunished.[2] That the laws in Denmark made very little mention of

[1] Cf., for instance, Fagrskinna, chap. xxxii; Norges gamle Love, I, 102; II, 35; Flateyjarbók, I, 59, 184; Steenstrup, Venderne og de Danske, pp. 42 ff.; Christian II's gejstlige Lov, chap. cxxiii; Statute, 1537, art. 19.

[2] I refer to the material that has been collected by L. Freund, Lug u. Trug (vom Standpunkt des Strafrechts und der Geschichte).

insults to one's honor is a matter of no consequence;[1] it was felt to be a difficult subject for legislation. In the realm of injuries an individual was adjudged free to rule according as he saw fit, to invent his own reparation.

Most of all, however, poems and ballads were feared, for they could flit about the country and leave an insulting rumor to germinate in every man's mind. Hence the mere notion of a false picture of events must have seemed dangerous.

Even in olden times, among the Norse, satirical verses were a much dreaded weapon. In the Grágás (an Icelandic law code) there is found a provision (c. 238) which forbade the composition of a poem on an individual, even though it contained no satire; two lines, however, were permitted. If an entire poem—namely, eight lines—contained satire, the author was fined three marks, and if the composition were longer, he was banished. For a strophe of four lines containing satire, the poet was outlawed, as well as he who composed lampoons in verse on the Danish, Norwegian, or Swedish kings. In other lands we find that heavy penalties were attached to the composition of satirical ballads;[2] it was even forbidden to compose new ballads on the political situation of the day. Accordingly the council of Breslau was obliged to take legal proceedings against the "neue Gesänge und Gedichte" when the

[1] On the far-reaching effect of a derisive word and on the grim revenge exacted, see Grundtvig, Folkeviser, Nos. 358, 363, 364, 366–368, 457; cf. also No. 391.

[2] Koegel, Geschichte der deutschen Litteratur, Vol. I, Pt. 1, p. 208; Paul, Grundrisz der germ. Philologie, Vol. I, Pt. 1, pp. 171 ff.; Gaston Paris in *Journal des Savants*, 1891, p. 680. Luc de la Barre composed and sang satirical ballads on Henry I, for which he was condemned to lose his sight; Luc killed himself in prison; see Orderici Vitalis, Hist. Eccles., ed. by Le Prévost, IV, 459 ff.

priests and the people raged against the newly chosen king, Georg Podiebrad (1457). His successor, King Ladislaus, reproached the citizens of Zittau for having composed and sung "neue Lieder." When Philip the Good would put down the strife in Holland between the two parties, Kabeljaus and Hoeks, he forbade the use of these party names and the singing and reciting of insulting ballads.[1] In fact, we have instances to certify that the magistrates prohibited the playing of melodies belonging to insulting ballads from the towers.[2]

There is found in Von Liliencron a German ballad (No. 119) which very characteristically illuminates the subject. Bishop Johannes, of Würzburg, had a valet named Haasz, "der konnte wohl singen," whose especial business it was to bring to the bishop the news of everything, important or trivial, that happened in the town. Meanwhile Haasz did not stick to the truth. He added something of his own, according as the person concerning whom he reported was friendly or inimical to him. Therefore it came about that many people who were innocent got into trouble, and many who were guilty escaped punishment. As a consequence, the arrogant valet was feared and hardly endured. On the bishop's death (1466), the valet at once thought of slipping away, but he was captured by the people and, amid many bitter jests, his hands were tied behind his back and he was thrown into the Main. "Now go to-day to your lord, sing him a song, and bring him the news!" The poem, made by some contemporary on the event, contains an account of Haasz's arrival before the bishop.

[1] Von Liliencron, Die historischen Volkslieder, II, iii, 339.

[2] Böhme, Altdeutsches Liederbuch, p. xxxvii.

The editor Von Liliencron sympathizes with Haasz: Even if he had been malicious in his songs and talk, "the popular justice executed against him was even ruder and more atrocious. He has therefore the claim to be remembered in a collection of historical ballads as a martyr to his verse." This is doing Haasz too great an honor. And the popular justice which was put into force is, in any case, a living witness of how such conduct was regarded. Opposed to such false charges the common people stood defenseless, and they felt that death alone was a fitting punishment. From the Danish ballads also we learn that grim and bloody revenge followed upon false charges and assertions.[1]

Thus I have shown how both the nature of things and the form of a ballad sung by the people would definitely restrict arbitrary distortion of contemporary events.

But above all, in the foregoing, I have had in mind only ballads dealing with contemporary happenings. When treating of that which lay a generation back in time, or with the distant past of the folk, the poets were not bound to stick so rigidly to the truth. And yet a closer examination may show that such a free dealing with historical experiences and figures of the past as poets of to-day allow themselves, did not obtain in the Middle Ages. At any rate, the great traditions, which were the common possession of the people and were known to high and low, were not suffered to deviate from the truth; the folk would not put up with poetic caprice, however much the poets had leave to fill out traditions and to invent happenings in the spirit of antiquity. I shall not, however, enter upon this comprehensive question.

[1] Grundtvig, Folkeviser, Nos. 262, 266; Nyerup og Rahbeck, Udvalgte Viser, III, No. 119; Kristensen, Jydske Folkeviser, II, No. 63.

CHAPTER VIII

RETROSPECT

In conclusion let us cast a glance back over the results obtained.

Throughout I have in essence attempted to show on internal evidence what is old and genuine, what arose during the Middle Ages and persisted on from that time unspoiled; I have tried to point out the contrasting color and tone which distinguishes the later, modern additions. It may reasonably be asked, however, whether we have no external guides toward identifying the age and aspect of the ballads with respect to definite dates. When Svend Grundtvig declares, as is frequently the case, a certain ballad to be a genuine ballad of chivalry belonging to the twelfth century, does he base his statements on belief alone? On this point our only answer is that we must depend substantially upon the ballad collections made by the ladies of the nobility in the sixteenth and seventeenth centuries, and that it is very difficult therefore to say just what a ballad looked like in the twelfth century. If, into the bargain, it is characterized as a ballad of chivalry, it deserves to be remembered that certainly nothing of chivalry proper is to be found in Denmark at that time.

We should endeavor to see, on purely external grounds, how far back in time we are in a position to trace the ballads. When we undertake such a retrogressive journey we light upon the following results. In the middle of the sixteenth century Laurentius Petri mentions the ballad of "Hagbard and Signe," and in a tract on the popish mass, dating from 1533, the precentor says that he will "cheer himself with the ballad of 'Rane,'" which was also known to the Swedish historian, Master Erik Olsen (ob. 1486); "quidam Rane, de quo canticum solenne frequentatur." Christiern Pedersen writes in 1534, "the old heroic ballad runs, 'Olger the Dane won a victory over Burmand'"; and the very same line is found introduced in a fresco painting in the Floda church in Södermanland, dating from the conclusion of the fifteenth century: "Hollager da(n)s(k) ha(n) wan siger af Burman [Holger the Dane won a victory over Burmand]."

But we can go somewhat farther back yet. In a manuscript in Linköping, of 1450, there is written a portion of "The Knight transformed into a Hart" (No. 67): "I dreamed all the night of a maiden"; and in a manuscript in the Royal Library of Copenhagen, belonging to the same date, occurs several times the refrain from the ballad of "Marsk Stig" (No. 145): "For this the land stands in danger."[1] At about the same time the geographer

[1] In a Latin MS., New Royal Collection 123 4to, which contains devotional and theological pieces, there are found written down at the bottom on the side or at the end of the piece the following scraps, which seem to be pen tests. On page 26, verso, at the bottom: "Hay ffre gudh giordh [God has made ?]"; p. 38, v.: "multi sunt prelati sive sacerdotes nomine sed pauci dignitate" (Augustinus); "Hay free gudh giord fforthy standh j waadh [God has made the land to stand in danger]"; "Non semper oleum"; p. 50, v.: "fforthy stand landh i waadh [51, r.] cogita ad quem finem posses venire"; p. 54, v.: "fforthy stand landh j waad"; "Non semper oleum hay hay." The assistant librarian, Mr. C. Weeke, came across these notes and kindly called my attention to them.

Claudius Clavus noted down the ballad verse which he used in an enumeration of a series of place-names in Greenland.[1] It has been mentioned above (p. 137) that a Swedish ballad verse is found in a manuscript of the first half of the fifteenth century.

But we can travel a whole century farther back, namely, to the stump of a ballad ("I dreamed a dream late last night"), which, together with its melody, is found in the Runic Manuscript of the Skaane Laws (c. 1300). When we consider next that we know of a verse from an Icelandic ballad of the thirteenth century which has a form altogether like that of the Danish, then we can well believe that our ballad poetry goes back to the thirteenth century.

Saxo repeats in his circumlocutory manner old ballads (such as the one on the sons of Armgrim, the one on the battle of Braavalla), which were written down in alliterative verse; but this does not preclude the possibility of ballads having been composed in the style of the heroic ballads. Their form could scarcely be recognized under a Latin dress, and there is nothing in the way of the two styles having lived side by side, just as was the case in England, where one finds alliterative verse existing in as late a period as the fourteenth century,[2] while at the same time we know that King Canute the Great is said to have composed the stanza:

> Merie sungen ðe muneches binnen Ely,
> ða Cnut ching rew ðer by;
> roweð, cnithes, noer ðe land,
> and here we þes muneches sæng!

[1] Björnbo and Carl S. Petersen, "Claudius laussæn Swart," in *Vidensk. Selskabs Skrifter*, 6th Series, Histor.-philos. Afdeling, Vol. VI, Pt. 2, pp. 149 ff.

[2] Rosenberg, Nordboernes Aandsliv, II, 446.

Perhaps the oldest example extant in Denmark of the use of end rime is an inscription in the Öster Brönderslei church in Zealand, dating from about 1200; but the inscription uses also alliteration.[1] The conclusion that we arrive at is this: there is a possibility that in Denmark ballads were composed after the style of the heroic ballads as early as the twelfth century; but that in every case proof must be submitted to show that any one ballad can be assigned to so distant a date.

Meanwhile my investigations in the historical ballads[2] have brought to light that we have no ground for regarding any given ballad extant as having originated in the twelfth century. These deal with events of that time, but they do not speak like contemporary witnesses, although, on the other hand, they do not appear to be much later. As far as the thirteenth century is concerned, the matter stands otherwise, for both Dagmar and Marsk Stig have been besung as well as events of the time of Valdemar the Great.

There exist moreover several ballads that I have not touched upon in the foregoing which surely date from the thirteenth century. These are Danish ballads, but they concern themselves with Swedish affairs, in that they sing of the abduction of women belonging to the family of Sune Folkesön. One of these, "King Birger's Sister Bengta" (No. 155), tells how Sune Folkesön's daughter Benedicte was carried off from the cloister by the

[1] See my treatise on the final period of alliteration and the first of end rime in *Histor. Tidsskrift*, 7th Series, IV, 121 ff.

[2] Johannes Steenstrup, Vore Folkeviser fra Middelalderen, chap. vii, 1891.

Ostrogoth Lagmand Lars. What the ballad relates agrees well with what evidence we can gather from scattered sources of various kinds. An annal gives us even the date of the event, — 1245, — but it seems highly improbable that the author of a ballad should have collected the diverse materials and from these formed a ballad. Another ballad, "Sune Folkesön" (No. 138), relates that Eline, the mother of the woman who was thus carried off, had suffered a similar fate, in that Sune had taken her away from the Vreta Cloister; here at any rate several of the actors are historical and the events themselves are by no means improbable. Finally there befell an abduction in the third generation of that family, when, according to the ballad "Folke Algotsön" (No. 180), Ingrid, a daughter of Benedicte by her second marriage with Svantopolk Knutsön, was abducted by Folke Algotsön, just as she was about to celebrate her wedding with the Danish lord high constable David Thorstensön. This event is recorded in the annals for 1287 or 1288, and it was one which had serious consequences for the sons of Algot (see Nos. 181, 182). In addition to the stamp of old age which distinguishes these ballads, historic reality pervades them to a remarkable degree, and the representation, on the other hand, is so independent of the sources that there is no question of their having been written down contemporaneously with the events.[1]

With the evidence thus brought forth agrees also the fact that a ballad verse was written down as early as the time of Erik Menved (c. 1300), and the ballad of "Niels Ebbesön" (No. 156) must have been composed immediately after the event, that is, April 1, 1340.

[1] Cf. H. Schück, Svenska Literaturhistoria, I, 118.

The fourteenth and fifteenth centuries apparently represent the period of flowering for the ballads, but it is possible that a great portion of the ballads of chivalry first date from that period which marked the transition to the Reformation or even from that age, so full of ferment, contemporaneous with Luther. Gaston Paris, in a learned dissertation, has set himself against the tendency to place the ballads of European lands far back in time, and he asserts that the great flowering of lyric-epic poetry begins in most lands in the fifteenth or, at the earliest, in the fourteenth century.[1] I believe, however, that in the case of Denmark this period may be set somewhat farther back; but the main development and the greatest part of the fruiting this poetry reserved for the later years of the Middle Ages.

It has thus been possible to trace the changes in taste and style which came over the ballads at the conclusion of the Middle Ages or in the period of the Reformation. When one sets himself to define accurately the general outer character and the contents of the ballads; when, for example, one investigates how closely ballad poetry approached to the realm of the lyric, or the degree in which the refrain and the text admit the personality of the singer; when one considers to how great or how small an extent religious belief, feeling for one's fatherland, or learning makes itself felt; when one scrupulously tests the ballad's external form and appearance: then he will have an opportunity to observe and to marvel over the way in which various ballads and groups of ballads constantly happen to stand as exceptions, and over the ease with

[1] *Journal des savants*, 1889, pp. 526 ff.

which they become exceptions in several of the directions named above. These deviations are in and for themselves remarkable, for within all folk poetry composition comes about easily, in the same manner, with the same basis, and in the same style; and the singer everywhere avoids asserting his own peculiar individuality and taste. Least of all will such a subjective attitude seek to maintain itself in a variety of ways, or to depart in several different directions from the common starting point, either, for example, in form or in content. Ballads which do this are in every case pushed out to the extreme limits of this kind of poetry; and suspicion against them is usually augmented by the very condition that the predominating taste and style of these exceptions prove to be exactly like those which prevailed during the Renaissance and the Learned Period — a taste and style that are highly significant for all those verses which were added in late manuscripts to ballads of the old type, which are recognized as belonging to old manuscripts.

In this way then a large number of ballads which obstructed the clarity of vision in folk poetry can apparently be removed and conducted to their proper place, that is, to learned poetry or more particularly to street ballads of the last few centuries.

But among the great number of genuine ballads which we can assign to a period preceding the Reformation we can find still other tokens which determine their earlier or later dates. We trace, for example, in the romantic ballads, where a false taste appears, the influence of a more learned or more artistic poetry; we notice in later ballads lyrical elements fused with the older, purely epic style; at the same time also, as in Germany, the melody has begun to get the better of the text. Furthermore there enters into the make-up of the ballads a new chord, a new grasp and dash; the note of patriotism constantly lets itself be heard more loudly; and whereas the earlier love songs were to a pronounced degree light, cheerful, and happy,[1] the songs of the time of the Reformation are in every instance concerned with rejected passion and distracted moods. Despondency here finds expression rather as a new mood than as an emotion arising from a changed conception of life.

It has already been pointed out to what degree the refrains form an inseparable, component part of the ballads. The contrast between the text and the refrain has also been emphasized. In the refrain the *I*, which is excluded from the body of the ballad, puts itself forward; it voices its joys and sorrows, and it invokes the listeners and sympathizers. Here feeling is not content with working under cover of the narrative, but breaks out directly. Here the singer shows his partiality for the beauty of nature and the flowers ("The woods are decked all in flowers"). Here words are addressed immediately to the auditors ("Guide ye well the runes"). Here moralizing finds a place ("Fair words gladden many a heart"), and wishes may be uttered ("May I capture one of the fairest").

[1] Böhme, Altdeutsches Liederbuch, p. xxxiii: "The older love songs are overwhelmingly cheerful and voice practically nothing but the victorious mood of love"; Talvj, Charakteristik der Volkslieder germanischer Nationen, p. 444; Rosenberg, Nordboernes Aandsliv, II, 444: "Love [in the ballads] is never pining; with slighted lovers the ballads have not the least sympathy, — a *Schillerish* Ritter von Toggenburg one would have found laughable or stupid."

Here one spoke truths of a general nature ("Sorrow is heavy when one must bear it alone"). In short, in everything from which he is otherwise debarred by the rigorous epic tone required of ballad style, the singer gives his voice free play.

By a series of investigations I have next established the influence which the use of the ballads in the dance has exerted on their make-up, together with the influence which their preservation by memory alone must have exercised. In addition I have sought to make plain how very often in later times, when the ballads were collected and noted down, learning and a new taste have set a stamp upon the style not original with them; how they became overlaid with new additions, such as, for instance, Catholicism. Thus it has come about that many rust spots and much dust have been removed, and thereby are brought into clearer light the incomparable simplicity and freedom from prejudice, and the plainness in style and expression which gives this poetry its greatest worth and keeps it alive among the people, while so much of the poetry of art has gone out of fashion or has become unintelligible.

Finally one aim of these studies has been to sever the connection of the ballad with the poetry of antiquity. To draw a genealogical tree or to build a bridge that will lead over from the one to the other is wholly impossible, for the two kinds are fundamentally distinct. The Icelandic lay, as far as its form is concerned, is constructed on the principle of word accent, while the ballad verse is based on words in relationship, that is, on the sentence or the sense accent. The lay has a slow movement, a measured sound, as if one had the swing of a pendulum before his eyes; while the ballad ripples melodiously or springs along as best it can according to its own sweet will. In the old lay the words stand shoulder to shoulder, appositives are found in abundance; while the ballads appear in no way so closely drawn together and are by no means so chary of words. And whereas the lay permits the most violent inversions and arbitrarily shifts the natural places of subject, object, and predicate, the ballads never venture on such extraordinary transpositions, but adhere to the natural order of speech.

Its manner of expression then fits perfectly the natural, simple narrative, which is so far removed from the frequently weighty, didactic contents of the lays. The lays use alliteration and are recited; while the ballads employ end rime and are sung, being accompanied by the dance, which the olden times knew not or scarcely at all. When in conclusion it is remembered that the lays with their kennings affect a difficult language, or even a language that belonged exclusively to poetry; while the ballads have no need of such circumlocutions and intellectual pictures, and, on the whole, use a language that does not differ from that in daily speech: then I well believe that it may safely be asserted that here we have before us two widely differing species of poetry, between which exists scarcely any spiritual affinity. It is quite another thing to say, however, that the range of ideas peculiar to antiquity in many ways lives again in the poetry of the Middle Ages, that the legends and myths of heathendom can here appear under new guises, and that even single expressions and images from the heathen lays bob up in the folk poetry of Christian times.

With this I conclude these attempts to lay bare the true spirit and form of the ballads. This book is now commended to all those who yet love the old, naïve art of poetry and take pleasure in it as in a fresh fountain and cooling shadows on a sultry day, and to those who still look upon the popular ballads as one of the unique and most valued treasures of our literature.

INDEX TO BALLADS

The figures in parentheses give the numbers of the ballads in Svend Grundtvig's collection, *Danmarks gamle Folkeviser*

Agnete and the Merman, (38), 97 ff., 223
Axel and Valborg, (475), 210, 213, 215

Bald Monk, The, (15), 119, 120
Ballad of Envy, The, (366), 22 ff.
Ballad of Isaac, The, 21
Ballad of Susanna, The, 21
Bedeblak, (63), 161
Betrothed in the Grave, The, (90), 31, 129, 167, 188, 190, 229
Bold Sir Nilaus' Reward, (270), 51
Boyhood of Jesus, Stephan, and Herod, The, (96), 99, 100
Bridal, The, (88), 177
Burd Ellensborg and Sir Oluf, (303), 200
Buried Mother, The, (89), 188, 220

Child Jacob, (253), 96
Cloister Maiden, The, (Grundtvig's Heroic Ballads, No. 20), 63, 223
Cloister Robbery, The, (476), 41, 210, 215
Combat with the Worm, The, (24), 47
Companion's Grief, The, (273), 51

Dalby Bear, The, (64), 180
Dalebu Jonsen, (Landstad, No. 24), 90
Dangerous Maiden, The, (184), 231
Daniel Bosön, (421), 90
Death of Alf the Lesser, The, (151), 226
Defeat in Ditmarsh, The, (170), 122
Dialogue of Two Maidens, (Unpublished No. 291), 97
Duke Henry, (334), 130

Elfen Hill, The, (46), 62, 74

Fair Annie, (258), 113 ff.
Faithless Bride, The (Kristensen), 172, 199
Find Lille, (123), 44
Flores and Margeret, (86), 40, 210, 211 ff., 215
Folke Algotsön, (180), 55, 256
Forced Consent, The, (75), 28, 46

Game at Dice, The, (238), 173, 181 ff.
German Gladensvend, (33), 44, 71, 139
Gralver the King's Son, (29), 89
Grimild's Revenge, (5), 101 ff., 133, 134

Hagbard and Signe, (20), 221, 231, 253
Hagen's Dance, (465), 13, 26, 130
Hedeby's Ghost, (91), 59
Henry of Brunswick, (114), 120, 121, 125
Hildebrand and Hilde, (83), 49, 93
Holger Dansk and Burmand, (30), 210, 253

In Chastity and Honor, (225), 201
Iron Wolf, (10), 162, 233

Karl and Margrete, (87), 210, 216, 229
King Apollonius of Tyre, (88), 210, 214
King Birger's Sister Bengta, (155), 30, 43, 255
King Christian II in Sweden, (172), 41, 192
King Didrik and his Warriors, (7), 160
King Didrik and Holger Dansk, (17), 210
King Didrik and the Lion, (9), 106
King Didrik in Birtingsland, (8), 29
King Hakon's Death, (142), 31, 48
King Hans' Wedding, (166), 21, 154
Kinsman's Revenge, The, (4), 217
Knight Transformed into a Bird, The, (68), 44
Knight Transformed into a Hart The, (67), 33, 253
Knud of Borg, (195), 42

Linden on Lindenberg, The, (205), 195
Lindworm, The, (65), 185
Little Karen, (101), 118, 128
Lombards, The, (21), 70

Magnus Algotsön, (181), 202, 222
Maiden at the Thing, The, (222), 203
Maiden in the Linden, The, (66), 184
Maiden in the Woods, The, (416), 173
Maiden transformed into a Bird, The, (56), 53, 175, 203
Maiden transformed into a Hind, The, (58), 50
Maiden transformed into a Wolf, The, (55), 50
Maiden's Defense of Honor, The, (189), 13
Maiden's Morning Dream, The, (239), 54, 196
Maiden's Punishment, The, (464), 63
Malfred and Magnus, (49), 162, 210, 211, 212, 214, 215
Marsk Stig, (145), 76, 77, 84, 225, 238, 253
Marsk Stig's Daughters, (146), 31, 94, 203
Meeting in the Wood, The, (284), 55, 96
Meeting of Kings in Roskilde, The, (118), 239
Memering, (14), 92
Mermaid's Prophecy, (42), 90, 135
Mettelil and Queen Sofie, (130), 151
Murdered Housewife, The, (110), 96

Niels Ebbesön, (156), 123, 151, 202, 218, 227, 238, 256
Niels Paaskesön and Lave Brok, (164), 48
Nightingale, The, (57), 61, 111 ff.

Olaf and Asser White, (202), 45
Oluf Gudmundsön, (Unpublished No. 306), 210, 215

Peder and Malfred, (278), 19, 95
Peder Gudmandsön and the Dwarfs, (35), 72, 73, 76
Poacher, The, 48
Proud Elin's Revenge, (209), 45, 130, 167, 195
Proud Ellensborg, (218), 201
Proud Elselille, (220), 12
Proud Signild and Queen Sophie, (129), 18, 31

Queen Dagmar's Ballad, (135), 70
Queen Margrete, (Vedel), 109

Rane Jonsen's Marriage, (48), 90
Rape of the Venedian King, The, (240), 19
Redselille and Medelvold, (271), 51, 84
Regin the Smith, 75
Ribolt and Guldborg, (82), 49, 118, 204, 217

Sacrilege, The, (112), 199
St. George and the Dragon, (103), 122
St. Gertrude, (93), 188
Series of Kings, The, (115), 104
Sir Bugge's Death, (158), 43, 161, 202
Sir Ebbe's Daughter, (194), 219
Sir Lave and Sir Jon, (390), 91
Sir Sallemand (Abrahamson, No. 153), 96, 214
Sir Stig's Wedding, (76), 13, 43, 44
Sir Tyge Krabbe's Fight in Skaane, (171), 220
Sivard and Brynild, (3), 129
Sivard Snarensvend, (2), 69, 70
Skipper and the Maid, The, (241) 21
Söborg and Adelkind, (266), 217
Son's Sorrow, The, (272), 51, 56
Soul at Heaven's Door, The, (106), 144 ff.
Sune Folkesön, (138), 141, 148 ff., 256
Svend Felding, (31), 126, 205 ff.
Svend Felding and Queen Jutte, (32), 154, 208
Svend Vonved, (18), 38, 152

Terkel Trundesön, (480), 210, 216
Test of Fidelity, The, (252), 198
Thor of Havsgaard, (1), 67
Trold and the Housewife, The, (52), 155, 185, 191
True as Gold, (254), 53, 116

Valraven, The, (60), 29, 163, 186, 187

Wager, The, (224), 200
Water of Life, The, (94), 185
Wounded Maiden, The, (244), 21

Young Man's Complaint, The, (53), 60
Young Ranild, (28), 89
Young Sir Thor and Lady Thore, (72), 143
Young Sveidal, (70), 228
Youth of Vollerslöv, The, (298), 197

SCANDINAVIAN BALLAD COLLECTIONS CITED IN THE TEXT

A. S. VEDEL. *It Hundrede vduaalde danske Viser.* 1591.

ABRAHAMSON, NYERUP, and RAHBEK. *Udvalgte danske Viser fra Middelalderen*, I–V. 1812–1814. Usually cited as Abr.

SVEND GRUNDTVIG. *Danmarks gamle Folkeviser* (completed by Axel Olrik), I–VIII. 1853–1899. *Danske Kæmpeviser og Folkesange fra Middelalderen, fornyede i gammel Stil.* 1867. *Danmarks Folkeviser i Udvalg.* 1882.

EVALD TANG KRISTENSEN. *Jydske Folkeviser og Toner, samlede af Folkemunde.* 1871. *Gamle jyske Folkeviser.* 1876. *100 gamle jyske Folkeviser.* 1889. The three collections are referred to in the text as Kristensen, I, II, III.

H. C. LYNGBYE. *Færöiske Qvæder om Sigurd Fofnersbane og hans Æt.* 1822.

V. U. HAMMERSHAIMB. *Færöiske Kvæder*, I–II. 1851–1855. *Færösk Anthologi*, 1–4 parts. 1886–1889.

SVEND GRUNDTVIG and JON SIGURÐSSON. *Islenzk Fornkvædi*, I–II. 1854–1885.

M. B. LANDSTAD. *Norske Folkeviser.* 1853.

SOPHUS BUGGE. *Gamle norske Folkeviser.* 1858.

A. I. ARWIDSSON. *Svenska Fornsångor*, I–III. 1834–1842.

E. G. GEIJER and A. A. AFZELIUS. *Svenska Folkvisor.* New, much enlarged edition, edited by R. Bergström and L. Höijer. 1880.

INDEX

Aabenraa, 147
Abrahamson, 200
Agerhus Castle, inventory of, 109
Alliteration, 138 ff., 141 ff.
"Alvíssmál," 38, 231
Ambroise, 244
Annals, Ryd Kloster's, 209
Arthur's Chase, 15
Arwidsson, 61
Assonance, 139 ff., 159
Atlikviða, 194
Aventiure, 230

"Backbiter," the, 235
"Ballad Book" of Bröms Gyllenmärs, 235
Ballad style, 216
Ballads, abstractions in, 234; accompanied by the drum, 25; and the dance, 9 ff.; "birdskin," 175; broadside, 120, 146, 150; Catholicism in, 146, 178 ff., 207; change in character of, 258, 259; Christianity in, 193; Denmark's store of, 6; dramatic structure of, 228 ff.; fairy hillock, 61; history in, 237 ff.; *I* in, 34 ff.; introductions to, 32, 40 ff., 228 ff.; inversions in, 216 ff.; kennings in, 233, 234; language of, 233; legendary, 178; lyrical elements in, 34, 35, 62; magic in, 188; manner of singing, 93 ff.; melodies, 163 ff.; meter of, 125 ff.; miracles in, 181, 185, 187; monologue in, 49 ff.; moralizing in, 198 ff.; nature in, 171 ff.; patriotism in, 202 ff., 259; proverbs in, 225 ff.; records of, 6, 7, 255, 256; religion in, 178 ff., 191; romance in, 210 ff.; satirical, 22; street, 247; supernatural in, 181

Battle of Brunkebjerg, 122
Bayeux Tapestry, 230
Benoît, 244
Berggreen, 166
Bergström, R., 118, 215
Bistev, 135
"Book of Ballads," Anna Urop's, 61, 199
"Book of a Hundred Ballads," Vedel's, 71
Bugge, Sophus, 59, 101, 118, 147, 153

"Chronicle," Svend Aagesön's, 239
"Chronik des Landes Dithmarschen," 11, 93
Clavus, Claudius, 254
"Cyprianus," 188

Dance, the, and the ballad, 9; accompaniments to, 25, 29; beginning of, 27 ff.; frescoes of, 14; in couples, 11; in the Faroes, 20; in Germany, 165; in Oberpfalz, 165, 166; in the open air, 12 ff.; kissing in, 19; of the nobility, 17; picture of Salome in, 16; with objects in the hand, 13, 46
Didrik Saga, 25, 101, 102
Dietrich of Bern, 136

Earl Gissur, 10
Edda, the Elder, 52
Efterstev, 135
England, historical ballads of, 245
Erotic poetry, 39
Erslev, Professor Karl, 237, 240

Faroes, the, ballads of, 7, 162
Finnish runic songs, 78, 79
"Fjölsvinnsmál," 38

Flensborg, 105
Foresinger, 27, 93
Fornyrdalag, 147
France, historical poetry of, 244
Frey, 100

Geijer, 87, 95
Germany, borrowings from, 97, 102 ff., 114 ff., 117, 118 ff., 136, 175, 176; heroic ballads of, 37; historical ballads of, 243 ff.; medieval folksongs of, 35 ff.
"Gertrude's Book," 188
Goethe, 38
Grágás, 249
Greek modes, 164
Grimm, Wilhelm, 86
Grönland, Peder, 93
Grundtvig, Svend, 1, 61, 64, 90, 97, 98, 111, 112, 113, 116, 118, 121, 122, 135, 146, 153, 159, 180, 181, 182, 187, 198, 199, 207, 209, 217, 218, 219, 220
Guild, statutes of a, 14
"Guðrúnarhvöt," 52, 194

Haasz, the valet, 250
Hansen, Professor Peter, 3, 223
Harald Hardrada, 242
Heiberg, 189
Heidrek's saga, 38
"Heldenbuch," 101
Hervor's saga, 38
Höijer, L., 118
Holger Dansk, 210
Hoppelrei, 15
Hovedstev, 135

Iceland, ballads of, 7, 8, 162, 173; lays of, 241, 260, 261; riddle poems of, 38; satirical ballads of, 130
"Illustrated History of Danish Literature," Professor Hansen's, 3
Indstev, 135
Ingemann, 56

Johannes, Bishop of Würzburg, 250
Jongleurs, 25

Jörgensen, A. D., 237, 240, 241, 246, 247

Kabeljaus and Hoeks, 250
Kalkar's Dictionary, 105, 106, 107, 109
"Karrig Niding," 18
King Canute the Great, 153
King Christian I, 209
King Christian IX, 240
King Haakon of Norway, 240
Kok, Laurids, 158
Kristensen, E. T., 61, 164, 232
Kviðuhátt, 136, 137, 138

Laale, Peder, 26, 227
Läffler, Professor L. Fr., 65
Laub, Thomas, 164
"Lay of Gudrun," 52
"Le Bourgeois Gentilhomme," 157
"Liden Gunver," 168
Liliencron, Von, 243, 250, 251
"Literary History of Sweden," Henrik Schück's, 204
Little Karen strophe, 128, 133
"Lucidarius," 107
Lykke-Dans, 19
Lyngbye, Pastor, 75

Magni, Archbishop Johannes, 26
Manuscripts of ballads, Anna Basse's, 60; Countess Christiane's, 149; Dorothea Thott's, 195; Karen Brahe's, 43, 45, 46, 85, 113, 121, 148, 196, 200; Langebek's Quarto, 114, 149; Magdalena Barnewitz's, 44; Rentzel's 148; Sophie Sandberg's, 204; Sten Bille's, 74, 113; Sten Miller's, 43; Svaning's, 136
Minnesongs, 236

"Name him to death," 49
Neocorus, 11, 93
"Nibelungenlied," 102, 103, 221; verse of, 103, 110, 128, 131 ff.
Nibelungs, ballad on, 101 ff.
Nithart, 85

"Oddrúnargrátr," 52
Öhlenschläger, 131, 132, 158, 213
Olrik, Axel, 96
Olsen, Master Erik, 253
"Om Kirkesangen," 164

Palladius, Peter, 178
Paris, Gaston, 245, 257
"Peder Paars," 214
"Persenober and Constantianobis," 75
Petersen, N. M., 135, 136
Petri, Laurentius, 253
Philip the Good, 250
"Players," the, 25, 26, 68
Plovpenning, Erik, 209
Podiebrad, Georg, 250
Pontoppidan, Erik, 99
Proverbs, 151, 225

Recke, Ernst von der, 125, 126, 132, 133, 136, 138, 142, 156
Refrains, 29, 31, 81 ff., 159, 172; alliteration in, 159, 160, 162; German, 84, 92; in the text, 92; nature of, 82 ff., 259; primary and secondary, 135; subjectivity in, 87; variable, 88 ff.
Rhythm, 125 ff.
Rime, 125 ff.
"Rimed Chronicle," 56
Romances, 75
Rosenberg, Carl, 3, 125, 126, 130, 133, 135, 137
Ruus, Laurids, 27

St. Sigfred's legend, 205
St. Stephen ballads, 99, 100
Satire, in Iceland, 249; laws against, 250
Saxo Grammaticus, 254
"Schnada-hüpfl," 22
"Sir Ro and Sir Rap," Baggesen's, 88
Skaane Laws, 65, 254
Skrikke-Rei, 15
Snorri, 241
"Song of Sigurd," 33
"Stadsret," 105
Stolt, Jonas, 13
Storm, Gustav, 147, 210, 242
"Sturlunga Saga," 130
"Svend Dyring's Hus," 189
Syv, Peder, 4, 30, 100, 118, 151, 186, 200, 217

Tagelieder, 36
Talvj, 42, 246
"Town Laws," Magnus Smek's, 204
"Tragica," Vedel's, 177
"Trymmekendans," 11

"Vafþrudnismál," 38
Vedel, Anders, 4, 67, 104, 136, 151, 176, 196, 217, 221, 226, 227
"Vie de Guillaume le Maréchal," 245
Vikivaki, 17
"Visitation Book," 178
"Völuspá," 136

Wace, 244
Wächterlieder, 36